Narrating Diaspora:

A Study of
Five Contemporary Jewish Auto/Biographies

Dedicated
in loving memory
to my mother and father

"Honor your father and your mother,
so that your days will be lengthened upon the land that
HASHEM, your God gives you."

Narrating Diaspora:

A Study of
Five Contemporary Jewish Auto/Biographies

Elaine Barron Mendelow

To Dr Alan Berger —
With deep gratitude
for being my committee
chair —
Your student Mendelow
Elaine Barron Mendelow
(Ph.D.) thanks to your
stellar guidance)

Prestige Books International
New Delhi

April 4, 2022
3 Nisan 5782

Published by
Prestige Books International
New Delhi 110 060
prestigebooks@gmail.com
Phone: 9818755529

Associate Office
11B, Broomwood Road
London SW11 6HU

Associate Office
P.O. Box 2250
Sydney 2001

© Author /Publisher 2021
ISBN: 978-81-943009-8-4

Printed in India

Contents

Appendices

Preface

When I began the writing and research of my work, I had in mind to review the Jewish diaspora as a backdrop for the contemporary diasporic life narratives. My subsequent review of the diaspora is informed by both secular and religious sources; i.e., postcolonial theory as well as rabbinic commentary. The Biblical *Megillat*/Book of Esther, an ancient quintessential auto/biographic Jewish diasporic narrative, is referenced significantly in the analysis of the contemporary narratives for synergies with its "Esther moment" of declaration and commitment to Jewish identity. The contemporary life auto/biographies which provide the most recent chapters in the Jewish diasporic story narrative proved to have several synergies with earlier aspects of the saga, as expounded by the application of Dr. Robin Cohen's common features of diaspora. As expected, Megillat/Book of Esther paradigms is also forefronted in the life events of the interviewees, as illustrated in the detailed examination of each of the stories of the principals.

With respect to the genre of auto/biography, the medium is often the message. In exploring the history of auto/biography from ancient to modern sources, I was struck by the universal need to tell one's tale, transcending the bounds of time and custom. Though the medium has changed throughout the ages, from scroll to printed page to recorded sound/image, the genre has remained constant, if diverse. From the Mosaic slave narrative to the more recent African-American versions, auto/biography has allowed the subaltern to speak, countering marginalization as an invaluable form of empowerment.

The discussion includes an examination of the negative and positive interpretation of the Jewish diaspora, from secular and religious sources, both ancient and modern. Additionally, the 1948 (re)founding of the state of Israel signals a physical end of the 2000 year exile; now that a Jewish homeland exists once more, staying in diaspora is a voluntary choice.

The research also yields an unexpected alternative to the anticipated binary options to terminate the diasporic journey by physically returning to the reestablished Jewish homeland and/or ending spiritual displacement in the diaspora with a deeply involving Jewish project: the concept of transnationalism. In the 21st century, the choice is no longer binary. For instance, Zmira Mozorosky has chosen to spend a good part of each year in Israel, with her Israeli family. So, too, the pull of family ties makes Rochel and George Berman frequent visitors to Israel. Sibyl Silver returns to Israel regularly, as does Isaac Jacob. They feel very much at home in both worlds, their chosen country of residence outside Israel as well as Israel itself. The United States, with its current environment of religious freedom and porous borders (for US citizens) is very conducive to a dual lifestyle. It is not possible to predict if this will be the case several decades from now; especially in light of the capriciousness of prior diasporic venues.

The characteristics of these diasporic stories are echoed in the lives of countless transnationals, though not necessarily in a Jewish context. For example, one of the subjects of the contemporary narratives, Jay Lauwick, pursued a secular transnational existence: he lived in the Gallic milieu and the North American environment consecutively and simultaneously during different phases of his life. The current political climate offers numerous examples of migratory populations, from the exiled Tibetan community of the Dalai Lama to the Syrian population fleeing the violence of their country's civil war. How these groups make their way through the process of creating a liminal space in an environment outside an original homeland will be a most telling diasporic story of the 21st century.

On a personal level, I credit the journey of writing this dissertation for helping me to find my Jewish voice, in both my academic and private life. It has informed me in ways I could never have foreseen when I began. Gaining acceptance into the Comparative Studies Doctoral Program was an opportunity that can only be described as golden. (Never too late is my mantra.) I eagerly look forward to the academic possibilities afforded this senior scholar; i.e., Chaucer's Clerk in *Canterbury Tales* who would gladly learn and teach. Attending and presenting at conferences offers the opportunity to travel both domestically and internationally, a favorite activity.

Additionally, I intend to pursue the advancement of creating life narratives in the commercial capacity of my venue, *Heritage Biography International,* whether as a lecturer aboard a cruise liner or on land in programs for students of all ages and disciplines. It is my hope that the publication of my book will inspire many other voices to record their life narratives, for themselves and the generations to come. Every life is a story worth telling.

I wish to express my heartfelt gratitude to all who helped me on my doctoral journey. To those of you who do not see your names in print, please forgive my unintentional oversight. It takes a (global) village to complete a Ph.D. program.

Special thanks go first to my advisor, Dr. Alan L. Berger, who encouraged me from my ambition's early beginnings. I remember sitting in his office, offering up my ancient transcripts and my recently retaken GRE scores. He gave me the guiding words of inspiration I needed to submit an application to the Comparative Studies Ph.D. program at FAU. The acting director of the program, Dr. Michael Horswell, now Dean Horswell, was welcoming from the very first advising appointment. His wise counsel was indispensable in helping me to form my stellar committee, which, with a little coaxing on my part, he agreed to join. Kudos goes to supportive committee member Dr. Miriam Sanua Dalin, an outstanding Judaic Studies scholar whose presence on my committee assured the highest standard of academic integrity.

I am eager to acknowledge an honorary member of my committee, my dear, dear friend Dr. Howard R. Wolf, Emeritus Professor and Senior Fellow, Department of English, SUNY Buffalo, who was always there to help navigate the inevitable shoals and challenges encountered after a hiatus of many decades away from the rhythms of a university program. "H," as I like to call you in our voluminous email correspondence, you were a steadfast presence and an unflagging source of support and counsel throughout the experience. I honestly don't think I could (or would) have done it without your treasured friendship.

My special gratitude goes out to my professors in the Comparative Studies Program, Dr. Taylor Hagood, Dr. Adam Bradford, Dr. Alan Berger, Dr. Regis Mann, Dr. Emily Stockard, Dr. Richard Schusterman, Dr. Eric Berlatsky, Dr. Marcella Munson, Dr. Steve Blakemore, and Dr. Faith Smith. Thanks also to all my cohorts in the program for their help and support, especially Lochard Noel, who always insisted on accompanying me to the parking garage, despite my protests.

Very special thanks are reserved for Gabrielle Denier, Administrative Paraprofessional of the Comparative Studies Department. As she has done with so many department cohorts, she came to my rescue many times: indispensably helping me in meeting swiftly impending deadlines, filling out vital forms, and surviving the experience of comps! Throughout these ordeals, she remained a model of kindness and patience, her usual sweet self. Thank you, Gabby for all you do. Thanks also to her counterpart, Bonnie Lander, Executive Assistant for Dr. Berger. Bonnie managed to schedule important dissertation advising appointments into Dr. Berger's busy calendar. She also made certain that numerous letters of recommendation were retrieved, sent and received in a timely manner; not always easy with such a peripatetic professor, not to mention printing out numerous copies of dissertation chapters.

I am grateful to FAU Graduate College for awarding me a 2015-2016 Graduate Diversity Fellowship and for the opportunity to participate in the Summer 2018 Dean's Summer Writing Workshop. Thanks especially to workshop leader Dr. Eric Berlatsky and my workshop colleagues Melanie Uribe, Jason Levan and Michael Dillon for their constructive comments, especially on the diaspora chapter. The whole experience helped me get to the finish line.

Many thanks go to Professor Roger Porter of Reed College, author and authority in the field of auto/biography. His reading suggestions provided me with the fruitful bibliography which played a key part in guiding the diasporic structure through the life narrative analyses. He also listened patiently to the early beginnings of my dissertation proposal defense with helpful observations.

When we moved to South Florida over twenty years ago, we became part of the Boca Raton Synagogue community. The synagogue was the source of so many secular and Judaic learning opportunities, offering speakers and lectures encompassing contemporary and cultural topics, often in very erudite presentations by world-famous personalities. The experience was academically so stimulating that it rekindled my desire to pursue a degree within an organized university program. I owe a great deal of thanks to Rabbi Emeritus Kenneth Brander, PhD, *Marah D'atra* Rabbi Efrem Goldberg, Associate Rabbi Phillip Moskowitz, the BRS faculty, staff and the many program speakers and course instructors, especially Rebbitzen Hassia Yehuda and Dr. Avigail Rock whose courses made such an impression on me. A special thank you goes to Mrs. Amy Horowitz, whose wise counsel was so supportive in the *Megillat*/Book of Esther chapter. Thanks also go to my *Shabbos davening* mate Avigail Andrea Alpern for her calm presence and sharp proofreading skills. Thanks as well to my loyal friends Penny Pearlman, Hena Aloof and Judy Schneider who sat together with me during all those illuminating Saturday afternoon *shirum* and even adjusted birthday celebrations to fit the immutable demands of my academic calendar.

My introduction through friend and community member Lisa Finestone to photographer and *mensch* Ed Reichenberg heralded the beginning of a family friendship and working relationship spanning nearly two decades. He served as the photographer for nearly all the recorded interviews. I am grateful for his technical support, discretion and calming presence; so helpful in capturing so many of the life stories we did together. Having him work on the video camera aspect freed me up to concentrate solely on the interview which certainly enhanced the results. Many thanks go to technical consultant Benjamin Weiss, whose youthful expertise was indispensable, for, among other things, uploading the interviews to create an easily accessible private online site for committee members.

The congregants of the Boca Raton Synagogue truly represent "the ingathering of the exiles." From their midst came the individuals who became the subjects of five contemporary auto/biographies: Isaac Jacob, Zmira Mozorosky, Rochel (and George) Berman, Sibyl Silver and (the late) Jay Lauwick, whose late wife Leah would surely have cheered me on in this pursuit. My thanks and gratitude to them for sharing their stunning stories is beyond measure.

Many thanks are in order for the members of my family. My darling millennial daughter Raquel Rein, my greatest and most loyal fan, offered her constant technical and moral support. Raqueli, I don't know where you found the patience to get your mother up to speed in 21st century technology, but I'm glad you did! Thank you, too, for our precious grandchildren, Jordana and Bibi whose sweet entrances into our lives put the project in perspective for me. Of course thanks to my son-in-law Jeffrey Rein, father of Jordana and Bibi, who wanted a bumper sticker that read: "My grandmother is an honor student." Thanks to the California faction, my youngest brother Dean Barron, always ready to lend an ear and be a valuable sounding board, and my son Ron Mendelow and his wife Sharon, for their moral support three time zones away. Thanks to my younger brother Dr. Martin Barron for setting the bar so high, and his wife Laura for her inspiring pursuit of her artistic studies. My cousins Barbara Rich, Susan Rosenberg, Joanne Burke and Linda Schneider constantly cheered me on, giving me strength to finish this special mission. "Never too late" has become our family mantra.

Last but not the least, I owe a debt of gratitude to my husband, Dr. Gary Mendelow, my beloved partner of forty-five years, who willingly assumed all manner of domestic chores so I could be free to read, write, and finish whatever assignment needed my full attention. With his fluent skills in oral and written German, he guided me through a challenging online German Reading and Research Course. I like to think that when we pored together over a complex passage of German literature after our Friday evening Sabbath meal, we had neatly defied the Final Solution. Gar, your unflagging support was instrumental in helping me realize my dream.

Introduction

Apropos to the subject, the genesis of the topic reveals an early autobiographical connection. Long before I had heard the word "diaspora" or knew what it meant, I was already thinking about the concept. I couldn't have been more than seven when I sat in the little playroom of our basement in Ohio, looking at some books my mother had given me. The one with the orange and blue cover was called *Bible Tales*, and had generously illustrated stories of the first five books of the Bible. All the principals were there; Abraham, Isaac, Jacob, Moses, the Matriarchs, along with their stories. I read through it eagerly, grateful for all the sketches to help tell the tales. Then I picked up the second book, with its wine-red cover and daunting title, *A Child's History of the Hebrew People*. The print was a lot smaller, so I examined the sparsely scattered photographs and illustrations. I remember a few camels, some maps and present-day pictures. I tried to put the two together: long ago, the Jews were in their land somewhere in the desert, and now some of them seemed to be back. I couldn't quite understand—I was Jewish and I lived in Ohio. My parents had been born in New York, where many of my aunts, uncles and cousins still lived. I knew that my religious grandfather had come to New York from Poland, but how did he get to Poland? Why weren't we in Israel? Searching for the answers to those questions became part of a quest—for my Jewish identity, and a map for, in the words of Edward Said, "the voyage in."

As I matured and became more knowledgeable about Jewish traditions and history, I simultaneously pursued an interest in journalism. Throughout secondary school and college, I was active on school papers, finding my "beat" often focused on some form of interviews. In the capacity of being an editor of the school paper, I was given the opportunity to interview the author Carl Sandburg when he came to take part in the dedication of his namesake junior high school in Levittown, Pennsylvania. It was an unforgettable experience. Later as a university student, I interviewed a steady stream of visiting international professors in an ongoing column of my own—complete with byline; heady stuff for a freshman. I was accepted into a graduate journalism program and would have pursued a career in journalism, if my foray into a student teaching experience had not proved so rewarding.

The arrival of the ubiquitous video camera in ever more user friendly permutations inspired what ultimately gave rise to this topic: the founding of the enterprise, Heritage Biography International. As explained on its website, www.heritagebiography international.com, my business specializes in life story interviews, recorded in a video/DVD format. (The popularity of the USB flash drive has offered another recording tool, as well as a private YouTube setting; the wonders of ever-evolving technology.) The interview is conducted with questions and answers derived from interviewee written responses to a chronological outline. The filmic format allows for visuals, including photographs, memorabilia, objects d'art, and performances of special skills and talents.

Through my professional involvement, it occurred to me that the conflation of auto/biography with 21st century technology would be a fruitful area of academic study in pursuit of a Ph.D., the next project on my life agenda. I applied and was accepted into the Comparative Studies program at FAU. In my statement of intent, I mentioned research on autobiography from Gutenberg to Google as a possible topic for my dissertation.

All cohorts entering the Comparative Studies CLL program in the fall semester of 2013 were directed to take a relevant seminar, Postcolonial Theory. The syllabus was daunting: almost thirty assigned texts written and edited by significant 20th and 21st century authors in the field, spanning many earlier centuries of the postcolonial experience. The course requirement was a 20-page term paper relating postcolonial theory to our proposed dissertations.

Because Jewish Studies was one of my areas of concentration, I had decided to focus on Jewish auto/biography for my dissertation research. While reading the required seminar texts, it had occurred to me that the Jewish people were the poster children of postcolonial theory; they had endured the full catastrophe of imperial power: warfare, plunder, colonization, enslavement, genocide, and expulsion, leading to a two-thousand-year exile/diaspora. A perfect match.

The resulting term paper was a series of diasporic introductions to introduce the Jewish life narratives of the dissertation. The ancestors of the interviewees had wandered all over the world in the wake of events including the Spanish Inquisition, the pogroms of Eastern Europe, the Farhud of the Middle East, as well as the diasporic aftermath of the Holocaust. Tracing the journey of the interviewees' ancestors illuminates and informs their own diasporic narrative. An overview of the ancestral diaspora provides perspective for analyzing the role of diaspora in an individual and collective context, spanning through chronology and geography.

Over 2500 years ago, a Jewish man and woman recorded the story of how a planned Jewish genocide was averted in the Babylonian empire. The woman convinced the members of the Sanhedrin to include it in the canon of the Bible, as a template for how to negotiate life in diaspora, should the situation ever arise again. During their long and winding exile, the Jewish people were able to reference this paradigmatic auto/biography, Megillat/Book of Esther in order to navigate life in the diaspora. The work is first discussed at length through the prism of relevant postcolonial theory, and then for synergies within the context of individual contemporary life story narratives.

One sought-for synergy is a version of "the Esther moment" in the modern biographies and how it engenders "the voyage in" (Said, *Culture and Imperialism* 239) for the diasporic personality. Within the various narratives, the "Esther moment" occurs when the principals prioritize Jewish identification through their projects. Though their decision may not involve a risk to life and limb, the declaration of commitment still qualifies as a life-changing movement. It can be seen as a virtual homecoming to Jewish roots, if not to the original physical homeland.

The five life narratives demonstrate the ease with which 21st century technology facilitates non-written auto/biographical production for the general public. No longer within the purview solely of the printed page, today's auto/biographical expansion encompass filmed interviews, social media, as well as blogs and websites. Computer technology has facilitated the writing process, as well as providing new platforms for recording life experience. Elements of classical auto/biographical theory are discussed in relation to these new genres, along with unique variances which challenge older theoretical tenets.

The book explores five selected life narratives in the context of the Jewish diasporic experience. Focusing on both form and content, it directs its analysis to include a thorough discussion of two equally significant aspects: (1) the diasporic elements of the life narratives, vis-à-vis the application of an early Jewish diasporic (auto) biography, Megillat (scroll of) Esther, through the prism of postcolonial theory, and (2) the innovation of modern technology and its effects on the production/form of the life narrative.

The first context, the examination of diasporic synergies, explores the hypothesis that reconnecting with one's Jewish roots repairs the many ruptures caused by diaspora, replacing a feeling of displacement with a (restored) sense of belonging and self-worth. The second context relates how significant developments in current auto/biographical/life narrative theory recognize the employment of 21st century technology to record one's life story, facilitating its efficaciousness and thereby its accessibility to members of the general public.

Chapter 1
*Megillat/*Book of Esther: Ur-Auto/Biography

W ith the inclusion of an account of an averted Jewish genocide 2500 years ago in the Babylonian Empire, the Biblical canon offers a template for how to negotiate life in diaspora/exile, should the situation ever arise again, which it did several times (Esther IX. 29-32).

My dissertation research begins with this paradigmatic account, known as the Biblical *Megillat/*Book of Esther. Before going into its analysis, here is a brief summary:

The Biblical story of Esther opens with an account of a lavish banquet given by King Ahasuerus, the Biblical Xerxes. During this banquet, with its abundance of food and drink, King Ahasuerus summons his beautiful queen, Vashti, to show herself off before the guests. (Vashti happens to be the daughter of Belshazzar and the granddaughter of Nebuchadnezzar; Ahasuerus had basically married the boss' daughter.) For various family/feminist-relevant reasons she refuses, which elicits her dismissal.

Not long afterward, a Cinderella search/beauty pageant begins with the mission to find Ahasuerus a new queen. The land is scoured for the most attractive young females, who spend several months in the seclusion of the harem as they prepare for their audition with the king. Esther is one of the chosen candidates. Orphaned when she was very young, Esther had been adopted and raised by her kinsman Mordechai, an advisor to the king. Mordechai, who is known to be a Jew, instructs Esther not to tell of her religion or their familial relationship. Like an obedient daughter, she obeys him.

Esther, who wins the hearts of all she meets, is chosen by Ahasuerus to be his queen. Shortly thereafter, Mordechai foils an assassination plot against the king by relating it to Esther, who tells the king in Mordechai's name. The matter is recorded in the book of chronicles in the king's presence.

Mordechai is not so popular with a recently promoted minister, Haman, whose advancement entitles him to have the king's servants at the king's gate prostrate themselves before him. Haman becomes so filled with rage at Mordechai's Judaic-based refusal to bow down to him that he obtains permission from the king to destroy all the Jewish people. The day of destruction is selected by randomly casting lots, or *purim*, to determine the month and year. Word is sent out to every province of the planned genocide to destroy the Jews in eleven months' time, and sealed with the signet ring which the king had given to Haman upon acceptance of the Final Solution.

When Mordechai hears of the edict, he goes into mourning mode: he tears his clothes and puts on sackcloth and ashes. Esther is informed of his behavior by her staff, and sends a mutually trusted chamberlain to speak to Mordechai. They carry on an intense back-and-forth exchange through the messenger, which results in Esther agreeing to what Mordechai implores her to do: to go to the king and plead for mercy for her and her people. She had not been summoned by the king for the past thirty days; to go in to the king unsummoned is an offence punishable by death. In preparation for such a dangerous endeavor, she sends word to Mordechai to assemble all the Jews in Shushan to fast for her, as she will also. Resigned to her fate, she declares, "If I perish, I perish" (Zlotowitz 19). This time it is Mordechai who obeys Esther.

After the fast, Esther dons royal raiment to go before the king, who extends the royal scepter to her and offers to fulfill her wishes. She invites the king and Haman to a banquet. The king readily accedes. At that banquet, she invites the king and Haman to a second banquet.

On the night between the two banquets, the king is unable to sleep. He has the royal chronicles read to him, relating how Mordechai aborted an assassination plot. (The king's inability to sleep was thought to be connected with something he had left undone as referenced in the chronicles; in this case, not yet rewarding Mordechai for his loyalty.) In a swift turn of fortune, Haman becomes the one leading Mordechai through the city, now dressed in royal raiment and riding on the king's horse.

That evening Esther holds the second banquet. This time when the king inquires what her request is, Esther pleads for her life and the life of her people, revealing her identity as a Jew. When the king asks who brought this about, she exposes Haman as the mastermind of the cruel plot. Haman is immediately hanged on the very gallows he had built for Mordechai. The king gives Haman's estate to Esther, who reveals her familial connection to Mordechai. The king slips off his signet ring, which he had removed from Haman, and gives it to Mordechai. Esther promptly puts Mordechai in charge of Haman's estate.

Even the pleas of his beloved queen can't rescind the royal order, but Ahasuerus can and does approve Esther's idea of a decree to countermand the one devised by Haman. To that effect, Mordechai writes an edict in the name of the king, sealed with the king's signet ring, giving the Jews permission to defend themselves against the genocidal military attack, which they very successfully do.

Eventually Esther and Mordechai coauthor an account of the events, which makes its way into the canon of Biblical writings. (Not only did Esther not perish, she published!)

A Jewish presence in the Persian Empire was forefronted by prior travels in the Jewish odyssey. As recorded in the first books of the Bible, Joseph, son of Jacob, grandson of Isaac, and great-grandson of Abraham, was sold into slavery by his brothers. After a series of events culminating in a rise to power in Egypt, second only to its absolute ruler Pharaoh, Joseph saved his family from famine in Canaan. Eventually, he was joined in Egypt for the duration by his entire family; brothers, father, altogether a band of seventy souls,

The Jews had sojourned in Egypt for eons, first as welcome guests, then as slaves, when Moses ultimately led them out of Egypt back to their land on a forty-year journey through the desert. On the way, they acquired the tenets of their religion and built a portable altar, which they assembled along the way. Several centuries after their return, a permanent Temple structure was erected by King Solomon, son of King David, in the 10th century B.C.E. Four hundred years later, the Temple was destroyed by Nebuchadnezzar, and the Jews were exiled; scattered throughout the Babylonian, and what would eventually be, the Persian Empire. A Jeremiad prophecy had circulated throughout the Middle East that the Temple would be rebuilt by the Jews returning to their land after seventy years of exile.

That time was drawing near, when the story of Esther takes place. As explained in Midrashic metatext, the banquet which opens the story celebrates what was thought to be the failure of the Jeremiad prophecy to come to fruition; a miscalculation on the part of the Persians. Nevertheless, the gold vessels and sumptuous fabrics referenced in the description refer to the spoils of the Temple, confiscated by Nebuchadnezzar at the time of the Babylonian conquest, 587 BCE. The reference to the vessels in Megillat Esther was sensitively non-specific for the purpose of political correctness; this account was going to be circulated among the conquerors.

In his book, *To Heal a Fractured World*, Rabbi Lord Jonathan Sacks has referred to the Book of Esther as "that paradigm of Diaspora life" (Sacks 155). In preparation for referencing specific synergies of the modern diasporic auto/biographies with this ur-auto/biography, I am going to draw on scholar/author Dr. Robin Cohen's categorization of common features of diaspora. For the purpose of this discussion, I have paraphrased all nine features. It is noteworthy how many of the nine features appear in some manner or form in *Megillat*/Book of Esther, both overtly and covertly.

The first feature involves dispersal from an original homeland, often traumatically, to two or more foreign regions. In this case, the First Temple was destroyed, Jews were exiled from their land, and scattered over the Babylonian/Persian Empire. Evidence of this scattering can be found within the text in the reference to the writing of the proclamations/edicts to the one-hundred-twenty-five provinces which made up the Persian Empire.

Another feature, a collective memory and myth about the homeland (location, history, suffering and achievement) is found within the text in the detailed nomenclature of Mordecai and Esther: Mordecai, and by association his relative Esther, are identified as being from the tribe of Benjamin.

Not only does this reference hearken back to the origins of the twelve tribes, sons of Jacob, but is also a reference to King Saul, a Benjamite, whose failure to follow divine orders to slay Agag, king of Amalek, allowed for the eventual propagation of Haman, an Agagite (1 Samuel 15:9). When Mordecai follows his pleas to Esther to go to the king with the observation that perhaps this is why she finds herself queen, commentaries to the Megillah note the exchange as alluding to the opportunity Esther has been given to make up for the shortcomings of a Saul, a Benjamite ancestor, in defeating Haman, a current Agagite (Esther 3:1). Saul's (in)action led to the dire situation in which Mordecai and Esther and the Jews of Persia find themselves. This history demonstrates another one of Cohen's features, "a strong ethnic group consciousness sustained over a long time based on a common history/fate" (Cohen 17). History is repeating itself, with an opportunity/necessity to change the outcome.

Cohen cites another feature of diaspora, the development of a return movement to the homeland, which, though not alluded to directly in the text, can be assumed to exist from another biblical source, the *Book of Ezra.* Written in the same time frame, Ezra recounts the ongoing return movement facilitated and financed by Cyrus. The fact that all the Jews of Persia did not rise up *en masse* to leave for their homeland can be seen as evidence of how fulfilling their lives in diaspora were. (Cyrus' motivation was probably self-serving; he was familiar with the Jeremiad prophecy and probably wanted no part of it; the death of Balthazar recounted in the *Book of Daniel* was a compelling cautionary tale).

Prior to going before the king, Esther instructs Mordecai to have the Jewish people fast for her, calling to mind another feature of diaspora, "a sense of empathy and co-responsibility with co-ethnic members in other countries of settlement" (Cohen17). The vast Persian empire is described as having one hundred and twenty-seven provinces (Esther 1:1), which would be loci of settlement. The people did fast for her, exhibiting their empathy and co-responsibility for Esther's daunting task. This demonstration of unity challenges the image that Haman calls to mind when he says to the king, "There is a certain people scattered abroad and dispersed among the peoples in all the provinces of your realm" (Esther 3:8). The term employed for involuntary dispersion in the Tower of Babel narrative from the Book of Genesis is structured from the same root as the term "scattered" cited in the prior passages from Deuteronomy. When the structure built to unify/avoid dispersion is divinely dismantled, its builders are described as being "dispersed . . . over the face of the whole earth" (Gen. 11:8).The word for dispersion is the verb *pazar*, meaning to scatter. It is this same word, "scattered," which is used by Haman in the Book of Esther to describe the loci of the Jewish people to Ahasuerus, echoing the Hebrew word "scattered" found in the story of the Tower of Babel. The use of this word conflates the connotation of the divine hand as the instrument of dispersal in the Tower of Babel with the fate of the Jews in Megillat Esther, subliminally echoing the divine concept. It is ironic for the anti-Semitic villain to employ a term which references an act of the Jewish deity; a testament to authorial/editorial skill?

The Jewish people may be fragmented, but they are not isolated from one another; Esther and Mordecai are able to write decrees and happy dénouements directly to them, though not with the speed of email; travel time is always a factor in conveying messages throughout the large area of the kingdom.

As is so often the case in the Jewish diaspora, the host society often exhibits ambivalence towards the Jewish people; the Persian host is no exception. Two of Cohen's features, "a troubled relationship with host societies/lack of acceptance/possibility of another calamity, and the possibility of a distinctive, creative, enriching life in host countries with a tolerance for pluralism" (Cohen 17) exist side by side in the text. Mordecai is a prime example; his position as a valuable government official does not exclude him from the punitive actions of another (higher) official, Haman, on the grounds of religious discrimination.

Living a "distinctive, creative, enriching life" can be achieved with a skill set accompanying an exile; as a member of the Sanhedrin, Mordecai had to know seventy languages "It was owing to his knowledge of languages that Mordecai was able to discover the plot of the two eunuchs, who conversed in the language of Tarshish, their native country, thinking that no one would understand it" (Meg. 13b; comp. Targum Sheni to Esth. ii. 22). To put it in terms of postcolonial theory, Mordecai was an eminent native speaker; locating him in Homi Bhabha's "liminal space." Mordecai managed to live in the intersection of two worlds, the Jewish and the secular, setting an example for subsequent exiles to follow.

For those who navigate the two worlds with difficulty, the diasporic identity challenge of Self/Other is forefronted, as with Esther. It is interesting to note that the two examples of Esther and Mordecai feature two different approaches on whether or not to acknowledge one's Jewish identity; the lesson for those in diaspora just might be to evaluate the best course of action to follow on a case-by-case basis. Rabbinical commentaries suggest that Mordecai advised Esther not to reveal her Jewish identity just in case there might be repercussions to the community should Ahasuerus become displeased with Esther.

A key lesson relating to language proficiency can be extrapolated from Mordecai and Esther. As has been mentioned, Mordecai was fluent in several languages, while Esther has been lauded by modern and medieval commentators on her oratorical prowess. The episodic events following Esther's unsolicited appearance in court to her accusation of Haman are referenced in detailed rhetorical analyses by the medieval 15th century Spanish philosopher, Rabbi Isaac Arama [1420-1494, Spain], illustrating how Esther's impressive oratorical skills were offered as a model for politically correct court behavior. In her cogent article, "Unveiling Esther as a Pragmatic Radical Rhetoric," Professor Susan Zaeske traces Esther's influence to influential figures of the abolitionist movement who invoked Esther as a model for speaking truth to power. On more than one occasion in the 21st century, opportunistic Israeli politician Prime Minister Benyamin Netanyahu has invoked Esther's model in order to try to draw an enthymematic parallel between himself and Esther, as well as conflating the anti-Israel threat of modern Iran and the genocidal edicts of ancient Persia.

Additionally, Esther's literacy allowed her to participate fully in the process of shaping the written account, and allows for the classification of this work as an ur-auto/biography, at the least a co-authored collaboration with Mordecai.

Auto/biography is less frequently written in the third person, though the eponymous author of the Torah, otherwise known as the First Five Books of Moses also produced an ur-auto/biography in the third person, including his own death. It has been strongly suggested by commentators that Joshua, Moses' successor, wrote the very last part after the fact, acting as an editorial assistant.

Additional support for the ur-auto/biography theory rests with the assumption that if *Book of Esther* is regarded as a generally factual account, the private conversations between Esther and Mordecai would have to have been related by the principals, since they would be the only ones with knowledge of what was said.

One of these private conversations will form the basis of an important synergy with the other auto/biographies: the "Esther moment," when Esther steps out of her liminal space firmly into a commitment to her own people to approach the king on their behalf.

In her 2003 book, *Esther and Ruth,* Professor Patricia K. Tull takes credit for coining the term, "the Esther moment. " She relates, "When teaching the book of Esther extensively for the Presbyterian Church (U.S.A.) a few years ago, I coined the phrase, 'having an Esther moment,' for the many times themes from the book seemed to rise up and envelop a moment of personal or community life. During that study, many women told me stories of their own lives, of moments when the world changed for them, when they were called upon to grow up in ways they hadn't needed to before, to dig down deep to find courage to speak up on their own behalf or on behalf of others who were even more vulnerable than they—'Esther moments' in their own lives (5).

The modern life narratives often exhibit a synergy with "the Esther moment," when the principals prioritize Jewish identification through their Jewish projects. Though the decision may not involve a risk to life and limb, the declaration of commitment still qualifies as a life-changing moment. The project becomes a *cause celebre/raison d'être,* commanding the better part of their time and attention.

The Esther moment and its modern counterparts have significant ramifications with regard to aspects of diaspora. As will be discussed in detail in the next chapter which deals specifically with diaspora, the locus of diaspora is psychological as well as physical. Even though the principals may not actually return to the original physical homeland, their affiliation with their Jewish identity signifies identification with their Jewish roots, a virtual homecoming. The discussion of diaspora's positive aspects will continue in the next chapter's detailed discussion bringing rabbinical and secular viewpoints into the conversation. Esther's rise to power holds resonances of the earlier rise to power of one of her Biblical forbearers, Joseph. Here is a brief synopsis of Joseph's story:

> Biblical patriarch Jacob, son/grandson of patriarchs Isaac/Abraham, fathered twelve sons by four women. His favorite was Joseph, eldest son of his favorite wife, Rachel. The other brothers were jealous of their father's preferential treatment, and decided to send him away with a passing caravan. They tell their father Jacob he was killed by a wild beast.
>
> During Joseph's subsequent enslavement in Egypt, he rose to a position of power second only to Pharaoh himself, and successfully oversaw the preparation of grain reserves before the onset of an impending famine. When the famine hit Canaan, the brothers went down to Egypt to buy food to stave off starvation.
>
> In a dramatic turn of events, Joseph reveals his Jewish family identity to his astonished brothers and ultimately brings the entire family down to Egypt to ward off the famine. The family lives (almost) happily ever after, until a new Pharaoh enslaves them.

What follows is the redemption and departure described in the Book of Exodus of what is now a large population of family descendants.

In his book, *The Queen You Thought You Knew*, Rabbi David Fohrman shares a synergy with Esther's declaration at the Esther moment, "ka'asher avadeti, avadeti," "If I perish, I perish," (Esther 4:16) and an identically formulated phrase, ka'asher shakolti, shakolti, "If I am to be bereaved, I am to be bereaved"(Genesis 43:14) in the story of Joseph. This phrase is uttered by Jacob when he finally agrees to send his beloved son Benjamin to Egypt as demanded by (as yet unidentified) Joseph.

These two instances serve as the only time that particular phrase formulation appears in the Bible, a sure exegetical sign that they share a commonality. It should be stated here that the identicality of the construction of the two phrases is an indication of the intertextual referencing of the story of Joseph, another diasporic paradigm, in the much later story of Esther. A full treatment of this fascinating topic would furnish sufficient material for another paper; Rabbi Fohrman promises to devote an entire sequel to "breathtakingly extensive literary links between Esther and the Joseph saga."(Fohrman 134 n.23). The volume is eagerly awaited.

In the broadest sense, the intertextual synergies between Esther and Joseph reference the reader back to the (also) paradigmatic story of a Jew in exile, one who, like Esther, rises to royal heights of rank and power in an alien land while still retaining ties to one's cultural roots/values, a powerful lesson for those in exile.

Chapter 2
Diaspora: A Long and Winding Road

Introduction

The life journeys of the subjects whose auto/biographical narratives are presented here actually began many centuries ago, with the diaspora of their Jewish ancestors. Before launching into a detailed discussion of these contemporary narratives, it is important to review the history and theories of the Jewish diaspora, which spanned thousands of miles and millennia. Looking through the prism of diasporic discussion is a necessary prerequisite to inform the analysis of the circumstances which shaped the narratives' life paths, illustrating synergies between events throughout the ages to the present day. Because these speakers are aware of the twists and turns in the diasporas of their ancestors, their personal life narrative must be seen as situated along a continuum which includes the entire journey. Anything less would be an incomplete rendering; one more in a long line of diasporic ruptures.

This chapter's discussion will include several diasporic topics to be discussed in more detail within the context of subsequent chapters specifically treating individual life narratives. Those topics include a discussion of relevant diasporic theory pertinent to the narrative subjects, the origins and concept of the word "diaspora" in a universal context as well as its applications to ancient and modern Jewish history, descriptions of the four Jewish exiles, contemporary Jewish diasporic models, and the 21st century diasporic option of transnationalism. Though diaspora is often regarded as a negative event, additionally, diaspora/exile will be presented as a positive event through ancient and medieval Talmudic teachings as well as modern scholars, in both a religious and secular context. Special attention will be paid to the analysis of diaspora scholar and author Robin Cohen, whose book *Global Diasporas* provides a cogent basis for insights into the role of diaspora within the lives of the auto/biographical subjects. This chapter's detailed analysis of the general topic of Jewish diaspora provides a vital directive from which to explore the role of past, present, and future diaspora in the narratives.

Definition of the Term "Diaspora"

In the introduction to the section on diaspora in *The Post-Colonial Studies Reader*, diaspora is described as "the scattering throughout the world from one geographic location" (Ashcroft 424). In the same section, the editors reference how the "*Shorter Oxford Dictionary* defines diaspora as 'the dispersion' (Ashcroft 424). "First used to describe the Jewish dispersion in Babylonian times and then after the Roman destruction of Jerusalem, . . . the term first occurs in Deuteronomy 28, Verse 25 which says 'the Lord will cause you to be defeated before your enemies you will come up from one direction but flee from them in another and you will become a thing of horror" (Ashcroft 424).

Cohen cites a different passage in which "diaspora implied a forcible dispersion" (Cohen 21): "If you do not observe and fulfill all the law . . . the Lord will scatter you among all peoples from one end of the earth to the other. . . . Among these nations you will find no peace, no rest for the sole of your foot. Then the Lord will give you an unquiet mind, dim eyes and a failing appetite. Your life will hang continually in suspense, fear will beset you night and day, and you will find no security all your life long." (Deut: 28:15, 64-66)

With their unsettling prospects of emotional and physical anguish, these two passages from Deuteronomy forefront the negative view of diaspora as "forced dispersion." A negative view of diaspora is not the only interpretation, as further discussion shall show.

Etymology of the Term "Diaspora"

The word diaspora traces its etymological origins to the Greek roots *dia* and *sperein*, "namely 'to scatter', 'to spread' or 'to disperse" (Cohen 21). In his succinct volume, *DIASPORA: A Very Short Introduction,* Professor Kevin Kenney explains that "The Greek words *diaspeirein* and *diaspora*, applied to Jewish history, came into widespread currency in the translation of the Hebrew scriptures known as the Septuagint (ca. 250 BCE) (Kenney 3-4).

As Cohen explains, the term is so closely associated with the Septuagint Greek translation of the word "scattered" in the passage found in Deuteronomy: 28 that the word's origins have been virtually lost.

Cohen also points out the how the connotation of *speiro*, "to sow," as in the dispersion of seeds could lead to "refashioning the old idea of diaspora" (Cohen xiv). This positive concept of diasporic dispersal as a seeding process was expanded in Richard Freadman's *This Crazy Thing a Life*: "Indeed the very word diaspora, which is derived from the Greek speirein (to sow) and dia (through), contains an ambiguity: it suggests dispersion from a source, but also fertility, seeds that will flower elsewhere" (Freadman 29). (The concept of a fruitful diaspora will be further explored later in the chapter.)

Diasporas, author/scholar Stéphane Dufoix elaborates: "In the so-called Septuagint Bible, 'diaspora' is used twelve times. But it doesn't refer to the historic dispersion of the Jews who were taken as captives to Babylon after the destruction of Jerusalem in 586 B.C., or to any other human historical event . . . Instead, 'diaspora' always meant the threat of dispersion facing the Hebrews if they failed to obey God's will, and it applied almost exclusively to divine acts . . . Martin Baumann shows that it was only in later Jewish tradition that the meaning of 'diaspora' changed to designate both the scattered people and the locale of their dispersion" (Dufoix 4-5). Building on Baumann's observation, Dufoix notes that the exilic Hebrew terms *galut, galah* and *golah* are often rendered as "diaspora," rather than exile, though they are translated with different Greek words in the Septuagint for emigration, settlement abroad, wartime captivity; a conflation of connotations.

A Tale of (at least) Two Diasporas

Finding spiritual positivity in the experience of diaspora rather than negative consequences is not just a modern concept. Within the commentary of ancient rabbis as well as contemporary religious and secular theorists, the Jewish diaspora has been read in both a positive and negative context. As seen from previously cited biblical passages, the Jewish diaspora can be interpreted as retribution for crimes against divinity. Conversely, 16th century Kabbalist Rabbi Isaac Luria and 21st century Biblical scholar and author Rabbi Jonathan Sacks see the diaspora as a divinely orchestrated opportunity to repair the world's ills. Sacks highlights the same idea in the teachings of the Arizal, Rabbi Isaac Luria, who "in the aftermath of one of the great human tragedies of the Middle Ages, the Spanish Expulsion . . . framed a vision of hope in the midst of catastrophe. The divine light that initially flooded creation proved too strong. There was a 'breaking of the vessels' as a result of which fragments of God's light lay hidden under the rubble and wreckage of disaster. It is our task, he [Rabbi Isaac Luria] said, to 'heal' or 'mend' the world by searching for those fragments and rescuing them, one by one" (Sacks to Heal a Fractured World 265).

The concept of scattering seeds which take root and grow as previously demonstrated in the etymological origins of the Greek term "diasperein," is echoed in the Kabbalistic concept of gathering in the scattered sparks. It is another example of conflating the process of sowing and reaping; the gathering of the sparks by those who were sent out to accomplish the task. Additionally, the Jewish concept of *tikkun olam*, "mending the world," pursued by Jews in fields ranging from social justice to ecology is cited as the mission of an exile brought about for just this purpose by divine ordinance.

In addition to the positive and negative context of Jewish diaspora, an underlying debate ensued over the diasporic model: is a return to the land of exile the paramount uniting objective of the dispersed peoples, or is the practice of Torah, God's law, the chief spiritual goal? The Zionist movement of the 19th and 20th centuries, which preceded the (re)establishment of the state of Israel in 1948, provided the theory and the opportunity to put that theory into practice: after a two-thousand year hiatus, it had become possible for the exiles to return to the land of their ancestors, now a Jewish national entity.

The prospect/existence of aviable Jewish national state did not unite all Zionist thinkers into a common cause. The development of Zionist movements in the nineteenth and twentieth centuries saw a recurring debate between "two established models of Zionist historiography—a centre in Eretz Israel surrounded by the diaspora as a surrounding circle, or the elliptical model of Babylon and Jerusalem proposed by the Diaspora nationalists" (Conforti 245). Authors included Simon Dubnow, Salo Baron, Yitzhak Behr, Simon Rawadowicz, and Ben Gurion, among others.

These writers were joined by 20th century authors Daniel and Jonathan Boyarin, who even went so far as to say that diaspora was a greater Jewish contribution to society than monotheism: "Indeed, we would suggest that Diaspora, and not monotheism, may be the most important contribution that Judaism has to make to the world, although we would not deny the positive role that monotheism has played in making Diaspora possible" (n.50). Exception could be taken that diaspora outranks monotheism in the hierarchy of world Jewish contributions, however, the importance of the concept of diaspora should not be undervalued, especially in light of challenging 21st century migratory issues.

In their essay, "Diaspora: Generation and the Ground of Jewish Identity," brothers Daniel and Jonathan Boyarin suggest that "diaspora, rather than the model of national self-determination, offers a vision of identity that might be utopic, but one that is also strong and free of persecution for all" (Braziel and Mannur 85). Boyarin and Boyarin assert that rather than espouse Zionism which is "predicated on a myth of autochthony . . . We will suggest that a Jewish subject position founded on generational connection and its attendant anamnestic responsibilities and pleasures affords the possibility of a flexible and non-hermetic critical Jewish identity" (Braziel and Mannur 92).

As an aid to promoting world peace, they recommend "Assimilating the lesson of Diaspora, namely that peoples and lands are not naturally and organically connected" (Braziel 110). They continue, "Diaspora can teach us that it is possible for a people to maintain its distinctive culture, its difference, without controlling land, **a fortiori** without controlling other people or developing a need to dispossess them of their lands" (Braziel 110-111). An extension of this issue would be the Palestinian response to the same.

What is/was the path to Zion? It could be argued that though autochthony, a frequently used term of the Boyarin brothers is an intrinsic part of the Jewish heritage, the connection between the people and the land provides an opportunity for (re)interpretation in every era according to individual circumstances and personal belief systems. These ideas are shown to be conflated by an etymological discussion of Sacks on the term, Tsiyun/Zion. Though the word "Zion" is often used in context with "Mount Zion," an actual location in Jerusalem, throughout history it has also been used as a referent to the land of Israel.

Sacks explains that the word tsiyun means "signpost," used in the context of the message of the prophet Jeremiah, who "told the Jews of his generation who were going into exile that they should set up signposts (tziyunim) so that they would not forget the way back to Israel. The sages interpreted this to mean that they should not abandon Judaism. Zion is not just a place. It is a way of life . . . Zionism is a matter of not only where we live, but also how we live" (Sacks, The Jonathan Sacks Hagaddah, 52-3).

In the 21st century, author Alan Wolfe follows this positive diasporic train of thought in his provocative and persuasive book, *At Home in Exile*. Wolfe's observations can serve as a springboard for the new (and old) ramifications of current 21st century Jewish diaspora/exile. Wolfe asserts that "The blessings of exile are older, and more enduring, than the evils of stateless-ness. By bringing back to life the universalist ideals developed during their long residency in exile, a new generation of Jews can offer the best hope for a revival of the Jewish future" (Wolfe 215).

To support his argument, Wolfe notes several 21st century conditions; among them, the ending of diasporic negation with the opportunity for religious freedom outside of Israel as well as the fall of anti-Semitism, existing concurrently with the rise of opportunity to participate fully in society. Devoting an entire chapter to the topic "Anti-Anti-Semitism," Wolfe cites many examples to support his claim that anti-Semitism has fallen, not-ing that "Dangers there will always be, but the reality is that the barriers once put in place to keep Jews out of the major institu-tions of gentile societies have crumbled in nearly all of the plac-es in which significant numbers of Jews live" (Wolfe 163).

As Yitzhak Conforti points out in his 2015 article, "State or Diaspora: Jewish History as a Form of National Belonging, "The previous models that explained the relationship between Diaspo-ra and state as two opposites, and even as two national centres, are insufficient in the postmodern age of multiple identities. As a result, contemporary historians emphasize the desire to reveal the multiple Jewish voices and identities of past and present, and tend to blur the borders between homeland and Diaspora" (Conforti 245).

So, can the diaspora exist without a physical centrality? Is it possible to claim diasporic identity without any acknowledgement of a spiritual centrality? What about the many Jews around the world who chose not to actively practice Judaism? What is their position and place in and on diasporic unity **vis-à-vis** Jewish identity? Finally, what is the context of the diaspora viewed within and without the five Jewish diasporic narratives? As will be explained in further detail, the relevance lies in the experience of being a Jew in exile. This detailed discussion of diaspora serves to situate the contemporary narrative in the important context of the greater diasporic saga.

The Abrahamic Diaspora

Before beginning an examination of the four Jewish exiles as they are cited in Jewish tradition, it is instructive to feature the diasporic experience of the earliest patriarch, Abram/Abraham. Within the Book of Genesis, the first patriarch, Abraham, begins by complying with a divine dispersal, a diasporic homecoming/journey: In Genesis 12:1, God tells him to "*Lech lecha*/Go for yourself from your land, from your relatives, and from your father's house to the land that I will show you." The reflexive *lecha*, "for yourself" has been interpreted to indicate that the spiritual quest is to be pursued by looking within oneself, an interior examination as well as an exterior journey.

Later in Genesis, 14:13, the exilic concept is instantiated by the eponym by which Abraham is identified, as the *Ivri*, "the other side.' Literally, this means that he came to Canaan from the other side of the Euphrates" (Scherman the Chumash 55). The word "*ivri*" forms the origin of the word, "Hebrew," used both to designate a language and a person, two strong forms of identification.

Biblical commentary observes that though Canaan transplants Sarah and Abraham had many devoted disciples in their new environs, "they were essentially alone; they could never blend into whatever culture surrounded them" (Scherman The Chumash 55), an apt comment that applies to several subsequent diasporic Jewish populations. It could be said that with its early appearance in the saga of so many of the early Jewish patriarchs, diaspora has long been embedded in the DNA of the Jewish people.

Additionally, the interpretation of God's covenant*al conversations* with Abram/Abraham and subsequently the Jewish people can be seen as synchronous with a productive, constructive presence among members of the other nations of the world:"and all the nations of the earth shall bless themselves by your offspring" (Gen. 26:4). Rabbi S.R. Hirsch explains this concept to mean that the Jewish presence is divinely guaranteed to bring good things to the nations in which they live; echoed by variations found in modern theorists, as has been explored earlier in this chapter.

The Four Jewish Exiles: #1 The Egyptian Exile

Taking a closer look at the characteristics of the four Jewish exiles will shed light on the mutuality and exclusion of the concepts. Tracing the path of these exiles recovers general ancestry; for most families of Jewish descent, including most of the interviewees, specific genealogy information is very nearly irretrievable. As has been earlier referenced in the Dufoix discussion, in the context of Jewish history, the terms diaspora and exile have often been conflated. In light of Jewish history, the Hebrew word for exile, *galut*, holds within it the connotation of a forced departure. Evidence of a forced departure can be inferred within the story of the first exile more than three millennia ago, the Egyptian one, recorded in the early books of the Bible. Joseph was forced to leave his home and family when his brothers sold him. He became enslaved in Egypt, ultimately rising to power, resulting in his family's residence in Egypt to avoid being starved by a famine. They remained in Egypt for over four hundred years; first as honored guests, then as persecuted slaves. That exile ended with the Jewish people's exodus, who, according to the Biblical narrative, led by Moses through forty years of wandering through the desert, eventually reached their promised land.

The Four Jewish Exiles: #2 The Babylonian Exile

The second exile occurred nearly 2500 years ago, in 587 BCE, with the destruction of the First Temple by Nebuchadnezzar. As was the custom in those times, Nebuchadnezzar continued to expel the Jewish people from their own land and scatter them into assorted alien territories, as did his predecessor, Sennacherib. Conquerors employed this technique to divide a people so as to prevent unity which could more easily lead to insurrection. When Nebuchadnezzar's empire fell to Persian conquerors, the Jews found themselves governed by a ruler, Cyrus, who facilitated return and rebuilding of the Temple. The seventy-year period between the destruction of the First Temple and the rebuilding of the Second Temple is known as the Babylonian exile. It is worthy to note that not all Jews returned; many chose to stay in diaspora rather than struggle to rebuild the ruins of their homeland.

The Four Jewish Exiles: #3 The Greek/Syrian Exile

Though it is described with the Hebrew word *galut,* or exile, a better terminology for the next exilic era would be the modern postcolonial term, "colonization." During this period, the Jews did not leave their land; they were colonized by a subjugating conqueror. In 138 BCE, a little over one hundred years before the Common Era, the Syrian/Greeks took control over Judea and its people. In addition to issuing edicts forbidding various aspects of Jewish worship, they defiled the sacred Temple by using it as a stable. When the Maccabee tribe's guerilla warfare regained control, the Temple was cleaned before being restored to its holy service. This victory originated the holiday of Chanukah, or "rededication." It bought the Jews two hundred years of autonomic self-government.

The Four Jewish Exiles: #4 The Roman Exile

In 70 CE, the Roman ruler/general Titus destroyed the second Temple, ending the Jewish people's 500-year sojourn in Judea. Once again, the Jews were dispersed, this time to Rome. This exile, which was to last for 2000 years, is known as the Roman exile, even though the Jews found themselves scattered to many more locations across the globe during the ensuing millennia of frequent persecutions. The Roman exile formally ended with the (re)establishment of the state of Israel in 1948. By then the condition of diaspora had become a state of mind as well as a state of being, as might be expected from the Jewish people's checkered 4000 year history.

Divine Land/Brand Covenant

For observant Jews who recite their daily prayers, it would be difficult not to be aware that they are in a state of diaspora. On weekdays, the Sabbath and holidays, the exiled Jews constantly beseeched God to remember the promised divine covenant, recitations that continue until today. References to the restoration of Zion and Jerusalem abound in the morning, afternoon and evening liturgy/*Shacharit, Mincha, Maariv* and in the Grace After Meals/*Birkat HaMazon*. Though the function of these supplications was to hold God, the recipient of the request, to an unfulfilled promise, the prayers also acted as an ever-present reminder to focus the supplicants on the longed-for end of their exilic state.

God's covenant involved more than a land grant. Though the promise of the land of Israel figures strongly, the divine bond contains other equal components. The acknowledged presence of other nations and their interrelationship with Abraham's myriad descendants, the Jewish people, is no less a part of the covenantal accord.

Rabbi Dr. Judah Goldberg parses the Abrahamic covenant as a tetrad: (1) the people of Israel [Gen.12:2], (2) the land of Israel [Gen 15:18], (3) the ethical life [Gen 18:19], and (4) the spiritual life [Gen 17:7]. While a part of the covenant undeniably involves the promise of land, other aspects, especially the spiritual life, transcend the boundaries of territory. "Keeping the way of Hashem, doing charity and justice" (Gen 18:19) aptly describes many a Jewish exilic pursuit. Living an ethical life is intrinsic to Isaiah's observation that the Jews will be "a light unto the nations" (Isaiah 49:6). Importantly, this non-land clause of the covenantal agreement might only be able to be fully carried out in the context of a diasporic locus; i.e., if the Jews sequester themselves, they cannot perform in an exemplary capacity.

Etymological Indications of Duality of Diaspora

This duality of diaspora can be seen as an intrinsic part of its word origin. "A fundamental ambivalence is embedded in the term diaspora: a dual ontology in which the diasporic subject is seen to look in two directions—towards an historical cultural identity on one hand, and the society of relocation on the other" (Ashcroft 425). This description of the diasporic locus precisely inscribes the position of the hybrid: straddling two worlds; a balancing act at best. The Biblical book of Exodus refers to the position of "Other" in an exilic context. The similarly worded passages appear in close proximity to one another in 22:20 and 23:9, "for you were strangers in the land of Egypt," recalling Israel's Egyptian exile.

Becoming a stranger is a crucial part of Jewish diasporic identity, so it is not surprising that a duality of interpretation appears in an entomological analysis of the Hebrew word for stranger, *"ger."* In her February 2018 lecture series at the Boca Raton Synagogue, Professor Avigail Rock of Bar-Ilan University offered the observations of two medieval commentators on the etymologic origins of "ger." Both have significant applications to understanding the concept of the diasporic individual. The Radak, Rabbi David Kimchi (1160-1235) cited the root *legar,* which means temporary dwelling. Ibn Ezra, Rabbi Abraham ben Meir ibn Ezra (1089-1164) traces the word's origins to *garger,* a berry taken from a cluster. Collectively, the etymological explanations capture the duality of the diasporic subject: displaced from one world, tenuously placed in another. This precarious national journey is described by Amos, an Old Testament prophet, in the imagery of a divinity that will "shake the house of Israel among all the nations, as [grain] is shaken out of a sieve, and not a pebble falls to the ground" (Amos 9:9). "Just as large items do not fall through the sieve, so the House of Israel, though they will be shaken from place to place, will never 'fall to the ground' completely" (Scherman 1368).

The relevant concept of temporal duality is found in Greek mythology: "Janus, the figure from the Greek pantheon whose gaze is simultaneously directed both forward and backward, suggests a certain temporality; the figure at once looks to the future and the past" (Braziel 9). Like Janus, the diasporic individual is often situated between the two worlds, both spatially and temporally. Attempting to find security by creating a liminal space can present a nearly unresolvable challenge.

Liminal Space vs. Israel

Moreover, how does one retain the religious connection to one's Jewish heritage outside of the state of Israel? Will the cultural bond be able to withstand the forces of assimilation? The issue is not one of religious freedom, but rather the level of personal commitment. It is not a philosophical issue, but one of momentum. In a state where Jews form the majority, the language and calendar will have a more Jewish orientation, simply making it easier to live a Jewish life by default, in terms of custom and culture, however varied or nonexistent the levels of worship may be. I would argue that being part of the majority of anational Jewish society preserves Jewish connection by default; i.e., language, Jewish calendar, geopolitical history, national monuments, etc.

A Special Subset: Post 1948 Israeli Diaspora

Robin Cohen's diaspora series includes a book devoted to a special subset of diaspora, *Israeli Diaspora*; anecdotal and theoretical reflections on the circumstances and consequences of leaving the territory of the Jewish state (re)established in 1948 after a two-thousand year exile. Within this work, two diasporic auto/biographies are discussed that foreground the experience of emigrating from Israel, the narratives of Isaac Jacob and Zmira Mozorosky. More detailed explorations of their very different emigrations will follow in their life narrative chapters. An aspect of their stories which deserves scrutiny calls into question the role of the newly established state's less-than-supportive national policy towards religious observance as well as the low priority given to preservation of ethnic cultural identity.

The concept of moving out of Israel carries negative linguistic as well as negative cultural connotations, in Alan Wolfe's term, "diasporic negation." Within the Hebrew word for emigrating from Israel, *yored,* is its root, which means literally "to go down." Conversely, the Hebrew word for immigrating to Israel is making *Aliyah,* or going up. The name of Israel's national airline is *EL AL,* "upwards," sharing the same root, "*al,"* with *Aliyah.* Interviewees within *Israeli Diaspora* often expressed an intention to return to Israel, despite the fact that during the decades in which they had been living outside the land they had established firm familial and economic roots. This position can be explained in part by the persistence of a native Israeli mindset of diasporic negation, however subliminal, in the *Weltanschauung* of the Israeli expatriate.

Ending Diasporic Exile through Spiritual Homecoming

Characteristically described as a condition of physical exile from a native land, I argue that the condition of Jewish diaspora contains a spiritual component whose exile can be ended in a virtual, rather than physical homecoming. One can return to one's Jewish roots in many ways other than making Aliyah; by renewing or reinforcing a connection with one's Jewish identity. This Jewish bond takes many forms of commitment: participation in a Jewish organization, an increased or sustained level of Jewish worship, or tackling a Jewish project. The five interviewees in this work exhibit variations on this theme. Rochel Berman and Sibyl Silver have taken on life-changing projects, Jay Lauwick made a marital commitment to espouse the traditions of Judaism, Zmira Mozorosky (re) connected to the observant practices of her Babylonian family ancestors, and Isaac Jacob made Judaism a priority in his life decisions: not working on the Jewish Sabbath, marrying a Jewish woman and educating their sons in Jewish schools.

To continue in the vein of Boyarin and Boyarin, I would argue that though autochthony, a frequently used term of the Boyarin brothers, is an intrinsic part of the Jewish heritage, the connection between the people and the land provides an opportunity for (re)interpretation in every era according to individual circumstances and personal belief systems. These ideas are shown to be conflated by an etymological discussion of Rabbi Sacks on the term, *Tsiyun*/Zion. Though the word "Zion" is often used in context with "Mount Zion," an actual location in Jerusalem, throughout history it has also been used as a referent to the land of Israel. Rabbi Lord Jonathan Sacks explains that the word *tsiyun* means "signpost," used in the context of the message of the prophet Jeremiah, who "told the Jews of his generation who were going into exile that they should set up signposts (*tziyunim*) so that they would not forget the way back to Israel. The sages interpreted this to mean that they should not abandon Judaism. Zion is not just a place. It is a way of life . . . Zionism is a matter of not only *where* we live, but also *how* we live" (Sacks, *The Jonathan Sacks Hagaddah,* 52-3).

The idea of looking to the liberated land of Israel as a center even by Jews who are not intending to make Aliyah is not a new one. Before World War II, the late Rabbi Yisachar Shlomo Teichtal shared strong anti-Zionist views with many of his Orthodox colleagues. During the war he experienced what can only be termed an epiphany. While hiding out from the horrors of the Holocaust, he managed to write *Eim Habanim Semeichah*. Quoting external texts without access to references, he refuted his prior opinions:

> Now, even though all of Israel will not return right away, it seems to me that the Land will become a universal center for the entire Jewish nation, by the very fact that there will be an assembly of Jews in Jerusalem and Eretz Yisrael. Even those who remain in the diaspora will keep their eyes and hearts on the Land. They will be bound and connected with all their souls to the universal center, which will be established in Eretz Yisrael. It will unite them even in the Diaspora, and they will not be considered dispersed at all.

Sadly, the author of these prescient words did not live to see the founding of the state of Israel in 1948; he perished at the hands of the Nazis in early 1945. His vision of a diasporic population with members so united by Eretz Yisrael that they will not be considered dispersed describes a spiritual homecoming without borders, an early form of transnationalism, a term to be discussed in more detail later in the chapter.

Liturgical Models of Diaspora

As has been discussed, the idea of Jewish diasporic unity through a connection to the homeland echoes through many a prayer in the Jewish liturgy. Additionally, some prayers serve to bond together the scattered groups. Long before Benedict Anderson imagined his *Imagined Communities*, the Babylonian sages living after the close of the Talmudic period in 500 CE (Barnavi 65) composed two prayers which are referenced to this day as "Yekam Purkan." The name comes from the first two Hebrew words of each prayer, "May salvation arise," and asks for blessings to be bestowed on those individuals involved with educational and leadership positions in the pursuit of Torah studies in the land of Israel and in the Diaspora. Diaspora is referenced as Babylonia. "The original [Aramaic] text of the prayer has been maintained throughout the centuries of exile—even when the great masses of Jewry no longer lived in Babylonia. By extension, however this timeless prayer refers to all Jewish communities; the word Babylonia is a general term for all Jewish communities outside of Eretz Yisrael" (Scherman *The Complete Artscroll Siddur* 449). Though the liturgy contains many prayers for the restoration of the Temple along with a return to Jerusalem/Israel, this prayer in particular includes and unites the diasporic exiles who maintain their connection through a community involvement with the study of Torah, acknowledging the reality that the land of Israel is not the only locus in which a Torah-true Jew can reside. Life in diaspora can even act as more of a catalyst to Jewish observance, as shall be explored in the auto/biography of Zmira Mozorosky.

Living (Well) in Two Worlds: Transnationalism

I would not completely remove Zionism and a return to the land of Israel from the Jewish equation as do Boyarin and Boyarin; previously cited commentary of the 21st century can be seen as pointing the way towards a more transnationalistic existence, where boundaries are not so much erased as figuratively moved to create Homi Bhabha's "liminal space," in which the bicultural hybrid can live and thrive.

Attention must be paid to the uniquity of the (North) American experience; on some level, everyone in the United States, with the exception of the indigenous peoples, is descended from people who came from elsewhere, whether voluntarily or involuntarily. For the Jews, in contrast to their prior emigrations/immigrations, where they were ever the foreigners in a land of native citizens, this circumstance of the American experience allowed them not to be the eternally different unwelcome strangers. Combined with the unequalled freedom to participate fully in the educational and commercial opportunities that America offered, the great wave of 19th and 20th century immigrant Jews were able to thrive and grow while taking their (equal) place in society, a privilege so often denied to them in their wanderings from country to country. As with other citizens of the United States, American Jews have the option to move freely from country to country. If they choose to live part of the time in Israel, they can do so, without relinquishing their rights as American citizens. Additionally, the technology of the twenty-first century in which we find ourselves now living affords the opportunity to travel great distances speedily and safely, easing the path for living in two countries: transnationalism through technology. One of the narrative subjects, Zmira Mozorosky, who divides her time between Israel and the United States, prides herself on enjoying the country in which she finds herself. Her view is echoed by West Indian author George Lamming, a resident of London, who remarks in "The Pleasures of Exile" that "The pleasure and paradox of my own exile is that I belong wherever I am" (Ashcroft 18).

In light of this increasingly familiar state for so many inhabitants in the world of the 21st century, Stéphane Dufoix has proposed a more nuanced analysis of transnationalism through "the

consideration of four ideal types that involve the structuring of
the collective experience abroad 'centroperipheral,' 'enclaved,'
'atopic,' and 'antagonistic' (Dufoix 62). For clarification, he rep-
resents the four models through a chart, to the end of a clearer
understanding of the phenomenon's aspects. He explains that in
the usage of the word "transnational," the concepts of "nation"
and "state" are often conflated, confusing meaning and understanding of the peoples/movements it seeks to represent. Dufoix'
analysis of the Jewish diaspora in the context of the four models
notes a change in mode after the founding of modern Israel, reinforcing the dichotomy between the new state-centric stance and
"all the groups for whom the essence of Jewish identity lay in
exile and dispersion." He continues, "This belief has survived
the creation of the State of Israel, notably within a current of
thought called diasporist" (Dufoix 69). Perhaps the 21st century
will see the coinage of the analogous term "transnationalist,"
along with further theoretical exploration and application in that
diasporic direction. Hugo of St. Victor, a twelfth-century monk
from Saxony, expresses a diasporic notion of transcending nationalism: "The man who finds his homeland sweet is still a ten-
der beginner; he to whom every soil is as his native one is already strong, but he is perfect to whom the entire world is a foreign land" (Ashcroft 441-42).

Conclusion

In order to supply the necessary background information to
the life narratives, this chapter has analyzed the concept of Jewish diaspora from several standpoints: linguistic, religious, historical, literary, liturgical, philosophical, theoretical, and political. It has presented its subject in great detail in order to situate
the five auto/biographical narratives along the historical continuum of an exilic experience spanning over four millennia. A full
understanding of the concepts and history associated with the
many aspects of the Jewish diaspora is essential in order to un-

derstand the five contemporary narratives as well as the men and women who live through them. These connections will be discussed within the chapters focusing on the individual narratives.

I choose to give the last word to Israeli art critic Itamar Levy. His comment appeared in the Boca Raton Museum of Art curator notes accompanying Izhar Patkin's installation "You Tell Us What To Do, a cinematic montage depicting diasporic events leading up to the 1948 founding of Israel. Levy observes, "Who among us does not live in several time zones, in several places, straddling different cultures, languages, history and mythology?"

Chapter 3
Methodology

T he modern diasporic auto/biographies are represented by an audio/visual recording of each subject's life narrative interview, based on answers to a questionnaire, which appears later in this chapter. Answers can form a chronological life story outline, with specific sections on family ancestry, childhood, love/marriage, career, children/grandchildren, relationship to Judaism vis-à-vis the Jewish State and words of wisdom for future generations, as well as questions on hobbies, travel, and health issues. Questions were designed to jog a subject's memory to provide an opportunity to share life details with present and future generations, especially information about earlier generations, preserving memories which might be known only to the interviewee.

Along with all the issues unique to the genre of written auto/biography (the past "I," the present "I," the "I" of the narrative, the oral/testimonial aspect of these life narratives should be addressed; especially the role and influence of the facilitator. The role can be problematical if the interviewer/facilitator "leads the witness," so to speak. As the interviewer, I saw my role as one of support in the process of eliciting information from the interviewee, especially helping to locate a sought-for word in English for those subjects for whom English was not their native tongue.

During the filming of the interview, the photographer and the interviewer function as a live audience. The interviewee experiences the immediacy of direct reception to his/her spoken words, a circumstance which can have varying ramifications. It can elicit a more animated delivery, both verbally and non-verbally, or, it can inhibit the subject from sharing information with people (interviewer, photographer) who may be simply acquaintances, rather than close friends or family. In the course of conducting life story interviews through my business with family, close friends, and "simply" acquaintances, I have found that whatever the association, in the course of the process the trio of interviewer, photographer and interviewee develop a closer relationship engendered by the experience of sharing intimate details of one's life story. In the telling and the listening, a bond is formed, analogous to the circumstance of sitting next to what was a stranger on an airplane who shares his/her life story; no longer a stranger, but a new-found friend. The interview is actually enhanced by the subject's motivation to share his/her life narrative, much like the stranger on the plane.

Though the stranger on the plane and the interviewees featured share some characteristics, they are differentiated what I have found to be a virtually essential part of the process—the written responses to the questionnaire/outline. The process of writing unleashes the floodgates of memory, allowing the interviewee to retrieve a reservoir of otherwise inaccessible material. It also provides the interviewer with important referential data, i.e., dates, names, loci, with which to prompt the interviewee to elicit accurate information.

Accuracy of information becomes an issue in the area of historical testimony. Reflections on past political rather than personal circumstances should be regarded as subjective, rather than objective. Even if the interview's purpose is to create a record of personal family history details, rather than a historical account of events, the product can only be enhanced with corroboration from reliable outside sources; newspaper reports, photographs, film, published and critically reviewed eye witness accounts, correspondence, etc.

What follows is the questionnaire/outline which acted as the basis and springboard for the interviews:

Heritage Biography International Questionnaire

A. Roots

1. What is your name?
2. Nickname? Jewish name?
3. What was your father's name?
4. Occupation?
5. When was he born? When did he die? How did he die?
6. What are some of your memories of him?
7. Did you know his parents? (your paternal grandparents)
8. What were their names? Nationalities? Occupations?
9. What was your mother's name? Maiden name?
10. Mother's date of birth? Death? Cause of death? Memories of her? What did she look like?
11. Did you know her parents? (your maternal grandparents)
12. Did you have aunts and uncles? Names, dates of birth/death, occupations, origins, fond memories?
11. How about brothers and sisters? Brothers-in-law? Sisters-in-law? Cousins?

B. "This Is Your Life"

1. When/where were you born?
2. What is your earliest memory?
3. Where have you lived?
4. Tell something about your first years at school. (location, size, public/private, teachers)
5. Tell something about your childhood and how times were different from today.
6. Where did you go to high school? When did you graduate? Who were your friends?
7. What was your first job? How much did it pay? What other work did you do?
8. Where did you go to college? Why? When did you graduate? How did you finance your education?

9. Tell us how you got your more advanced degrees. (M.D., Ph.D.)

C. Love and Marriage

1. Where and when did you meet your spouse? Was it love at first sight?
2. Tell us something about your courtship. When and where did you get married?
3. Where did you go for your honeymoon? Where did you set up married life?

D. Military Experience

1. When did you start? Were you drafted? Did you enlist?
2. What branch of the armed forces were you in? Where were you stationed? What was your closest call? Did you emotionally/intellectually reference any part of your family's diasporic history?
3. When were you discharged?

Children

1. How did you pick your children's names? Any unusual circumstances of their births?
2. Tell the story of the day each one was born. Who do your children look like? Are there any traits in them that you saw in your parents, siblings, or other relatives?

E. On the Streets Where You've Lived/Career Moves

1. List all your addresses in chronological order, also telling where you worked at that time.
2. Share some highlights of your career.
3. When did you retire? What are you doing now?

F. Travels

1. Recount some of the places you have been.
2. Best trip? Worst trip?

G. Health

1. Operations?
2. Allergies?
3. Life-threatening diseases?

4. Chronic illnesses?

5. Mental health issues?

I. Religion /Israel

1. How would you describe your affiliation with Judaism? (Orthodox, Reform, Conservative, Traditional, secular, cultural, familial)

2. Have you ever encountered any anti-Semitism in your public or personal life?

3. Has your outlook on/practice of religion changed in the course of your life? How and why?

4. What is the role/influence/function of Judaism in your life?

5. Recount any special religious celebrations or family holiday rituals from your childhood.

6. What role does the existence of the state of Israel play in your life?

7. Have you ever lived in Israel or plan to make *Aliyah?* If so, what do you like/dislike about life in Israel?

8. Do you have family in Israel? How/why did they make the move?

9. Describe the igniting of your Jewish spark. How has it affected your own view of your place in Jewish American culture?

10. What do you see as the future of Judaism in America and in Israel?

J. Words of Wisdom

Expound on your philosophy of life. If you could communicate with the generations to come, what advice would you give them to help meet life's challenges?

K. Meaningful Mementos

List and organize any cherished certificates, keepsakes, china, jewelry, art, memorabilia that you wish to display and explain.

L. Favorite Things

Share your preference of poem/book/color/movie/song/food/actor/flower/author/number

M. Hobbies

Show and tell about your arts and crafts avocations, i.e.; knitting, crocheting, sewing, woodworking. Display and explain your collections; coins, china, posters, art. Share the story behind the object; how it was acquired, and why it's special in and of itself and/or to you.

N. For Posterity

Communicate any special requests to family and friends regarding memorial services, bequests, directives, etc. (When your family/friends view this, they will be able to consult with you to make certain they understand and so will be able to honor your wishes.)

Chapter 4
Found in Diaspora: Iraqi Tales of
Two Thousand and One Millennia

W hether part of the Babylonian Empire, the Persian Empire, or the Ottoman Empire, a Jewish presence endured in Iraq. The Jews there spoke to one another in a unique language that they had developed: a Judeo- Arabic dialect, written in Hebrew. Those Iraqi Jewish ancestors who survived the genocidal edict of Haman nearly 2500 years ago would have received the missives of Esther and Mordecai, who wrote to the satraps, governors of the one hundred twenty-seven of Persian provinces "to each province in its own script, and each people in its own language, and to the Jews in their own script and language" (Esther 8:9), implying that the message would have been sent to the ancient Iraqi Jews in their own Judeo-Arabic dialect.

Between 1781 and 1817, Sheikh Sassoon, president of the Jewish community in Baghdad, was chief treasurer of the Ottoman pashas. Sassoon was a member of the Sassoon family, known as "the Rothchilds of the East," who rose to great fame and affluence in India and directed an enormous commercial empire from Bombay (Barnavi 178).

Ezra Jacob, the father of interviewee Isaac Jacob, became part of this same Sassoon commercial enterprise when he began to work for them in Bombay in the late 1800s, and was later sent by the Sassoon family to Shanghai, where Isaac's parents met, married and raised their family. During their time in Shanghai, World War I saw the end of the Ottoman Empire. In 1948, Iraq was under British mandate when Isaac and his family left

Shanghai, which generated their British/Iraqi passports. They were supplied with visas by an Israeli government representative, leaving Shanghai the month before the Communist takeover)

The travel trajectory of the Jacob family, from Baghdad to Shanghai to Israel to England and the United States, removed them from the anti-Semitic events which took place in Iraq following their departure: the Farhud in 1941, the enforced exodus of the majority of the Jewish population in the early 1950s, not to mention the public execution of nine Iraqi Jews in 1969, which caused most of the rest of the 2500 Jews to leave. More detail on these events will be found concerning the diasporic auto/biography interviewee Zmira Mozorosky, a woman from Iraq whose family left hastily in 1951 after earlier persecutions.

Chapter 5
Shanghai Breezes:
The Isaac Jacob Life Narrative

The life story of Isaac Jacob holds several of the diasporic characteristics cited by diaspora scholar and author Robin Cohen. Their application and explanation will offer important synergies between theory and practice, resulting in a fuller understanding of the family's journey.

Isaac Jacob's maternal grandfather was able to leave Iraq because he had an attractive job offer in Bombay from the Sassoon family, who also was responsible for the subsequent move to Shanghai, illustrating Cohen's ninth characteristic of "expansion from a homeland for work, trade or colonial ambitions" (Cohen 17).

Isaac's father Ezra left Bagdad not solely for work reasons; he wanted to avoid conscription. Isaac relates:

> IJ: Iraq was under the Ottoman, the Turkish Empire, and they wanted to conscript all young people into the army probably at 16, so he had to leave. His brother left before him, and his father had passed away I don't know when in Bagdad, and his mother was still alive, and they all moved to Bombay and then to Shanghai. The brother moved there first and then he told his brother, told him to come . . . IJ: They had a potential job at ED Sassoon company. They were a very, very wealthy Jewish Bagdadian Jews who came there in the 1850s and established very big businesses, actually importing opium and exporting . . . goods, like cotton goods, a tremendous job.

Half a century after Isaac Jacob's father Ezra left Iraq for India, Isaac and his brothers left Israel for the United States for the same reason: "Expansion from a homeland for work, trade . . . " (Cohen 17).

Israeli bureaucracy inhibited business growth of the Jacob radio store/repair shop:

> IJ: We opened this radio store—the red tape is so . . . They used to come to the store and check all the radios—checked for the excise tax, a red tag, and if it didn't have a red tag, they would confiscate the radio. For instance, there was no tape recorder at that time; we had a wire recorder. That was the first kind of recorder that came out in the fifties. The recording is made on a very thin steel wire. We didn't have tape recorders, a wire recorder . . . the tape is made . . . we had that from Shanghai and they said where is the excise tax? [we said] We don't have it; we got it from Shanghai. [they said] Well, we'll have to confiscate it . . . That's what killed everything, my outlook on Israel.

When Isaac's brothers began the family's emigration, the United States was an attractive destination because of the brothers' fluency in spoken and written English acquired from their British schooling in Shanghai. Isaac also related that the siblings always spoke to each other in English. English could be considered the primary language of that generation of Isaac's family, although conversations with his father were a bilingual mélange: his father spoke to him in Judeo-Arabic, which Isaac could understand better than he could speak it, and Isaac answered his father in English, which his father could understand better than he could speak it.

Though they may have been scattered across the globe, Jews from Iraq always thought of themselves as part of a distinct entity. Cohen cites the diasporic characteristic of "a strong ethnic group consciousness sustained over a long time based on a common history/fate" (Cohen 17), which describes the mindset of Isaac's family.

The Iraqi Sephardic Jews were just such a closely knit community, within and without Iraq. In Shanghai as in Bombay, they lived near each other, worshipped together and married one another. When relatives from Iraq/Bombay visited their Shanghai cousins, engagements would often result, as took place with Isaac's family.

Memory of a common history/fate is forefronted by the assistance of the Shanghai Iraqi Jewish community to the Jewish refugees during World War II. Isaac describes their plight:

> IJ: We were not in the same areas as the refugees that came, the refugees from Europe and all the other refugees that came. They had houses where they could find houses. Then with the instigation of the Germans, who came to the Japanese authorities, they tried to convince the Japanese authorities that all these refugees who had escaped—they wanted to annihilate them. The Japanese authorities refused. They compromised. They said they would intern them in the ghettos. They didn't say Jews, they said all who came between 1937-9 would have to move into this ghetto and this was, it was a very dilapidated place. It was near the Japanese occupation section part of China, where these people had to go the housing was impossible, ten families cramped into one house, dysentery, typhoid, all kinds of diseases. There was one person, one Japanese official in charge of giving the visas to exit the area. He was a very nasty person. They had a hard time trying to get out, to do business . . . She [my mother] was the kindest person, very, very kind. She tried to help everyone, against my father's wishes.

With the arrival of Ashkenazi Eastern European Jews fleeing the Holocaust, Sephardic Shanghai Jews offered essential assistance to the newcomers, making it possible for them to survive the harsh conditions of Japanese occupation. Though the needy Jews were not Sephardic or Iraqi, the universalism/shared Jewish identity, forged by the bond of membership in *klal Yisroel*, the Jewish people, superseded the particularism of any individual cultural subset. At great personal expense, the resident Iraqi Jewish community provided those snatched from the fires of the

Holocaust whatever was needed for survival, a proud moment of *Yichud,* or Jewish unity.

Having lived through the troublesome years of Japanese occupation during World War II, the Jacob family now faced another looming crisis: the impending Chinese communist takeover of Shanghai, which motivated the Jacobs family to resettle. They left for Israel, ending the diaspora of over two millennia.

The state of Israel was established in May of 1948, the existence of which made it possible for the Jacob family to make *Aliyah* in April of 1949, just one month before the Communist takeover in May, 1949. A family member, Rose Jacob, remarked on the fortuitous timing: What if the years had been reversed and the Communist takeover had occurred in1948 and the state of Israel had been established in 1949? The wheel of fortune in the diasporic lottery had spun propitiously in their favor; a person of faith would see *hashgacha pratis,* divine providence, in the equation. The Japanese Occupation and the anticipated Communist takeover of Shanghai perfectly illustrate another of Cohen's diasporic characteristics: "a troubled relationship with host societies/lack of acceptance/possibility of another calamity" (Cohen 17).

The journey to Israel from Shanghai involved an ocean voyage to San Francisco followed by a cross-country train ride to Ellis Island before proceeding to Israel. Isaac relates the circumstances of their journey:

IJ: From China, we landed in San Francisco and took a train to New York. It took 4and 1/2 to five days. It was a sealed train; the windows were not open more than an inch or inch and a half. The FBI agents, many, many FBI agents in the cars to make sure that nobody gets off the train. They used to count at night to make sure that everyone was there. One day my brother was fed up with sitting on the chair to sleep, so he decided to find a place where he could sleep horizontally, so he went to the baggage car on top of the baggage and to sleep. The agents came at night, and realized

one person was missing. They asked us who it was, and I said my
brother was sleeping in the baggage car. They were very angry.
We got to New York and we went on a small boat to Ellis Island,
we were there for four or five days, the immigration center. We
were grateful to be there because we hadn't had any kosher food
for a very long time, and the Jewish Agency brought us kosher
food. So we were very appreciative of that kosher food after five
days.

From Ellis Island, the family proceeded on to Israel via Italy:

> IJ: We went from Ellis Island on a ship from NY to Italy. We land-
> ed on the west coast of Italy, a city called Tradi. We stayed in Italy
> for two to three weeks. They were processing us to see if we had
> any illnesses, contagious diseases just to make sure there was no-
> body sick going to Israel . . . My father had eye problems, glauco-
> ma, so my father had to get treated for glaucoma and my brother
> stayed behind with him. We went from Italy to Israel landed in
> Haifa, Haifa port. The authorities came on board. They found I was
> almost 18; they said, "We need everybody in the army—you're go-
> ing to be in the army right away!" So, they separated me from my
> family and took me to an army base.

Isaac served in the Israeli Army for two years. (His mother
didn't know where he was stationed for nearly two weeks.) He
has a picture of himself in a cap modeled on one worn by members of the French Foreign Legion; replaced shortly after by the
still-worn Israeli army beret.

An overview of the Jacob family saga perfectly illustrates
the last of Cohen's nine characteristics: "the possibility of a distinctive creative, enriching life in host countries with a tolerance
for pluralism" (Cohen 17).

The Jacob family grew and prospered in Iraq, India, England
and the United States. The post-Shanghai generations include
physicians and rabbis, who took advantage of the educational
opportunities open to them in pluralistically tolerant host societies. Very few family members live in Israel, but those living

elsewhere continue to maintain a strong connection with Israel; visiting often, attending school/seminary as well as keeping open the possibility of *Aliyah*, or emigration. Isaac's sons and their families are Sabbath observant; Isaac and his one of his sons live close to one another in the same community, within walking distance to their local synagogue. They are able to celebrate Shabbat and the holidays together. Their pluralistic synagogue holds both Ashkenazi and Sephardic *minyanim*/services, so they have the opportunity to *daven*/pray in the Sephardic tradition, in keeping with the Iraqi custom. He describes an Iraqi custom that the family keeps in the Passover Seder to this day:

> IJ: Well the way that we celebrate the Passover. Before we said the Manishtana the young kids, the Israelites when they left Egypt they tied it on their back, and before Manishtana, we went out. We knocked on the door. My father said, "Who's there?" and we said "Israelim." Where did you come from? Mitzrayim. We came inside and then we said the Manishtana. . . . I try to do it with the kids.

It is interesting to note that the Jacob family saga also contains several diasporic characteristics found in the Esther story. The two families share a common Mesopotamian locale, if several centuries apart, which might account for the similarities. Esther's family lived in the time of the Persian Empire and Isaac's family lived in the time of the Ottoman Empire, which placed both under the rule of a dominating power. The word for ruler, *pasha,* shares Old Persian and Turkish roots. There are also commonalities of loci and population.

Jewish Spark/Esther Moment

Within the paradigmatic story of Esther, the example of her relative Mordecai had been forefronted to subsequent diasporic populations for his loyalty to the tenets of his Jewish faith: when ordered to bow down to Haman, he refused, on the grounds that a Jew bows down only to God, certainly not to a mere mortal.

Even when Mordecai's refusal led to Haman's genocidal edict, he did not waver.

Though not as dire, a synergy can be found in Isaac's decision not to take a job that would require him to work on Saturday, the Jewish Sabbath, even for a higher position and an increased wage:

> IJ: Of course it's challenging, because looking for a job, saying you're not going to work on Shabbat, you're not going to work on the holidays. For instance, I worked in a place and somebody came, there was a salesman, and he said, "I can give you a better job, because I'm going to be a supervisor in this new plant." Great. He told me what my salary was and I was looking forward to getting a bigger salary. So he invited me for an interview and I went to the interview. He liked what I was saying. I did repairs for the machinery, the quip, photo equipment, the printing things, some. So he said, "The biggest day is Saturday when we do all the repairs." "Uh, oh," I said, "I don't work on Saturdays." So he said, "Sorry, I can't hire you.

Isaac's sons continue to carry on the tradition of observance. One of them became a rabbi. Isaac felt no pressure to assimilate/not observe Shabbat; for him, as for Mordecai, it was not even an option.

Isaac's "Esther moment" took the form of a sustained commitment to an observant, Torah-based Orthodox lifestyle. Family loyalty was paramount in both the Jacob family and the Benjamite descendants, Esther and Mordecai. In his interview, when he was asked to speak "words of wisdom," Isaac Jacob said that family was the most important thing in life; shown by being close to them and ready to help out when needed. Isaac relates this guiding principal of family loyalty:

> IJ: Well, The main thing is to stay with the family, to communicate, not fight with family, get angry; just be cordial with your family and family is the most important thing to think about.

So, too, Mordecai kept a watchful eye on Esther when she was in the king's palace, inquiring daily after her. Esther also kept an eye out for Mordecai; when she heard that he had rent his clothes and was wearing sackcloth and ashes, she sent him new clothing and sought to inquire as to the cause of his distress. Additionally, Isaac advises,

> IJ: Just to be very strong and think of the future. You see, you know time will be better, like they say in Israel, y'hiye tov, it will be good.

Within the saga of Esther, language proficiency plays a crucial part. Mordecai's facility with understanding several languages for his position as a member of the Sanhedrin enables him to foil a plot against the king's life: the conspirators were speaking aloud to each other in public in their native tongue, thinking that no one would be able to understand them; Mordecai did, and reported them to the authorities. Isaac's family spoke Iraqi, which allowed them to communicate with family members across the generations and miles. In Shanghai, Isaac went to English-speaking schools run by the colonial British authorities, as well as learning Chinese and Hebrew. When it came time to emigrate from Shanghai to Israel, the family was equipped to speak to Iraqi Jewish émigrés, as well as residents who had learned English when what would become Israel was governed by Britain from the end of World War I to 1948 statehood. Their proficiency in English which the Jacob family had learned in Shanghai stood them well when they emigrated to the United States and England. Isaac explains his schooling in Shanghai:

> IJ: It was in English, because it was sort of a British school. They had two exams, there was 6th form and six upper. In 6th form, they had an exam not from the school, from Cambridge University, in England. You went to an auditorium. You went to a special auditorium; they opened a package, a special [package].

Isaac relates a World War II memory from his high school days:

IJ: My brothers had cars, but in the Second World War, from 1941 to 1945 you couldn't get any gas. I went to school opposite a military camp, occupied by US soldiers before 1941, the Marines there, a big base. They knew that the war was coming, so they left. I don't know exactly when they left, but the Japanese Army took it over. My school was right across the street from this base. I used to watch from my window of the school. The way they trained was amazing. They used a wooden rifle, the same size and weight of a rifle.

When Isaac was in his 80s, he went back to Shanghai with his son, Marty. According to his family, he was treated like "a rock star." With the help of a Jewish woman they met at a Friday night Sabbath dinner at the local Chabad House, Isaac was able to locate some of his childhood sites:

IJ: The first thing I tried was to look at my house, where I had lived for seventeen, eighteen years. We went to the area there, and we were looking, and it started to rain we were going in that area, I knew it was in that area and we were walking around and I couldn't find anything, I couldn't find it, we were walking around and I couldn't find anything. Then we went to Chabad, there was a Sephardic Chabad, we had dinner there, it was very great, the first meal we had and it was a real good meal. A couple of people were serving; there was a Jewish guy and his wife, they were serving, they were working for the Chabad. We ate there two nights in this Chabad, and Marty got very friendly with the guy. So Marty said, "Maybe we should go out for a beer together." So we left the group, the group left, or whatever, they went back to the hotel and we stayed with this couple. . . . We couldn't find the house. So this woman said, "I'll find it for you." She ordered the Uber to come and took us to this area, and she speaks Chinese, obviously. . . . So she went to the corner, almost where I lived and there was a forty-story Four Seasons Hotel there near where I lived. So she went to the guards in the hotel and she spoke to them in Chinese and she said to them that they had a house where seven houses were attached and she explained to them. They said, "Oh we remember that. It was knocked down and they built a garden in the area."

At that point, Isaac and his son left the tour for a day so they could go exactly where they wanted in order to revisit places from Isaac's life in Shanghai:

> IJ: Yes, so we decided not to continue with the tour for one day. We hired actually a tour guide to take us where WE wanted to go. So we went to the school. And everything besides the school that I went to from kindergarten to twelfth grade was still standing there and the shule that I went to was still standing there. We tried to go into the shule, and they said "You can't go." So the guide she spoke to them. She said, "He was here," so they said, "Okay, you can go walk outside, you can't go inside." So we went to the shule. That's where Hillary Clinton when she went to China, she visited the shule . . . They said they made it into a museum, a museum for the past Jewish life. Chabad uses it once a year for Rosh Hashanah and Yom Kippur; they allow them to come and use it.

They also saw the school, a school no longer where Isaac (re)shared a high school memory that had made it difficult to pay attention to his studies:

> IJ: No, it's a government business. I was telling Marty and the group that we went with, the private [tour] that my classroom when I was a student there was overlooking the street and across the street previously was an American Marine barracks. So when the Japanese took over Shanghai, they had their army base there in this place. And I used to watch from the window how the Japanese used to train, with bayonets, make believe bayonets, made of wood. They really tried all out to kill the other guy. They had masks, like real fighting . . . And now there's a Starbucks café in that area.

There were a few areas which he found visually unchanged:

> IJ: there's an area called the "Bund." The Bund is an industrial place where very, very big buildings were built, huge, huge solid stone buildings. One of the buildings was built, was a hotel, by the Sassoon family, the Sassoon was a Sephardic banking family. . . . so, they were very wealthy. So they built this hotel on the Bund,

it's a unique kind of building, many, many rooms, a unique structure. . . . They changed the name, they made it the Peace Hotel
they called it now. Also the Bund which was founded in Shanghai,
a Hong Kong and Shanghai banking company. There was HSBC,
you know, HSBC was founded in Shanghai, and the building is
still there.

Though Isaac didn't meet anyone from his childhood or any of
their descendants, he did get to speak his no-longer-in-current-
use Shanghai Chinese vernacular:

> IJ: on this private tour, she [the Jewish woman from Chabad] took
> us to a Confucius Temple; Confucius is one of [the gurus, the main
> people]. I saw a janitor who was sweeping the floor and I asked
> him in Chinese, I thought that maybe he might know, and it turned
> that he understood me, and we were conversing. He understood
> what I was saying, and he was laughing his head off, because he
> couldn't believe a foreigner could speak [Chinese].

Isaac's trip to China illustrates a diasporic experience termed a
"pilgrimage," where the diasporic subject revisits the scene of a
forced departure, often with family. (Holocaust survivors usually
visit the loci of their childhood, as well as concentration camps
where they had been interned.) The pilgrimage provides a form
of closure, especially by sharing the experience with descendants. No longer just a memory, they have found their way back
to what once was their home. Being brought full circle to their
geographical origins gives perspective to reflect on the diasporic
journey as destination.

Chapter 6

By the Waters of Babylon:
The Zmira Mozorosky Narrative

Befor delving into the complex topic of diasporic synergies in Zmira's narrative journey, an overview of the tripartite Jewish population model is relevant. Two thousand years after the Babylonian exile, the wandering Jews found themselves literally all over the world. Some Jewish populations fleeing the marauding Crusaders of Western Europe, especially in parts of Germany and France, made their way to the less politically hostile climes of Eastern Europe, especially Poland and Russia, where they remained until the upheaval of the Holocaust and World War II. This demographic group came to be known as *Ashkenazi,* or Eastern (European) Jews.

In 1492, the Spanish Inquisition mandated an expulsion of Jews from Spain, which led them to flee to Turkey and parts of North Africa; i.e., Morocco, Tunisia, Algeria. Members of this group are referenced by the term *Sephardic,* or Spanish Jews.

A third group draws its name from the geographical locus of the Babylonian/Persian empire which they continued to occupy from the time of Nebuchadnezzar's forced exile more than five hundred years B.C.E. until World War II and the (re)establishment of the Jewish state in 1948. These Jews, originating from what is known as modern-day Iraq and Iran, are called *Mizrachi*, or the Jews of the East.

Beginning with the early 20th century Zionist movement and extending to the establishment of the state of Israel, Ashkenazi members occupied leadership roles and positions in the newly formed government. The prevailing attitude at the time towards the Sephardic and Mizrachi populations considered their Middle Eastern culture inferior to its more "Westernized" counterpart, a sentiment that is still being addressed and redressed to this day. East and West were vying in the Jewish world in the same Orientalist vein that Edward Said claimed for fields like anthropology and archaeology. In their zeal to create a modern society, the founders of the new state of Israel were determined to assimilate the new citizens into a culture of non-observant kibbutzim, an alien reality for the Mizrachi population.

The Bagdadians felt themselves part of a long, illustrious line of Jews. Zmira explains the heritage which she felt the Ashkenazi leaders did not appreciate:

> Yes, it's Iraq, Bagdad, Avraham Avinu, it's Ur Kasdim, it is Abu Talmud Bavli, it is the dynasty of David HaMelech, Rosh Galuta, and all this, all this was, although the Persian did take over afterward . . . But we were the "Al naharot Bavel, sham yahshavnu v'gam bachanu"/When they asked us to sing the song of the field, they cut their thumbs, and they say it as a bracha which you say on Shabbat, Shir Hama'alot, but really there's a weekday [song] to say before you say the bracha, "Al naharot Bavel, sham yashavnu v'gam bachanu,b'zochranu b'Zion"—so since then, they live in this place. How many Sifrei Torah was written, how many Rabbonim came out, the culture. The holidays were really holidays— what I remember from Pesach, Sukkot, and all this, nobody in our time, my children or grandchildren, they don't experience that. There's no way they could experience how we lived with my Saba and everything, before Pesach and achanot. So to them, to go to Kibbutz and everything gets wiped, who has the right to do that? You know, many times the Israelis talk about *k'fiadatit*, like you force the religion on them, but you really did a *k'fiadatit* in the worst way, to your parents, first of all you left the tradition, and you broke their heart, and now you take people who are not even prepared to understand what you're doing, and really *kufim Aleichem*, to be like without all this wealth, like the tradition/wealth that they came with. Who gives you this right? Who has a right to do that? Nothing was recognized in our culture, something we had to forget quickly and blend.

The issue of the thousands of immigrants from Arab lands is currently a hot topic which has generated a spate of books and films, which requires its own thorough discussion which time and space do not permit here. Among the issues being discussed is the possibility of reparations. When they fled Iraq due to the government repercussions following the establishment of the Jewish state, the Iraqi refugees arrived in Israel penniless, leaving behind millions of dollars in assets confiscated as Arab state property. Nearly seventy years later, the problem has only recently been addressed by the Israeli government; restitution is still pending.

Seven-year-old Zmira and her family were among the 140,000 Jews who were forced to leave Iraq between 1948 and 1960. Though they were returning after a 2,500 year absence to Israel, the land of their ancestors, their experience bore the earmarks of a diasporic dispersal rather than a return, or homecoming. (Of course, the exception proves the rule: Zmira's mother, an avowed Zionist, insisted on going (back) to Israel rather than Iran or Turkey, even though it meant great financial hardship; she happily adjusted to any and all adverse circumstances in the new Jewish state.)

Though the family's immigration to Israel ended a 2500 year diaspora, their emigration from Iraq, a place they had lived for all those years, was a secondary diaspora as well as a return. Looking at the Fetaya/Khalif family's departure from Iraq through the prism of Robin Cohen's common features of diaspora yields interesting synergies:

1) Traumatic dispersal: The family's dispersal was traumatic: their financial resources and property were confiscated by the Iraqi government, and they were forcibly expelled. The expulsion was made even more traumatic by the radical change in living accommodations. Zmira explains the circumstances:

> Jews did not feel anymore safe. And when you see somebody who is so established, suddenly packing and leaving, and this one is

missing, so the government of Iraq said like this: "Whoever wants to go to Filestine (Palestine) has to register. By the way, we were called "traitor" by then. And then, whenever you registered, you basically give up your passport and citizenship. One Shabbat, when the registration was like, exhausted, was like, slowed down, they closed the registration. One Shabbat, my uncle comes home and says like that to my mother, "Do you know this table? It's not yours. Do you know this silver spoon? It's not yours." She says, "What are you talking about?" The news came, already, on Shabbat, they did it on Shabbat because the Iraqis knew very well Jewish people would not desecrate Shabbat. So, one Shabbat, they put a stamp on every business, the houses didn't belong to us. We heard after we left, that it turned into a local hospital, that's how big it was. Anything in the house, nobody wanted to buy anything, because it's theirs anyway. I would like some time to describe or find some house like that, I didn't find yet, I found something similar in Or Yehuda that described a little bit what a house in Iraq was, in the museum. Anyway, my mother comes to Israel after this, after going through such—devastation. Some people committed suicide. In a matter of 3-4 hours—they had a tent—who lives in a tent? No running water. Some people committed that because they couldn't handle it. No language, nothing. And then it was a whole different thing.

2) A collective memory/myth about the homeland (history, achievement)

Iraqi Jews pride themselves on their success in government and business and are united by their common memories of prominence and prosperity.

3) A strong ethnic group consciousness based on a common history/fate.

The Mizrachi Jews of Iraq consider themselves a special subset with customs and traditions all their own as well as unique shared experiences.

4) A troubled relationship with host societies/lack of acceptance: Being regarded as "second class" in Israel initiated resettlement in the United States.

5) A sense of empathy and co-responsibility with co-ethnic members in other countries of settlement: Zmira's close Iraqi friends whom she met in the United States have become like family, much more than acquaintances. Their shared heritage forms an instant, automatic bond of understanding.

These examples allow the conclusion to be drawn that, under certain circumstances, the departure from a diasporic locus can take on the characteristics of a diasporic dispersal, even if returning to the country of origin. This conclusion is especially relevant to modern diasporic populations whose younger members, born in the diaspora, are more familiar with the adopted country's culture than that of their parents' country of origin.

As Zmira relates, when they arrived in Israel, the Iraqi immigrants were housed in makeshift tents before being moved to newly-built tin huts. Extended families that had lived under the same roof for generations were housed far away from one another and long-standing neighbors, intentionally dismantling the communal infrastructure as well as communities of worship. (Sabbath observance required synagogues to be within walking distance; in Iraq neighbors would worship together at a nearby facility.) Hastily built schools with barely qualified instructors only reinforced her acquired feelings of inferiority as a "second class" citizen; Mizrachi as opposed to Ashkenazi. These feelings propelled her to continue her diasporic journey to the United States, where she would be recognized as equal to other Israelis. As she explains, her positive experiences in the US also engendered a return to the age-old religious traditions of her ancestors, ending a spiritual diaspora brought on by the family's forced exodus from Iraq:

In contrast to the first diaspora/return to the original homeland, Zmira's second diaspora, a voluntary move, exemplifies at least two of Cohen's common features of diaspora:

6) A troubled relationship with host societies/lack of acceptance/possibility of another calamity: (Cohen 17)

At the heart and soul of Zmira's decision to leave Israel for America was her feeling of being treated as a "second-class" citizen, ironic in a country founded to provide a safe harbor for a population that has faced a lack of acceptance/rejection and the more threating reality of a(nother) calamity throughout its long diasporic history.

7) The possibility of a distinctive creative, enriching life in host countries with a tolerance for pluralism (Cohen 17):

During its first decade, the new state of Israel's treatment and attitude towards Iraqi/Jews reveals a regrettable "intolerance" for pluralism, which in turn diminished the opportunity to pursue a fulfilling, productive life. This timely issue is all too relevant in a world of fleeing migratory populations where a direct causal relationship can be seen between the opportunity to rebuild one's life and the acceptance of the host country. Zmira also contrasted the worldly environment created in Jewish Bagdad homes from family members being employed all over the world to her perception of the Ashkenazi environment:

> I feel pity for people who came from a certain place, they were not as open like the Bagdadian, they went to India, they went to China, they went to this, and there are people all over the world, like if somebody had eight boys, eight children, and it happened, and they lived in Japan, or they lived in China, in the British Empire, they sent a child to England, and one in Switzerland, and one in India, and one everywhere—they were Empire, they didn't have to do any paperwork—do you understand how they grew up? All our house was full of China, of food, of things that come from India. What did they know of in Europe? They couldn't even talk loud, because next door is the cardboard wall, and you were afraid from the goyim, and you were suppressed by the goyim, and feel afraid and whatever. The Enlightenment—they want to be like goyim. We want to be like goyim? The goy [would] shake my hand from my father and make a business for half a million dollars, nothing signed, he would say, "I trust you, you are ibnes Sabbat." [son of Sabbath; expression for a Jewish person]

The Jews were highly respected by the Iraqi Muslims. Zmira continues:

> ZM: Yes, so the goyim had respect for us. So which Jew want to be a Muslim? Which Jew want to be an Arab? So we—and also they [the Jews] had very key positions in Bagdad. I remember that one time that somebody said not only that.the treasurer of Bagdad was a Jew, but they insisted that he would be a Jew. I mean, I [haven't] researched this, this is something I heard, I mean, they were in schools, they were in the government, they were in the banks, they were translator—I had an uncle who had seven languages—he was a translator, Turgeman, he was from the Turkish time. By the way, he spoke also Farsi. So remember when we were trying to figure out—Hebrew for sure, Arabic for sure, English, because of written English, French—Well, I take it as Arabic, Persian and Turkish. And he was a translator in the government. So, they [Ashkenazim] come from a place where, like a box, and they finally with all the Enlightenment and losing children, and hating each other, the Jew against the secular, and the—we didn't know what it means to hate a Jew, we didn't know a different Jew. We had Rabbonim that they wouldn't eat in weddings, in nobody's house. You know what they would say? "I eat only the cooking of my wife." But not the Chasidic, this Chasidut, this [other] Chasidut, there is more the Rabbinical, and more the other, but we did not have hate for another Jew. We didn't know that. So, coming from there, bringing this to Israel and not necessarily the people who kept tradition—on the contrary, the people who did not kept (sic) tradition—they were close to Christianity, they were willing to wipe the name of Hebrew—coming, making, capturing the land, and we are now, they think, we are just like Arab. They don't speak our language, they don't know our mentality—we are very close to Avraham Avinu—Avraham Avinu put matzelet, he put the food on the floor, and I assure you, he gave them a beautiful Hachnasset Orchim. Yes, we did not have all the forks that's written in the books, and we did not learn from the German all the perfectness— But is it better? Is it necessarily better? Different. So when something is different, you cancel it like it's not existing?

8) Expansion from a homeland for work, trade or colonial ambitions (Cohen 17):

After being in Israel for a decade, the Khalif family had managed to buy a small home, from the earnings of her mother and older sister who found jobs in a factory, working many long shifts to save up the necessary funds. The sister ultimately was promoted to work in the factory office, where she met her husband-to-be. Her father, the patriarch, thought that Zmira would follow in the footsteps of her sister by getting a job in the factory after she finished high school; Zmira had other plans. She took advantage of the opportunity in America to get a teaching certificate, which launched her career as an educator, which she continued when she returned to Israel.

A point of interest: In Zmira's interview discussion she voices an opinion about the 1951 Bagdad synagogue bombing incident being perpetrated by a Jewish faction, which the Iraqi government claimed was the case. She believes the assertion of the Iraqi government. This assessment is not universally shared; evidence continues to mount, placing the blame on the Muslim Brotherhood (Segev haaretz.com). Zmira's choice to opt for the Iraqi government version witnesses the extent of the attachment to her family's 2500 year "homeland," making the events of her diasporic journey all the more remarkable.

Jewish Spark/Esther Moment

Zmira insists that if it weren't for the diasporic opportunity to live in the United States, she never would have found her way back to the level of religious observance that she had experienced as a child living with her extended family in Iraq. She relates that she has "patched the path" back to the spiritual traditions of her mother and grandmother, "all the way back to Avraham Avinu." She explains,

> [if I hadn't gone to live outside of Israel] I want to tell you, I'm convinced almost 100 percent, almost 90 percent, I would not be

back traditional, understanding Tanach, understanding Torah, connected—my mother used to say she has the first cordless telephone, before everybody had a phone, [talking to] Rabbonah Shel Olam. My mother used to talk to HaKadosh Baruchu straight, connected. So I got this back. In Israel I would have had the peer pressure. [not to be observant] How do I know it? Because when I got married and I became religious and my husband is religious, that's the time I didn't want to go back to my own friends, to my own circle.

[Growing up in Israel] I made a detour, and I went back exactly, patching the path, going straight to the path of my mother, grandmother, saba and all of this, and I feel I'm connected to Avraham Avinu through them.

As she explains, Zmira's "Esther moment" took the form of a renewed religious commitment to the traditional modes of worship of her Bagdadian ancestors. The dual commitment encompassed Torah observance of the Law as well as the Mizrachi tradition.

Chapter 7
"O (Yiddish) Canada!"
The Rochel Berman Narrative

Award-winning author Rochel Berman was born and raised in the city of Winnipeg, located in the province of Manitoba, in the cold reaches of northern Canada. During a conversation prior to the interview, she termed the neighborhood in which she lived a "bubble;" she grew up entirely within a Yiddish-speaking community. Yiddish, the historic language of Ashkenazic (Central and East European) Jewry, is characterized by a synthesis of Germanic with Hebrew and (Jewish) Aramaic (Katz 143). Rochel describes the experience nostalgically:

> RB: Oh, well, first of all, it was a total environment. We lived just around the corner from the Yiddish day school that I went to, and it was like a seamless place, being at home and going to school, and my mother was in the *Mutterfahrein*—I haven't used that word in a thousand years—that's like the Sisterhood. The teachers were all our friends, and Yiddish was my primary language, and this is what I spoke at home.

In addition to her first language of Yiddish being spoken at home as well as attending a neighborhood Jewish day school taught in Yiddish, she and her friends spoke Yiddish to one another and to the people they encountered in their daily lives. Her Yiddish name, Rochel, which she was and is known by, does not appear on her birth certificate; an unused, loosely anglicized version takes its place. As she explains,

> RB: My name is Rochel Udovitch Berman, but that's not on my birth certificate. My birth certificate is Ruth Roselyn Udovitch, but

I was named for some kind of Tanta Rochel, and here I am, "Tanta Rochel." And since I grew up in a Yiddish-speaking home, that's the name. . . . And I chose to carry it through my life—oh my God!" (Laughter)

Though she attended secular high school and college, her life and name had been indelibly informed by her early experience in Yiddish.

The little Yiddish *shtetl* nestled in the environs of Winnipeg was not a Canadian cultural outpost; it had been established by immigrants from Russia and Eastern Europe, among them Rochel's parents, who brought little else with them to their new home besides their Yiddish language and Jewish traditions. Charlemagne is attributed with the observation, "To have another language is to possess a second soul," which aptly describes the deep connection between language and culture in Rochel's world.

To fully trace the journey of the Yiddish language to its arrival in 20th century Manitoba is beyond the purview of this discussion, but a brief review of the language's path highlights the Jewish diasporic route of Rochel and her ancestors, migratory details that have been lost to the family in the passage of time. Originating as a Judeo-German dialect, the Jews of Germany brought *loshn Ashkenaz* ("Language of Germany") to Eastern Europe when they began to emigrate nine or ten centuries ago (Barnavi 192). The events of the Crusades, the Plague/Black Death, persecution for blood libel and the eventual expulsion from France, England and several German cities in the 13th and 14th centuries led to the emigration of Yiddish-speaking Jews to Eastern Europe, a less hostile environment at that time. Eventually, the anti-Semitic climate of early 20th century Eastern Europe would lead to immigration to the *goldene Medina*, "the golden land," as America was known in Yiddish. Many, like Rochel's parents, who wanted to come to the United States, were restricted by quotas, but were able to gain entry to Canada; they settled there and raised a family.

Rochel would voluntarily continue her family's diasporic journey by leaving Canada when she married her husband, George, an American, taking her Yiddish/Jewish background with her. It guided her marital, personal life and professional pursuits in her new adopted country, leading eventually to her experience as a member of the Jewish burial society, the writing of her book and its subsequent curriculum project.

Her book *Dignity Beyond Death: The Jewish Preparation for Burial* was an outgrowth of the experience of viewing her father in his hospital bed shortly after his death, and wondering, at the funeral the next day, what had happened to him in the interim. She describes the experience:

> I walked over to the bed, and I put my arms on his shoulders, and I kissed his head, and I noticed that it was getting cold, and I never had had that experience, of embracing my father and his not being warm. And then they took him out of the room, and I remember I went out and did I cry! You know, here I was in a strange environment, and I felt so bereft. Anyway, the next morning he had a graveside funeral, and when you live to ninety-five, there aren't many people around who are gonna come, the children live far away, so their friends aren't gonna come. Anyhow, we had a graveside funeral, and I kept thinking, where did they take him? What happened to him from the time I saw him till now? I didn't have a clue, so where did I go to with my head?, I went to—I knew there was a Chevra Kadisha, and I knew the Chevra Kadisha had tended to him, but what was my idea of a Chevra Kadisha? Chevra Kadisha were asocial, tiny little gnomes, who came out only in the dark of the night—well, that didn't bring me any comfort at all. I didn't know a single person who had been in Chevra Kadisha. Anyway, so, when I came back to New York, our shule had the beginnings of a Chevra Kadisha, and they needed more women, so I signed up so I would find out. And from the very beginning, it was

very clear to me that this is something I could do and that I should do.

What she learned from joining the *Chevra Kadisha,* the Jewish Holy Burial Society, would inform her knowledge about her father's posthumous passage and, in turn, the egalitarian ritual of Jewish burial preparation .

Through explaining and implementing the course outline and her book all over the world, Rochel is far from occupying a spiritual diasporic space; she lives and works within the positive Jewish context of sharing her Jewish knowledge and experience.

Jewish Spark/Esther Moment

For the parameters of my auto/biographical research, the circumstances of the "Esther Moment" will be expanded to include subjects who, unlike Esther, may open about their (strong) Jewish connection. Their moment may come with a commitment to a life-changing Jewish project, as in the case of Rochel Berman. Other variations will be discussed within the context of the individual life narratives.

Within Rochel's life narrative, the analogy with the "Esther moment" manifests itself as a commitment to an aspect of Jewish tradition, preparation for burial, which eventually evolved into the writing of her book *Dignity Beyond Death* and its outgrowth, a study guide/course being taught internationally in Jewish high schools. (In the interview I commented that for Rochel, fanning the flame of a Jewish spark was more like intensifying an already lit pilot light!)

When prompted to explain the role that Judaism has played in her life, she explains:

RB: Well, it's been the cornerstone, you know. It's what informs my moral compass. It informs what I do. It informs how I make decisions. Let me tell you something. I don't know if you know, but a couple of months ago we were robbed. Weird. While we were home. It was one of the—it was written up in the Sun-

Sentinel. They come, (gestures the outline across the forehead of a cap with a visor) they say they're from Florida Power and Light, and if they don't check our water immediately, we're gonna get poisoned. So I let them in. There were two guys; they're very professional beyond belief. They keep us busy, George was upstairs, they sent him down to help with the water, what water, there was no water, cleaned out all my jewelry and ran away. Anyway, there's another part of this story. My next door neighbor is president of the association, he has nothing else to do, he's forever wandering around, and he had seen them, and he knew that they were up to no good. And then he saw them coming to our house. And he says, "Oh, I should let them know. No I won't—I had a disagreement with George." Now, since then I have not dwelled on the robbers—they were making a living. Were they entitled to what they took? No. But they were making a living. He [the neighbor] That was a Chilul HaShem, because he put our lives in danger. What did he know? What if George—George was lying down upstairs—could have refused to come down? He could have said, "I'm sleeping, leave me alone." [The robber] He'd- a knocked him out, and taken his goodies. Now, so I ask myself, "If the guy next door—he has a very bad heart; he could drop dead any time—if I saw he was in need, what would I do? There is no question—I don't have to think about it twice—I would do whatever had to be done to save his life. So, that's how it [Judaism] informs.

In her interview, Rochel shared her insight that the process of *Tahara* Jewish burial preparation conflates her father's (very Jewish) core values of human decency and equality. That type of insight is not atypical of the life narrative interview process; I think of it as an "autobiographical moment," when the verbal (re)telling elicits an observation of connections. That these lessons were conveyed in the context of Yiddish conversation, with its metatext of Jewish wisdom, only further strengthens the importance of the family bond. She also expressed these thoughts in her book's introduction: "Participating in the egalitarian customs and ceremonies of burying the dead reaffirms an important personal tenet I learned from my father, a lifelong champion for equality and justice . . . On a communal and spiritual level, I have come to consider work with the Chevra as the most profound expression of my Judaism" (Berman 22).

Though Rochel and George Berman continue physically to live in a diasporic society outside the state of Israel, they have a strong transnational connection through their oldest son, Rabbi Dr. Joshua Berman, who immigrated to Israel/made *Aliyah* thirty years ago. The means by which the parents/grandparents stay in touch with Josh, his wife Michal and their four almost grown children led to the collaborative effort, *Oceans Apart: A Guide to Maintaining Family Ties at a Distance.* Through modern technology and parental wisdom, a close relationship has been engendered and preserved, both with the land and with the family. When presented with the observation that they have successfully bridged the distance between, Rochel observed,

> RB: Well, we've certainly tried very hard, and I would say, "Yes, we have," because there's nothing any of them want more than to come visit. And if there's one piece of advice I can give is you have to be proactive. It doesn't happen all by itself. I remember somebody in the community with whom I'm friendly, has children in Israel, said to me, "You have to teach me how to talk to my grandchildren in Israel." Well, you know, you have to work at it.

Rochel collaborated with her husband on several projects: George contributed photographic illustrations, and participated in the co-writing a biography. Entitled *A Life of Leadership: Eli Zborowski, from the Underground to Industry, to Holocaust Remembrance,* the book relates the life story of Eli Zborowski, immigrant-turned-successful-entrepreneur who was responsible for organizing the first *Yom Hashoah* commemoration in the United States in 1964.

Towards the end of the interview with Rochel, George returned home and consented to say a few words. George credits his wife with being his Jewish and spiritual spark; he considers their meeting "*bashert*," destined, and attributes it to some sort of divine plan. Before he met Rochel, he and his American-born parents led a typically assimilated life. Meeting Rochel changed all that; their union continues to inform his strong commitment to many aspects of living a Jewish life, bringing his spiritual diaspora to a fruitful end. He credits Rochel with being his Jewish spark:

> GB: I said that Rochel is my proof of God, my evidence of the existence of God; because when you look back and you see our events, so improbable, it had to be guided by something. (Rochel laughs in the background.) It certainly wasn't guided by me. It might have been guided somewhat by Rochel. But in the end—and the feeling I have is that we were bashert. That's it. I didn't want to get married, but I didn't see any other way to spend my life with her, kinda thing. And since then, some other things have come about that made me feel it was so right. And I didn't anticipate them, I didn't analyze them as I normally would—very analytical of the whole process—that I have to say, when you see a sequence of things that happen, that wouldn't have happened without some guidance, you have to believe there was [divine]guidance.

In the span of three generations, Rochel and her family have covered important milestones of diasporic life. Referencing Robin Cohen's common features of diaspora throughout this discussion evinces the family's gamut of diasporic experience.

The first of Cohen's features, "Dispersal from an original homeland, often traumatically, to two or more foreign regions" (Cohen 17), can be applied to Rochel Berman's family: their diaspora began several millennia ago with the Roman expulsion of the Jews from their homeland of Judea.

Rochel's parents' emigration from Russia, the land of their birth, to Canada, was the latest in a long string of generational migrations, as discussed earlier in the context of the centuries-long journey of the Yiddish tongue. In the early 20th century, the pogroms of Czarist Russia were followed by Bolshevik anti-Jewish restrictions. As historian Eli Barnavi notes, "at that time

[1920] over a third of East European Jews had left their countries of origin." A chart illustrating the migration of Jews from East Europe between 1899 and 1914 shows the original population of Jewish immigrants to be over a million (Barnavi 205). Rochel's parents were among this demographic.

With her marriage to George, an American citizen, Rochel immigrated to the United States. Though her native Canada and her adopted country share a common language, English, which eliminates the need to learn a "new" language, the move from the Yiddish-speaking community in which she was raised signals a definite diasporic linguistic shift.

Cohen's fifth common feature of diaspora finds both a political and religious resonance in the long Jewish journey: "the frequent development of a return movement to the homeland that gains collective approbation even if many in the group are satisfied with only a vicarious relationship or intermittent visits to the homeland" (Cohen 17). A recent movement of the 20[th]century, Zionism, advocated a return to the Jewish homeland, but it was not the first. During the same era in which the Book of Esther takes place, the Jewish leader Ezra, with the financial support of the Persian king Cyrus, spearheaded a successful movement 2500 years ago which culminated in the (re)building of the Second Temple. The religious context motivating a return movement can be found within prayers recited by observant Jews several times daily asking that the Jewish people be speedily returned to their lost homeland. The Hebrew word for the process of going back to the homeland is to make *Aliyah*, which literally means "to ascend." (Conversely, the Hebrew word for leaving Israel is *yored,* which means "to descend; with the connotation of diminished status.) George and Rochel's oldest son Josh made permanent *Aliyah* after finishing college. They felt they had done a great deal to facilitate the move by deciding to send their son Josh to a Jewish day school, where he formed associations with several *Aliyah*-minded teachers and students. Additionally, the curriculum informed his decision thirty years ago to move to Israel by featuring courses in Jewish cultural and religious history, as well as an opportunity to learn the Hebrew language. When asked if she could trace anything in his upbringing that became the source of his decision to move to Israel, Rochel replied,

> RB: Oh, yah, well, he went to yeshiva day schools, Orthodox yeshiva day schools, where it, you know, Zionism and making Aliyah was the goal. And, with regard to the SAR Academy in Riverdale, all his teachers made Aliyah.
>
> The principals made Aliyah. . . . At RAMAZ similarly, and at RAMAZ, they encouraged kids to go to Israel for a year before they went to college. They were already accepted; then they got deferments. Now, this was a big shock to us. If you go to Israel, you're never gonna go to college. How can you do this! We were educated and all his friends were going, that kind of thing, but after a year all his friends came back, except he decided to stay another year. So we said you could stay another year, only if Princeton would offer you another deferment. And they did . . . He did come back, to get his undergraduate degree in religion. He did it in three years because he had a lot of AP's, and then he went back immediately. And that's where he met Michal, and the rest is history.

Jewish diasporic life was informed by the characteristics cited in Cohen's sixth feature of diaspora; "a strong ethnic group consciousness sustained over a long time and based on a sense of distinctiveness, a common history, the transmission of a common cultural and religious heritage and the belief in a common fate" (Cohen 17). The aspect of "a common cultural and religious heritage" aptly describes the process of *Tahara* and how it was transmitted from generation to generation. Jewish burial traditions are linked with ancient and medieval practices in the commentaries and writings of Judaism, as Rochel explained:

> RB: Well, there's not too much about it—it's supposed to date back to the death of Moses on Zion Adar. The birth and death of

Moses is on the same day. And since there wasn't a Chevra Kadisha, it is said that God performed that. Now what we do now dates back to 15—I can't remember—15—[1500s] To the Chevra Kadisha of Prague. They're the ones that formalized all the things that we do, and it's essentially what we do.

Rochel interprets Cohen's sixth common feature of diaspora, 'the belief in a common fate" (Cohen 17) in the context of the relationship between American Jews and other Jews in the diaspora with Israel. When asked what she sees as the future/interplay of Jews in America and elsewhere with the state of Israel, Rochel replied,

> RB: You know, I see that Judaism has tremendous strength, and it will survive, wherever it is, in whatever form it is. [Israel's] the one thing that binds all the streams of Judaism, so. And then the fact that Israel has triumphed under such extraordinary adverse circumstances to be a respected democracy and economic success and every success. I mean, it's astounding. (Laughing) And only the Jews could do it, I don't know if only the Jews could do it, but the Jews did do it.

As a successful author and educator as well as a social worker, Rochel Berman exemplifies Cohen's ninth feature of diaspora: "the possibility of a distinctive creative, enriching life in host countries with a tolerance for pluralism" (Cohen 17). Berman's accomplishments attest to her enriching life in the United States; son Josh's emigration is a testament to the strength of two generations of sustained Jewish commitment and the freedom of choice granted by the host country.

Aliyah, however, is not always the end of the saga, as is seen in the autobiographies of Isaac Jacob and Zmira Mozorosky. The story has yet to be written for future migratory paths of Israelis and diasporic Jews growing up in the 21st century, and their (re)interpretation of Jewish commitment.

Chapter 8
Vive La France!
The Jay Lauwick Narrative: A Citizen of the World Sails the Jewish Atlantic

L ike many other parts of France, the city of Rouen has had a checkered Jewish history. Jews were expelled (twice) from France in the fourteenth century: in 1306 by Philip IV, and again in 1394 by Charles VI, following their readmission in 1315 (Frank 23). After the Spanish Inquisition in 1492, they trickled in, living furtively as Marranos, or crypto-Jews. "Starting in 1550, under the guise of being "New Christians," these Marranos were granted letters of protection by Henry II, who permitted them to live in France wherever they desired (Frank 24). They settled in Bayonne and Bordeaux and some went north to La Rochelle, Nantes, and Rouen. The 1648 Chmielnicki *pogroms* in the Ukraine caused Jews to flee to France, Poland and Russia. After the Treaty of Westphalia in 1648, Jews were allowed to remain in Lorraine. For the first time since 1394, Jews were legally permitted to live in France (Frank 24). The late seventeenth century brought the welcoming arms of Jean-Baptiste Colbert, finance minister to Louis XIV, who felt that Jews would bring business skills to France, which they did. In 1732, Sephardic Jews were formally recognized by royal decrees and permitted to practice Judaism (Frank 24). After the French Revolution, the National Assembly granted civil rights in 1791 to the Jews of Alsace and Lorraine. The emancipated French Jews were further assisted by Napoleon's creation of institutions designed to integrate the Jews into the French state

system (Barnavi 160). Emancipation and acculturation, to varying degrees, were accompanied by assimilation.

The subject of my next interview, Jay Lauwick, was born in
Rouen, France in 1933, to a mother from an assimilated Jewish
family; one sister had chosen to become a nun. Jay/Gerard is a
unique *juif-errant,* or Wandering Jew, with an extraordinary life
story to tell. An apt title might be, "A Citizen of the World Sails
the Jewish Atlantic." The "Jewish Atlantic" as a conceptual term
is used here in an analogous manner to Paul Gilroy's "Black Atlantic," forefronted as the route of forced diaspora for the enslaved African population. Limits of time and space do not permit a fuller comparison of the terms within the purview of this
discussion.

Jay, or Gerard as he was known in France, the country of his
birth, lived in France for the first forty years of his life, including
the difficult years of World War II. He grew up, pursued a mari-
time career, married, had a family, and subsequently divorced.
As a crew member on a cruise liner, he met his second wife, an
American. They decided to live in France, where their daughter
was born in Paris. A few months later, on the request of his second wife, they moved to America. After thirty years of marriage,
his wife passed away in 2004. He continued to live in their South
Florida condominium for the next thirteen years, until moving
back to France, where he spent the last few years of his life, until
he passed away in March of 2018. (The interview was conducted
in 2005, a belated 70th birthday present.)

Jay's Jewish connection is a story in itself. Though Jay and
his siblings were aware of their mother's Jewish ancestry, the
family had never practiced Judaism or identified in any way as
Jewish. He had once remarked that he thought his family had
come to Belgium and France via Holland; to Holland from
Spain, a well-known post-Inquisition Jewish diasporic trajectory;
there is a possibility that his father's family also had remote Jew-

ish roots. By becoming a practicing Jew during his marriage to Leah, he repaired a rupture of generations.

Jay's first close encounter with the land of Israel occurred long before he met Leah, in the course of his military service. As a young Frenchman, Jay was drafted into the military forces. He explains:

> JL: Yes, at that time, I was drafted like everybody; every young man was drafted in the military forces. As a professional merchant marine, I was drafted in the French Navy, and the draft at that time was for eighteen months, but, it was the end of the Indo-China War, and the beginning of the Algerian War, and instead of eighteen months, I was drafted for thirty. . . . In 1956—let me try—yes, in 1956 I was on board a destroyer, and we were dispatched to Haifa, to provide fire for anti-aircraft fire power to protect the city, because the Israelis did not have anything. They didn't have the land power and the marine power. So we stayed there probably for two or three weeks, turning around in front of Haifa. Then, at the same time, there was the Suez Canal operation against the Egyptians, with the French and the British. And then we stayed for several weeks; my ship was as an escort to aircraft carriers.

Jay also mentions that Israel was one of his favorite countries:

> And, [not] having anything to do with Leah or Judaism or anything, Israel. I was very impressed by Israel when I was there; I was there twice in 1956. First time in May was some kind of courtesy visit with the French navy, to Israel, and, we had some tourism, it was fine. The second time was during the war, several months later. But I was very impressed with the attitude of the people.

During the time he spent in Israel in the mid 50s, Jay mentioned that he did not identify himself as Jewish, either externally or internally. It is ironic that even though Jay's family did not acknowledge their Jewish ancestry, his relatives would have had more than enough "Yiddishkeit" to be assigned to annihilation in Hitler's gas chambers. It is also ironic that Jay had a part in defending the new state of Israel, not in the context of a Jewish fighting force, but as an unaffiliated member of the French merchant marine.

Jewish Spark/Esther Moment

The concept of the "pintele Yid," the inextinguishable Jewish spark that lies hidden deep within even the most secularized Jew has an interesting twist in the Jay Lauwick narrative. What ignited his Jewish spark was the love for/of a Jewish woman. The life he lived with Leah was a Jewish one; for Jay it was the first time he had openly espoused and practiced his Jewish heritage. Discovering his "pintele Yid," the inextinguishable Jewish spark said to burn in every Jewish soul, no matter how assimilated, would come about through the igniting of the more universal flame of love. Jay related how it happened when he first met Leah:

> The ship was alongside in La Guaíra, and I was not on duty or anything like that, I remember, and I was in the swimming pool, with friends, with colleagues, and it was noon, time for lunch, and we left, and we saw that woman, who was on a chaise lounge, you know, next to the pool, and reading and sunning, and I was looking at her, and I say eh, that's a nice girl, you know, and that's it, there was nothing else. And in the evening, we sailed, and we were on our way to Grenada, and I was on—I think I was on—my watch was from eight to twelve. And around ten-thirty—it was night, and you know how it is on board ship—you have the chart room with light, you need light to do your job—and the bridge is up front, and there's a curtain; and it means that the bridge is completely dark, it must be dark to keep your sight available for outside. So I was in the chart room, and the door opened, and the captain's maître d' came. He said, "Mr. Lauwick, the Captain would like you to give a tour of the bridge to Mrs. Goldstein, there, and, came that lady that was at the pool. And I had the time to look at her, and she was lovely, all dressed up, very nice, she had dinner with the Captain, and, so, that's fine. So, we talk a little bit about all the things, the

equipment, you know, the tour, you know, is very technical. And now, let's go to see the bridge. But the bridge, the bridge is completely dark, with no light. So I say, "You will be completely blind, so let me take your hand and guide you. And I know the place, but you don't. So, I took her hand, and I immediately felt that (makes the sound of a crash of a lightning bolt) that tension, you know that ah—[that electric spark] Yah. Anyhow, so we went outside, it was completely dark, she was blind, I knew my way around, we were on the wings outside, eyesight adjusted, and we spent a good hour, talking, and it was just more than a normal tour. And she left. And before leaving, we made an appointment to meet on the following day in Grenada, at the pool, after lunch. Fine. And after lunch I met her. She was there, so, she say, "I would like to—I would like you to give me a tour of the ship." "Let's go!" So, we went all over the ship, and we went in the fo'c'sle, in the back, the kitchen—I introduced her to the chief cook, you know, and she was delighted, and so we went all over the place. And that was the beginning.

Jay's Jewish spark was kindled by love: his second wife (unlike his first) was Jewish, and she, and he, became more observant as they raised their daughter, who was educated in Jewish schools. When they moved to Florida in the late 1990s, they chose to live in a Jewish community within walking distance of an Orthodox synagogue. As part of their observant life, they hosted many guests in their kosher home on Sabbaths and holidays. Jay and his wife were living as traditional Jews.

It is interesting to compare Jay's Judaic journey with Esther's: originally, both were not known as Jewish by those around them. In Jay's case, his new-found friends and acquaintances in the United States knew him to be Jewish, but they were not the people in his former home of France who did not know he was Jewish! When he returned to France after a forty-year absence, he was once again "unobservant," though his Jewish connection was evidenced by his observant Jewish daughter, who visited him frequently. With the bond to his daughter, he forged a lasting connection to Judaism. She will observe the traditional Jewish rituals of mourning and remembrance, i.e., when his daughter lights a candle on the anniversary of his passing, as is the custom, he will be remembered in a Jewish context.

Robin Cohen's Common Features of Diaspora

In reflecting on Jay's diasporic journey through the prism of Robin Cohen's common features of diaspora, the larger Jewish diaspora is subsumed by a secondary diaspora from Jay's native France. For several generations the family enjoyed what Cohen termed "a distinctive, creative, enriching life in host countries" (Cohen 17). His two shop-owning grandfathers, his businessman father, his mother's musical career as a pianist, his maternal aunt's successful design atelier as well as his own career in the Merchant Marine attest to the productive, constructive life led by these (covert) Jewish transplants.

Jay's expansion from his homeland was a variation on Cohen's feature #2, "Expansion from a homeland for work, trade or colonial ambitions" (Cohen 17). In this case, the expansion was motivated by love. After Leah had moved to France and given birth to their daughter, she told Jay she felt she had to return to the United States:

> JL: Leah one day told me, "I want to go back home. I want to move back home . . . She told me that—I think it was in September '75, just a bit later, because when Yocheved was three months old, Thanksgiving, Leah and Yocheved went to New York for Thanksgiving, and they stayed there a few weeks. And when she came back, she couldn't readjust, she say, "I want to go back home." I say, "Okay, let's go." So we sold everything we had. We sold the house—not the house, it was rented. We sold the car, we sold—we sold everything we could.

That was the beginning of Jay discarding his identity as a Frenchman and reinventing himself as a Jewish-American husband/father. His life in America forefronted Cohen's ninth feature of diaspora: "a distinctive, creative, enriching life in a host

country with a tolerance for pluralism" (Cohen 17). Jay was able
to find good employment opportunities:

> JL: So I got a job first in Paris, just after leaving the ship. I was in-
> volved with a marine electronic company, Raytheon. Yes. It was
> the national dealer for Raytheon. I was managing the Raytheon
> part of that company. And when I moved to United States, I had
> some contact, and I found a job, a similar type of job, and I got that
> for one year, I think. And after one year, a friend of mine, who was
> a captain, also a traffic manager for a French company in New
> York was killed in an accident, and his company offered me his
> job, usinore, and that was it. I took the job which was a very good
> job; I liked it, paying very much, a lot of travel, until 1987 when
> the company disappeared, for political reasons. And for several
> years I kept going on my own, all related to ship and steel.

He also explained other reasons for his successful adjustment:

> When I arrived here, I had—I was French, okay? But, I had a
> background, a professional background that helped me a lot. I'd
> been changing horizons for twenty-five years on a constant basis,
> meeting different people constantly, every day; dealing with Japa-
> nese, Hispanic people, German people, going places, hot weather,
> cold weather, you know? So it means that even living in France at
> that time, you felt not really assimilated, because you don't live in
> your city. Yes, you spend two weeks, one month, three months, but
> you leave—and you go places, to see different countries, different
> people. So, when I arrived in this country, I had that as a back-
> ground, you know. I was not just. I did not have too many prob-
> lems to adjust, for several reasons. First, the background that I'm
> talking about. Second, Leah, who was American. So it was easier
> for me to adjust because of her. She helped me.
>
> And I will say another reason why I had adjusted myself easi-
> ly: not only Leah helped me, but she insisted I was not allowed to
> make mistakes, or ignore. I was forced into it. This being said, I
> did not have major problems. I know the United States before—
> I've been—the first time I was in New York was in 1953, and I've
> been there many times in between, so it was not a shock.

World War II: Civilians in the Line of Fire

Jay L's narrative trajectory is unique in the inclusion of traumatic inter-Europe dispersals caused by the German WWII occupation of France. The displacements which his family suffered were not related to his Jewish identity, but to a war in what was his native France. The family bounced from place to place in an effort to find a place away from the bombs and fighting, a "safe harbor" for their growing family. He relates some harrowing memories. He describes a walk in Rouen in the throes of the battle-filled war's end:

> I remember at the end—it was in September, we moved back to Rouen, to go to back to school and things like that, and I remember, alone—I have never understood how my parents allowed me to do that—but I was alone on the river quay, that was the docks—covered with German equipment—trucks, tanks, all kind of things, and they had been completely destroyed by the planes, the Allied planes. Everything was completely destroyed, and I remember, looking out on—I was not interested at that time, but I could have taken all the arms and weapons I would have liked—the smell of dead corpse was impossible—I was twelve, I could not imagine that my parents let me do that, and I remember, I was alone! Almost nobody there, anyhow.

Jay relates another war memory from the spring of 1944:

> after April 1944, when there was a big bombing of the city. And, at that time, the Allied forces were trying to destroy all communication, bridge, in order to prepare for D-day. On the 19th of April, they were aiming the bridge at the boat—there were three bridges[s] in Rouen, on the river, and they came with, I don't know how many planes in the middle of the night, and they let go of the bombs and everything fell, you know, it was—it was a mess. And I remember we were all huddled, bunched together in the kitchen, and the bombs were coming down, was noise, there was fire, we could see fire, we could see, smell the powder, the dust, the smoke—it was a big thing. No bomb reached our vicinity, our ar-

ea—it was one mile away, you know. The following day, I went to school, and, of course, I had to go through the—rubble. And the fires, and the streetcars' wires down, you know, that stuff. And that was the last day of school. And I remember that school, in the playground, there was a cobblestone that came—nobody knew where, but thrown away by a bomb someplace, you know, and, anyhow, that was the last day of school, and we immediately moved back to Montenis, that was still at that little house, and we lived there for—until the end.

As a young adolescent, he came face to face with dying Germans:

On that day, I was on my way to the road, I don't remember, and a German truck loaded with food and stuff was attacked by a fighter, I don't remember which type of fighter it was, but I was in the line of fire. I was not shot at, because the truck was there, [gesturing] and I was a little bit further, but the noise of the gun was—I was terrified! I remember I fell on the ground, and—it was, I don't say close call, because the bullets were hitting the ground 200 feet from me or something like that—

But the noise, the noise, and the truck was destroyed, Germans were killed, I remember a German was in a dungaree, without shirt, just a jacket—he opened the jacket, and a bullet came through, completely through—he died a little bit later. Anyhow, that was a big thing.

JL: And sometimes we had the German patrols coming at night, waking everybody up, they were looking for paratroopers or anything, they were inspecting the house. That was a little bit scary, but not dangerous, really.

Wordsworth's observation that "The child is father to the man," is pertinent in the creation of a heritage biography; a time for looking back on childhood to find traces of the person one becomes. Jay was able to relate the stirrings of his interest in sailing the world to a childhood experience:

That began, that anecdote about books, happened in 1940—let's says 1945. I was twelve, and my father bought a collection of books—they were a very luxury at that time—leather bound, things like that—about different countries in the world—and of course, there were two books for the United States, and New York was in that book. And I remember reading that book about New York and being fascinated, absolutely fascinated. I knew everything in that book about New York. I knew everything— Manhattan, Fifth Avenue and Battery, everything. I was twelve, thirteen. At the same time, my bedroom was under the roof, on the three-story home that we had, a three-story house, and from my window I was able to see a huge panorama including the river and the seaport of Rouen. Rouen is inland, but it was a very active seaport with cargo ships coming in and out, and that was the beginning of my interest, yah.

Jay's peripatetic journey/return bespeaks the transformation of diasporic subjects to transnationals; living in two (or more) worlds. During the interview, Jay reflected on whether he felt more "American" or more "French." A strong indication of his status as a bi-cultural citizen was his reply when asked if he felt more like a Frenchman who lives in America, or an American who began his life in France:

I don't think I can answer that question straight-way. When I arrived here, I had—I was French, okay? But, I had a background, a professional background, that helped me a lot. I'd been changing horizons for twenty-five years on a constant basis, meeting different people constantly, every day; dealing with Japanese, Hispanic people, German people, going places, hot weather, cold weather, you know? So it means that even living in France at that time, you felt not really assimilated, because you don't live in your city. Yes, you spend two weeks, one month, three months, but you leave— and you go places, to see different countries, different people. So, when I arrived in this country, I had that as a background, you know. I was not just [in one place]. I did not have too many problems to adjust, for several reasons. First, the background that I'm talking about. Second, Leah, who was American. So it was easier for me to adjust because of her. She helped me.

In marrying a "native" Jay was able to acculturate. The price he paid to assimilate was the forfeiture of "Frenchness." He explains,

> Now, was I a Frenchman living in America? No, I gave up France, maybe not easily, but Leah forced me to give up France. She couldn't cancel who I was, okay, but she didn't like it. So, because of that I had to tone down my French "ship," and I did it, I had no problem, I had accepted that. That was part of my agreement to settle here. In fact, I am much more French now than I'm alone. I have renewed so many contacts in France.

After the death of his wife in 2004, he managed to recover his "Frenchness" with several trips back to visit relatives and former colleagues, ultimately going back to France to take up full-time residency, ending his voluntary French diaspora. During the several decades which he spent outside of his native France, he still kept and renewed his French passport, a sign that he still wished himself to feel on some level a part of a French milieu. It is a testament to the strength of the connection with his early French life, French siblings/family, language, culture, cuisine, as well as comrades from his life at sea, however long it lay dormant.

Postscript

In the decade following the interview, Jay enjoyed his life in south Florida, punctuated by annual visits to family and friends in France. Despite health challenges, i.e., bladder cancer, and a stroke in the eye which affected his depth vision, he remained always the intrepid traveler. He enjoyed a rigorous excursion to Greenland. When at home, he hosted visits from his sister Brigitte and her husband Charles, his son Stephane and his daughter Severine. He visited his daughter Yocheved in the summers; she visited him frequently in Florida during the long cold New York City winters.

As his vision deteriorated further from macular degeneration, he became unable to drive, a factor which created challenges to living independently in suburban Boca Raton. He was also an insulin-dependent diabetic, another health issue. He ultimately decided to move back to France, where French residency and his French work history would entitle him to fully funded health care, subsidized assisted living accommodations, and French social security benefits. To receive French social security, one must be a resident of France with a permanent French address; because American Social Security does not have a residency requirement, Jay was able to continue to receive his United States Social Security payments in France.

Jay left the United States in June, 2016, almost forty years to the day after his arrival. During the last few years before his death in March 2018, his daughter Yocheved would visit him every few months. Photographs posted on her Facebook page would show a happy blended family, usually enjoying a sumptuous repast—this is France, remember—often at Brigitte and Charles' cottage in Brittany.

A Round Trip Ticket? The Journey Back:
Maybe You Can Go Home Again

After being interviewed in 2005, Jay was inspired to take on the project of writing a small auto/biography of his career at sea. Guided by his little "diary" notebooks from his years on board ship, he wrote a 50-page account of his adventures at sea, both in French and English. I was privileged to edit the English version. He brought a copy to his merchant marine's 50-year reunion. The ending sums up not only his nautical career, but a life well lived:

> As far as I was concerned, April 3rd, 1974 brought also the end of my marine activities under the French Line flag. It is without too many regrets, even so, that I brought my bag ashore to begin a new life in a new world that will bring me to the New World. It will

take more than thirty years to retrieve a little bit of who and what I had given up. However, there were other ships under other skies and other flags, for other adventures. A way of life that ends without regrets and of which I am still very proud.

Chapter 9
From Russia with Love:
Sibyl Silver and the Torahs of Nizhny Novgorod

T he grandparents of the next interviewee, Sibyl Silver, immigrated to the United States around the turn of the 20th century. For her grandfather Ivan, emigrating from Mother Russia was the only way he could avoid conscription into the Russian army, which involved a twenty-five year tour of duty.

Avoiding a long and potentially dangerous military draft certainly qualifies as one of Cohen's common features of diaspora; leaving to escape a life-threatening situation, but non-military/civilian life for Sibyl's grandparents was also fraught with trauma and stress. A cursory glance at some high points of Russian anti-Semitism in the last four centuries will explain why more than 2.5 million Jews migrated from Eastern Europe between 1881 and 1914. (Ben-Sassoon 861)

In addition to the mandatory military service initiated for all Russian males between the ages of twelve and twenty-five by Nicholas I in 1827, Jewish boys as young as eight faced being kidnapped, or impressed (*khopped* in Yiddish) by government-sponsored agents, who would put them in Russian "Cantonist" schools until they were old enough to enter the military. Conversion was "encouraged;" many Cantonists never saw their families again.

Perhaps Empress Catherine II had paved the way for the easy apprehension of young Jewish boys; in the late 1700s she issued the edict which formally established the Pale of Settlement. The area, acquired from Poland, had a large Jewish population. Jews were not permitted to live outside of this area, in large cities like Moscow or St. Petersburg.

Residency restrictions, however constraining, pale (excuse the pun) in comparison to Russian *pogroms,* or riots. Carried out with the complicity of the Russian government, these massacres inflicted on Jewish towns and villages were frightening in their frequency and intensity. It is not difficult to see why Russian Jews would be eager to leave the land of their birth for a more promising future in a new land.

Though Sibyl's grandparents left long before the Revolution of 1917 (her mother was born in America in 1911), a cursory discussion of some 20th century seminal events which occurred after they left is helpful to set the stage for Sibyl and the Jewish project which took her back to the land of her ancestors.

As egalitarian as the Communist Revolution of 1917 promised to be, it did not wipe out Jewish persecution; the purges of Stalin included the execution of Jewish author Isaac Babel and the imprisonment/death sentence of his Jewish physicians. Just weeks before the date for their execution, the doctors were spared by Stalin's death. (The date coincided with the Jewish holiday of Purim, which celebrates the averted genocide of Persian Jews twenty-five hundred years ago.)

A hundred years after the 1917 revolution, an (ongoing) investigation of the 2016 American presidential election gave rise to accusations against Russia for hacking, and thereby influencing the outcome. In a March 2018 televised interview, Russian president Vladimir Putin's remarks to Megyn Kelly indicate that Jews are still looked on as outsiders/others. Putin observed that the accusations against Russia for hacking the 2016 American elections may actually apply not to Russians, but rather to non-Russian demographic groups within Russia, like "Ukrainians, Tartars or Jews" (Megyn Kelly, interview). *Plus ça change.*

In the middle of the twentieth century, Russia found itself fighting in the Second World War. Russia's ultimate victory over

Germany was not without great human cost; millions of human lives were lost, in defense within and without the borders of the Soviet Union. Moving through Eastern Europe, Russian troops pushed the German army back to Berlin. Somewhere on the way, they encountered a German train, carrying looted valuable Jewish artifacts, among them the Torah scrolls. The Torah scrolls wound up in a back room of the Military Library, where they were all but forgotten, until a Hungarian rabbi (re)discovered them decades later. So begins the story of Sibyl Silver and the Torahs of Nizhny Novgorod.

My personal experience with Sibyl and the Torah began in February 2015 when the Jewish Heritage Foundation brought a Scholar-in-Residence, Rabbi Dr. Shlomo Koves to the Boca Raton Synagogue. At the February 27th Friday night dinner, he explained how a few Jewish books arrived back in Hungary from the Lenin Scientific Library in Nizhny Novgorod. He followed the trail, and wound up discovering the 118 Torahs. Word quickly got around to other Chabad rabbis; Sibyl Silver heard it from one of them. In her interview, she tells how it happened:

SS: In the fall of 2012, our granddaughter Alexandra was a senior at NYU and was spending the year in Prague, so we decided to go to Prague. It was [the holiday of] Sukkot, and the kids were building a Sukkah. . . . It was during one of the Seudahs [festive meals] of Sukkot that Rabbi Barrish told a story of Rabbi Koves from Hungary who went to Russia and found these Torahs that were stolen by the Nazis. He was not able to get them out of Russia, but perhaps with some American help, maybe it would work. And I turned to my husband and said, "Wouldn't that be a great thing to do?" And he said, "I worked all my life. I want to go home and play my golf. You want to do it? You do it. I give you my full blessing."

We came back, and unfortunately, a few months later my husband got very sick, and everything was put on hold. He passed away on December 27, 2014. In February, 2015, I invited Rabbi Koves to come to the Boca Raton Synagogue and tell about the Torahs that are sitting in this library in Nizhny Novgorod and from here on in it just took off.

This project is the brainchild of Sibyl Silver, a self-described "girl from Brooklyn," who now lives in Boca Raton, Florida. Sibyl's "Esther moment" occurred as soon as she heard the Torahs' story and was drawn to try to rescue them. She experienced a raised level of commitment and purpose to her Jewish heritage. With her creation of the Jewish Heritage Foundation, she has made it her mission to spearhead an effort to bring the Torahs out of Russia, restore and return them to their rightful owners; communities or individuals or their descendants. If no one can be found from the original communities, they will be given to Jewish communities around the world in need of a Torah.

All this is indeed coming to fruition in ever-unfolding and unexpected ways. In the spring of 2016, Sibyl made a trip to Israel to meet with experts at Yad Vashem and Machon Ot, a school for scribes. (By the way, whenever the Torah travels via air, it flies first class, in its own seat!) The Torah was examined by experts from both institutions. Pictures of the meetings were posted on its Facebook site, JewishHeritageFoundation.com.

The findings of the experts were astonishing. Using a database of every letter of the Hebrew alphabet and the permutations of individual scribal styles throughout the ages, one Torah was identified as being from Italy, exhibiting letters in both Sephardic and Ashkenazi style. Previously, it had been assumed that the Torahs were from Hungary, though the exact details of where the German train carrying the Torahs was headed and how/when/where it was intercepted by the Russians are not yet known. I am hoping to do some in-depth research with my recently (re)honed German language skills into German war records in preparation for the book project that Silver has proposed. A work in progress.

Three Torahs have been fully restored. One sponsor family used a Torah in Israel for a family Bar Mitzvah at the *Ko-*

tel/Western Wall in Jerusalem. Another Torah went on the Spring 2016 March of The Living, a trip to Poland/Auschwitz for Jewish high school students. Sibyl accompanied the Torah on that march, along with then Dean Heather Coltman, FAU/Dorothy F. Schmidt College of Arts and Letters. While they are were in Poland, meetings took place with members of the Polish government for the purpose of trying to get the authorities to release (stolen) Jewish artifacts that have been in their possession for decades.

In true 21st century style, the story of the Jewish Heritage Foundation and the Torahs of Nizhny Novgorod is unfolding on the Internet through the Foundation's website and, of course, Facebook. Print news media also disseminate the details of the latest events. Additionally, Silver has also spoken with administrators of FAU's Center for Human Rights and Holocaust Education, in order to plan programs for local high schools. Though Sibyl describes herself as "just a girl from Brooklyn," she seems indefatigable.

A quiet military library in Nizhny Novgorod, a city well outside the Pale of Settlement, provided a safe, sheltered 70-year residence for 118 Torahs wrested from their towns and villages whose Jewish inhabitants, murdered in the Holocaust, had not survived to retrieve them. Though the rupture caused by the Holocaust can never be fully repaired, the restorative Nizhny Novgorod Torah project is an act of reparation for its participants in honoring the memory of those who were lost. The task of bringing the Torahs home has been taken on by Sibyl, who is determined to restore them to descendants of their original owners, whenever possible, or to communities of Jews around the world who are in need of a sefer Torah. The irony of the situation is not lost: the descendant of a Russian ancestor forced to live within the Pale of Settlement has made her way to a city off limits to her Jewish grandparents to rescue 118 Torahs, all but forgotten. Their original owners, murdered in the Holocaust, had not survived to retrieve them. Thanks to Sibyl's efforts, they have been brought to life, in services all over the world.

Along with the 118 Torahs discovered in the archives of the Lenin Scientific Library was a *Megillah*, a scroll of the Book of Esther. The Yiddish expression, *a ganze megillah*, "the whole megillah," is usually used in the context of a long-winded story which begs to be truncated. In the case of the Nizhny Novgorod megillah, the whole megillah is a blessing and a wonder. It was brought to the library in the mid 2000s by a family who discovered it in the wall of their home during renovations. (The library was known to have a collection of old manuscripts, so the family thought to bring it to the library for further inspection.) The scroll was rolled and stored in a cylindrical metal casing, a typical mode of storage. Gerard Genette's observations on the importance of paratext take on new meaning; the strong metal case certainly helped to preserve the scroll from deterioration. Very little work was needed for a *sofer,* a Hebrew scribe, to restore it to full working order. After so many years of lying hidden and unused, in March 2016 the members of the Boca Raton Synagogue proudly read from the Megillah to celebrate Purim 5776. I was there to participate in the thrilling event. The holiday of Purim is celebrated by hearing the Book of Esther read aloud from Megillat Esther. Megillah means "scroll" in Hebrew, and though there are other megillahs, i.e., Megillat Ruth/Book of Ruth, the term "Megillah" has come to refer generally to the Book of Esther. Its story of a hitherto unknown-to-be-Jewish Persian queen who risks her life to save her people from annihilation, a survival saga against all odds, is one that often resonates within the context of the 5000 year Jewish narrative.

Before the reading, Rabbi Goldberg explained the Megillah's lost-and-found history. He remarked that the initial prayer said before the reading, the *Shechiyanu* which thanks God for sustaining and bringing one to this occasion holds special significance for the return and recovery of this long-lost scroll, a survivor in its own right. It is not possible to know the last time it was read before a congregation or the circumstances that necessitated it to be secreted within the walls of a home for safekeeping, but it is certain that its restoration by Sibyl Silver brought it back to life.

If the Megillah can be regarded as a paradigmatic model for navigating Jewish life in diaspora, then the Torah, the Five Books of Moses, is looked to as a blueprint for every aspect of life (and death) for its Jewish adherents. Sibyl Silver observes,

> Without the Torahs, we are not a Jewish people. The Torah is—is the thread that binds us, the Torah is a book of ethics, the Torah is the mainstay of Judaism, the Torah is read on a Monday, on a Thursday, on a Saturday. It is read at a Bar Mitzvah, at a Bat Mitzvah. It is danced with on Simchas Torah. The Torah is—it's what HaShem, God gave to Moses for us, the people. But it symbolizes all people, be it Jewish and non-Jewish. Laws, our own constitution, things come from our Torah. The New Testament looks back onto the Torah. It is just the mainstay of life. It is our bread, it is our water, it is our existence. (Interview 14-15)

The Nizhny Novgorod Torahs serve an additional function. As survivors of their lost communities, they are witnesses for those who perished. When asked about how the Torah symbolizes and unites the people who perished with the future, Sibyl continues,

> It is the only thing left of those communities that one can lay their eyes on. It is the—when one sees it, one can witness what it's all about. It's one thing to look at rubble; it's another thing to see the written word. We all know that we can go to a cemetery, and there are plenty of cemeteries and plenty of shtiebels in Eastern Europe, where you can barely read the stones, or whatever, but these Torahs—you can read them, you can see them. It is so important to keep them alive (Interview 17).

For observant Jews, the Torah functions as the covenantal link, an inextricable bond between God and the Jewish people. Within its text are the rules and regulations for leading an ethical, Jewish

life, along with the God-centered story of creation and the creation of the Jewish nation. As Sibyl remarked, portions of the Torah are read aloud to the congregation on Mondays, Thursdays,
Saturdays and holidays. This performative aspect, the ritual of
reading the Torah aloud, is especially significant in the context
of a Holocaust Torah. At a February 2016 FAU program featuring the Nizhny Novgorod Torahs, Dr. Alan Berger observed that
these Torah scrolls act as "witnesses speaking for those whose
voices have been silenced" (Berger February 25, 2016).

On one level, the public readings function as a *tikkun,* or
healing for the Nazis' public display of the destruc-
tion/desecration of Torahs as performance and spectacle. As
Jenna Weissman Joselit, another speaker noted, the Nazis pur-
posely staged "a deliberate inversion of Jewish ritual practice."

This theme of destruction and renewal is found in Elie
Wiesel's book, *A Jew Today*, a story about a Holocaust survivor,
a sofer, a Torah scribe whose post-war life is dedicated to restoring Torahs rescued from the Holocaust, much like the Torahs of
Nizhny Novgorod. The observations of the sofer aptly describe
the relationship between Torah, memory and the Jewish people.
He explains to his visitor: "The Torah, that is true memory:
mine, ours" (74). The visitor relates what the scribe says next:

> And now he speaks to me of the love that Jews have nurtured
> for the Torah from the beginning. If someone drops a scroll, the
> entire community does penance.
>
> The presence of the Torah sanctifies; it warms the coldest of
> hearts. Jews never abandon it, never part from it. The scrolls are
> linked with the events that punctuate and enrich the life of a com-
> munity. One kisses them with passion, one dances with them, one
> communes with them. One honors them, one protects them. Impos-
> sible to unroll them without trembling; impossible to read in them
> without becoming a child again. All this the enemy knew; that was
> why he trampled them, dragged them through the mud and the
> blood, exhibited them like trophies of war and victory. With every

letter he retrieves, the scribe is healing living creatures, survivors." (Wiesel, A Jew Today 74)

Sybil describes the renewal of one of the Nizhny Novgorod Torahs:

> One Torah in particular has been restored by one family. This Torah will be going on the March of the Living, this Torah will be read by his son for the first time at the Kotel in Jerusalem in June [2016]. I mean, it's amazing to think that this Torah is alive, it's coming alive! And it symbolizes all that was destroyed, or they tried to destroy, they could not destroy. We have a scribe that has restored the Torah. It was in pretty good condition, so it didn't take a lot of work. So this Torah is going on this March [of the Living]—a second Torah, another family has dedicated it in memory of their parents. That Torah will also go on the March of the Living, and the first Torah, the last four words will be completed at the synagogue in Krakow where the scribe is coming from Jerusalem to do it, and it will be read on Thursday, May 5th [2016] in a synagogue, and I can't tell you the last time that Torah was read in a synagogue; we have no idea, but what a wonderful thing to think of!

In its relationship with the Jewish people of diaspora, the Torah has served to unite disparate populations in much the way postcolonial theorist and author Benedict Anderson describes the "imagined communities" of "print capitalism." Through the performative aspect of scheduled public readings, listeners can "imagine" the listeners in the loci of simultaneous public readings, as well as the commemoration of holiday festivals. This "link" provided members with a sense of nationhood which transcended geographical boundaries and cultural differences of language and custom, relating to elements of Robin Cohen's sixth common feature of diaspora: "a strong ethnic group consciousness sustained over a long time and based on a sense of distinctiveness, a common history, the transmission of a common cultural and religious heritage and the belief in a common fate" (Cohen 17). The actual content of the scriptures as well as the way in which they are employed in religious rites serves to reinforce the notion of community.

Though the celebrants may never meet one another, they are united in their shared religious observances. Dr. Howard R. Wolf, educator and author, observed that the Torah could be regarded as a virtual world wide web, perhaps the first facsimile of the Internet. (The Torah's empowering network prefigured its 21st century technology counterpart by several millennia.)

In her seminal book, *The Generation of Postmemory,* author Marianne Hirsch explores many facets of the second generation's reception of parental survivor memories. In her fascinating discussion of photographic images, she uses a term, "affiliative postmemory" (161). This term seems particularly appropriate for the way the Nizhny Novgorod Torahs are associated with events of the Holocaust; the artifact is an independent physical entity in and of itself, but the Holocaust exercised an existential influence that nearly caused its destruction. The surviving Torahs summon up the history of past events which becomes part of the witnesses' collective memory.

Though the Torahs survived the Shoah, the events of the Holocaust did sever the connection between the community members and their Torahs. Hirsch references Aleida Assmann's *Der Lange Shatten der Vergangenheit (The Long Shadow of the Past)* in the context of "the role of objects and places as triggers of body or sense memory" (211, n.14). The Torahs of Nizhny Novgorod trigger what could be termed the memory of history. Like the authors of neo-slave narratives, modern-day readers and viewers of the Torah have to fill the lacunae of the communities' past history with a composite version of facts gleaned from survivor testimonies, not knowing if they actually represent the lost communities. As complex technological methods of identification are used to identify the communities from which the Torahs came, the lacunae will be filled, allowing the Torahs to be linked to corroborated events, acting as silent though now more specific witnesses. The Torahs would act like "triggers of remembrance" (Hirsch 212) to the lost communities while simultaneously being read from in a community setting.

Hirsch also references Assmann's use of the metaphor of the classical Greek legal concept of the *symbolon*. She explains, "To draw up a legal contract, a symbolic object was broken in half, and one of those halves was given to each of the parties involved. When the two parties brought the two halves together at a future time and they fit, their identity and the legal force of the contract could be ratified" (Hirsch 211). Though Hirsch places the metaphor in the context of return journeys and the release of memories, she poses a question: "But can the metaphor of the *symbolon* cover cases of massive historic fractures, such as the ones introduced by the Shoah?" (Hirsch 212).

I would offer that in the context of the Nizhny Novgorod Torahs, the Greek metaphor works to express the essentiality of the partnership between a Torah and its Jewish community, a partnership torn asunder by the events of the Shoah; a relationship reforged by the Torah's rescue, restoration, reinstatement and functionality within a Jewish community. The appeal of the word *symbolon* lies in its ability to stand for something beyond itself, much as the Torah stands for the Jewish people's covenant with the Creator. Much secular and spiritual reflection has been given to the role of the Holocaust as the cause of a "massive historic fracture" between God and the Jewish people. Hirsch questions, "Would not contracts lose their legal force in such cases, so much so that the pieces would no longer be expected to fit together again?" (Hirsch 212).

And yet, to borrow Elie Wiesel's oft-used phrase, somehow the pieces do fit together again. United in a quest to recover, return and restore the once-lost Torahs of Nizhny Novgorod to remnants of their lost communities, modern Jews find that they experience a connection with the past, present and future—and it all began with an artifact. Wiesel remarks on the Torah's power to reconnect Jews when he sees the *Simchat Torah* celebration of Soviet Jews in Moscow: "Men who had not seen a Torah all year long were embracing and kissing it with a love bequeathed to them from generations past" (Wiesel *The Jews of Silence* 45).

The power of an artifact to connect Jews with past history and communities can also be seen in the "Violins of Hope": the project/book dealing with violins of the Holocaust that have been lovingly restored by Amnon Weinstein, a second-generation Israeli luthier/maker and repairer of string instruments. Earlier this year the violins have been exhibited at the Maltz Museum of Jewish Heritage in Beachwood, Ohio and played in concert by the Cleveland Orchestra. The back cover of James A. Grymes' book, *Violins of Hope* explains, "Today, these instruments serve as powerful reminders of an unimaginable experience—they are memorials to those who perished and testaments to those who survived." The same could be said of the restored Nizhny Novgorod Torahs. In the words of Cathy Caruth, "History is not only the passing on of a crisis but also the passing on of a survival that can only be possessed within a history larger than any single individual or any single generation."

To grasp the importance of the Torah for the Jewish people, one need not look any further than Freud, a secular Jew who was forced to flee Vienna in the wake of the *Anschluss.* In his powerful book, *Zakhor,* author Yosef Hayim Yerushalmi cites the message Freud sent in August 1938 to the "psychoanalytic diaspora assembled in Paris for the fifteenth International Congress:"

> The political misfortune of the [Jewish] nation taught them to appreciate the only possession they had retained, their Scripture, at its true value. Immediately after the destruction of the Temple by Titus, Rabbi Yochanan ben Zakkai asked for permission to open at Yabneh the first school for the study of the Torah. From now on it was the Holy Book and the intellectual effort applied to it that kept the people together (Yerushalmi 111n.7).

Not surprisingly, it is the words of Wiesel which most fully express the intersecting themes of Torah, memory and Holocaust survival so relevant to the Jewish Heritage Project and the Torahs of Nizhny Novgorod.

Rena Finder, a Schindler child, spoke in the Chabad of Central Boca Lecture Series. The youngest Schindler survivor, she and her mother were sent to work at Emalia, Oskar Schindler's enamel and ammunition factory. Finder was ten years old. Now in her late 80s, she delivered a stirring message of courage and hope: "Don't ever underestimate the power of each of us to change the course of history" (Finder March 9, 2016, Boca Raton). By her determination and perseverance, Sibyl Silver is doing exactly that with the Jewish Heritage Foundation Project. With the Torahs as witnesses, she is assuring that those communities who were silenced by the Shoah will not be forgotten.

Chapter 10
The Message in the Medium: Auto/Biography and 21ˢᵗ Century Life Narrative Technology

This chapter deals with the development of the genre of auto/biography and its relationship to the filmic life narrative form of the interviews in this work. From a short historical summary of the genre of autobiography to its present-day permutations, the discussion will conclude with some indicated speculation for the future direction of the genre. Relevance to the dissertation's diasporic narratives informs the content of the discussion; time and space do not permit a fuller treatment of the many aspects of autobiographical production.

The etymology of the word "autobiography" and its reference to the genre serve as an apt springboard for this historical discussion. In *Reading Autobiography: A Guide for Interpreting Life Narratives,* co-authors Sidonie Smith and Julia Watson relate that "In Greek, *autos* denotes 'self,' bios 'life' and graphe 'writing.' Taken together in this order, the words *self life writing* offer a brief definition of autobiography" (Smith 1). An examination of the three Greek word origins and the word's modern permutation indicate the direction the genre has taken. In her general introduction to *The Routledge Auto/Biography Studies Reader,* editor Ricia Anne Chansky explains the origin over three decades ago of the slash between auto and biography: "It is important to note that Timothy Dow Adams originally created the term *auto/biography,* with the slash, for the name of our journal as well as a way to refer to scholarship that encompasses both autobiographies and biographies. He and other founding members of *a/b: Auto/Biography Studies,* wished to connote interest in how lives are narrated and identities constructed without privileging self-life writing over life writing" (Chansky xxi).

The term "autobiography" is cited by Smith and Watson as first appearing in English in the review of Isaac Disraeli's *Miscellanies* by William Taylor of Norwich in the *Monthly Review* (1797). A first sighting is often attributed to Robert Southey's anglicizing of the three Greek words in 1809. American author Robert Folkenflik observes, "The term *autobiography* and its synonym *self-biography* . . . appeared in the late eighteenth century in several forms, in isolated instances in the seventies, eighties, and nineties in both England and Germany with no sign that one use influenced another" (Smith 2). Fast-forwarding to the 21st century, the modern term "selfie," like a phoenix rising out of its ashes, brings to mind the earlier term "self-biography" with their shared context of autobiographical production. *Plus ça change.*

In the 21st century the term auto/biography has been joined by other referentials, namely, *life writing* and *life narratives.* "For instance, the term *life writing* has come into use to designate the many genres of life stories that emerge from diverse communities, such as memoirs, letters, cookbooks, diaries, blogs, Facebook posts, song lyrics, documentaries, and reality television . . . a very useful umbrella term to conceptualize this vast and vibrant field" (Chanksy xx). These genres include but are not exclusive to formats originating in online production. So, too, the term "life narratives" can denote written and non-written forms of autobiography, "reflexive of the multiple modes through which individuals commit auto/biographical acts" (Chansky xxi). These five recorded/filmed life story narratives would find a place in this category. Referencing Julie Rak, Smith observes, "This shift from genre to discourse opens to the scenes of autobiographical inscription beyond the printed life story" (Smith 3).

In his introductory essay, James Olney situates the early stirrings of the genre's literary criticism: "In the beginning, then,
was Georges Gusdorf" (Olney *Autobiography: Essays Theoretical and Critical* 8). (Olney's dedication to the volume reads,
*"The editor dedicates his part in this volume to Georges
Gusdorf, mentor and friend,"* an indication of his high regard.)
Olney was ideally suited to translate Gusdorf's essay; quite un-
wittingly and unbeknownst to one another, he and Gusdorf had
written about similar autobiographic observations. Olney shares
his surprise: "In translating *Conditions et limites de
l'autobiographie* into English for the present volume, I have
been repeatedly astonished at the overwhelming similarities between that essay and my book, and after reading the translation,
Professor Gusdorf responded in kind: "I have the impression that
the translation is all the better for the reason that the thought is
not at all foreign to you. These ideas are yours also. The thesis of
Metaphors of Self [Olney's work]even turns up, toward the end
of the essay" (Olney 10). He goes on to note the "the ideas and
the general argument" as well as "specific details, examples, and
turns of phrase are identical" (Olney 11).

He emphasizes, " . . . I know for a certainty that Professor
Gusdorf was entirely unaware of my book in 1975—as unaware
as I was of his essay in 1969" (Olney 11). The coincidence of
multiple invention, or simultaneous discovery, as the phenomenon is sometimes referred, has occurred in mathematics and science as well as in the field of autobiographical criticism. I mention it here because it speaks to the universal experience that is
autobiography and why these observations ring so true to critics
and readers alike.

Olney's introductory is followed by his insightful translation
of Gusdorf's seminal 1954 essay, "Conditions et limites de
l'autobiographie/Conditions and Limits of Autobiography."
Gusdorf observed: "autobiography is a second reading of experience, and it is truer than the first because it adds to experience

itself consciousness of it" (Olney 38). He goes on, "Autobiography appears as the mirror image of a life, its double more clearly drawn—in a sense the diagram of a destiny" (Olney 40).

The next watershed moment in autobiographical literary criticism occurred with the 1973 publication of Phillipe Lejeune's "The Autobiographical Pact." In this seminal essay, Lejeune offered a definition of autobiography: "*Retrospective prose narrative written by a real person concerning his own existence, where the focus is his individual life, in particular the story of his personality*" (Lejeune 4, italics Lejeune) "The autobiographical pact is the affirmation in the text of this identity, referring back in the final analysis to the *name* of the author on the cover." (14). He continues, "What defines autobiography for the one who is reading is above all a contract of identity that is sealed by the proper name" (19).

In the ensuing five decades, Lejeune has been a continuing prolific presence in the field of auto/biography theory, embracing technological change. In a collection of essays from *Identity Technologies Constructing The Self Online*, Lejeune's essay entitled "Autobiography and New Communication Tools," explores 21st century auto/biography: "My first observation is that it [auto/b] has withstood the arrival of the Internet. Autobiography uses the resources put at its disposal by all other literary forms and no longer clings to the classical unifying narrative. These new forms often express troubled and problematical identities, but is that not the raison dêtre of autobiography. . . ? Could it be that our 'accelerated' world has found the forms demanded by our new 'narrative identities,' be they paper or electronic?" (Poletti 255-57) Perhaps Lejeune's visionary stance explains why his essays so often forefront conversations on the future of auto/biography. He is to be found within the pages of significant editorial collections presenting the spectrum of current autobiographical theory, in addition to the previously mentioned essay collection by editors Rak and Poletti, *The Routledge Auto/B*

Studies Reader, as well as Spring 2017's special issue of the Journal of the Autobiography Society, *What's Next? The Futures of Auto/Biography Studies.*

In the history of the genre, St. Augustine's *Confessions* is often cited as one of the earliest examples of autobiographical production. Gusdorf ranks *Confessions* as "a brilliantly successful landmark right at the beginning" (Olney AET&C 29), followed by Rousseau, Samuel Johnson and the modern Western explosion of autobiographical text. Olney credits the shift from *"bios"* to *"autos"* for the increased output. "This shift of attention from bios to autos—from the life to the self—was, I believe, largely responsible for opening things up and turning them in a philosophical, psychological, and literary direction" (Olney *Autobiography and the Cultural Moment* 19-20)

I would like to cite a far earlier, ancient example (8th century B.C.E.) of a narrative which contains what can be termed an autobiographical episode. Within Homer's *Odyssey,* the character of Odysseus/Ulysses reflects on his journey in an extended soliloquy delivered before an audience; ancient stirrings of travel writing, to the degree of historicity with which the Homeric account is credited. In claiming his own narrative, Odysseus enacts a textual reauthorization, from Homeric narrative to auto/biography. Additionally, Book Nine's recounted adventure of Ulysses/Odysseus and his men escaping the blind shepherd's cave by clinging to the underbelly wool of sheep can be seen as a metaphor for the transmission of autobiography via narrative: covertly carried along until discovered/uncovered.

Several thousand years after the *Odyssey,* another ancient text, the Biblical Five *Books of Moses* offer an eponymous authorial reference to an auto/biographical production presented in the third person, more a narrative format. Moses can add the designation of auto/biographic visionary to his list of attributes. These early books of the Bible are replete with conversational exchanges, affording the reader a less moderated view of the principle figures. As has been discussed in detail in a prior chapter, the later Biblical book of Esther stands as an early example of auto/biography couched in third person narrative, with important conversational exchanges.

Frequent and lengthy discussions within the literary genre of autobiographical criticism on the primacy of the narrative function in the living and telling of a life story attest to its essentiality. According to many critics like Rak, Poletti, and Turkle, it remains to be seen how the narrative will structure, or restructure itself in digital life story production; i.e., vlogs, Facebook, etc.

As described in the preface to the second edition of *Reading Autobiography: A Guide for Interpreting Life Narratives*, editors Sidonie Smith and Julia Watson have compiled a comprehensive guide in their examination of the life narrative genre, "the wide ranging field of autobiographical texts, practices, and acts" (Smith ix). Topics cover the comprehensive history of autobiography theory, as well as the expansion of autobiography studies into unique 21st century Internet additions. One section particularly pertinent to my project is Appendix A, "Sixty Genres of Life Narrative." Reading through the descriptions of life narrative genres identified several aspects within these variants of diasporic Jewish biography, including, but not limited to, Autoethnography, Collaborative Life Writing, Digital Life Stories, Ethnic Life Narrative, Oral History, and Spiritual Life Narrative. In attempting to categorize my own heritage auto/biography format, I was struck by its unique conflation in the context of the previously cited genres.

Exploring these genre descriptions will demonstrate important synergies as well as the inability of one category to envelop the many significant characteristics of the heritage biography format. Though the filmic media forum used to record and share these interviews places them firmly into the classification of *digital life stories,* my chronological outline questionnaire similarly places the project into the *collaborative life writing*

category. Originated by me, the interviewer, and completed by
the interviewee, the finished questionnaire exhibits an essential
collaborative aspect of the project. Additionally, the interviewee
is encouraged to add any material/information that s/he does not
find included in the outline. With its aspect of an inter-
view/conversation, *oral history* is another essential category.
However, the "oral" aspect is only part of the "aural" experience
of the history; the audience will be *listening* to the voice of the
subject (as well as "seeing" the speaker speak!), minimizing the
effect of mediation, persistent in any written version, in which
"the one who speaks is not the one who writes, and the one who .
writes is often an absent presence in the text who nonetheless
controls its narrative" (Smith 275).

Diasporic emphasis serves to situate these auto/biographies
into the category of *ethnic life narrative.* The exilic experience
traced in several of the interviews is referenced in the description
of a subset of the category: "Narratives of exile inscribe a no-
madic subject, set in motion for a variety of reasons and now
inhabiting cultural borderlands," This genre also references essays by William Boelhower and Sau-ling Cynthia Wong, which
appear in Eakin's *American Autobiography*, situating immigrant
autobiographies (Smith 269). Though the traditional genre of
spiritual biography involves confession and/or conversion, these
diasporic biographies feature an element of spiritual awakening
in the recognition of an individual mission, which situates the
individual in a satisfactory locus of resolution, a homecoming of
sorts, bringing closure to the process of unsettled diasporic wandering.

The challenge of genre categorization finds a counterpart in
the examination of the heritage biography format. Ultimately
represented in digital media, the writing component plays a significant developmental role. Often, it is the process of writing
down the responses to the outline queries that acts as a release to
revisit memories of long-ago events. Interviewees have remarked

that the simple act of writing the "answers" to the questions re-leases the floodgates of memory, a vital step in reflecting on the course of one's life journey in order to describe it. Medium and message are both intrinsically essential to the defining character-istics of this auto/biography format. This essential relationship of interdependence is probably the most significant characteristic of the heritage auto/biography; the intersection of the long-standing genre with 21st century technology.

Editor Margaretta Jolly's oversized two-volume work, *Encyclopedia of Life Writing: Autobiographical and Biographical Forms* approaches genre categorization through contributory essays by experts within the entry fields. While proving illumi-nating and expansive, the individual texts are also well-written, piquing and sustaining the reader's interest. In succinct, articu-late terms, several issues are explored pertinent to aspects of these heritage auto/biographies; specifically under the headings of *Interviews, Israeli and Modern Hebrew Life Writing, Jewish-American Life Writing, Judaism and Life Writing, Narrative, National Identity and Life Writing, Oral History, Orality, Per-sonal Narrative, Sound Recording and Life Writing, Survival and Life Writing, and Testimony.* What follows is a sampling of rele-vant synergies from some of the prior sections.

In the *Interview* section, author Wendy Webster offers a co-gent definition: "The interview is an oral exchange between two or more people that is distinguished from conversation by the division of roles adopted—one side questioning, prompting, or probing, the other providing answers" (Jolly 471). Mary Mar-shall Clark's comments in the *Oral History* section address the complex issues intrinsic to the role of the facilitator, i.e., ques-tioner/prompter: "While oral history, as a life-writing genre, bor-rows from autobiography, it is centered on the collision between autobiography and biography" (Jolly 677)." Though Clark de-scribes the relationship between autobiography and biography as a "collision," I would argue that with reference to the auto/biographies conducted for this research, the relationship is, rather, one of conflation, or merger. I regard my role more as one of prompter/recorder, rather than interpreter, especially through the participation of the interviewee in determining the topics to be discussed. Items in the questionnaire act as prompts. Importantly, whatever an interviewee does not wish to discuss is omitted from the videotaped conversation.

In his section on *Orality*, John Laudin calls to mind those signifiers not present in a printed text, i.e., "paralinguistic, extralinguistic features: gestures, facial expressions, postures," (Jolly 681), unseen in a voice recording, but very much evident in the videography format. Those features serve to enhance the performative aspect, present in sound/voice recordings; even more so in aural/visual media. A personal narrative can be seen as a performance of identity. According to *Personal Narrative* author Kristin M. Langellier, "people 'get a life' by telling their stories" (Jolly 700). Wendy Webster reinforces this idea in *Sound Recording and Life Writing:* "The narrative told, however personal or confessional is addressed not only to an immediate interlocutor, but also to a wider audience" (Jolly 823).

Life narratives are replete with a history of bearing witness and giving testimony, from slave narratives to Holocaust survivor projects. In their production centuries ago, slave narratives were constrained to the medium of written transcription, exhibiting the characteristics cited by Smith: "In oral history the one who speaks is not the one who writes, and the one who writes is often an absent presence in the text . . . a mediated form of personal narrative that depends on an interviewer who intervenes to collect and assemble a version of stories" (Smith 275-276). This concern is echoed by Sandra Lindeman and Krista Roberts (Chansky 385,411).

A stunning turn in technology is featured in a project from Conscience Display, a California-based firm that specializes in interactive digital storytelling. The project is headed by Heather

Maio Smith, managing director of the firm and wife of Shoah Foundation executive director Stephen Smith. Life-size, two/three-dimensional images of holocaust survivors projected onto monitors interact with visitors in sessions with a docent. For example, Holocaust survivor Pinchas Gutter's responses were recorded over a period of five days, with 52 cameras, yielding 30,000 different versions of questions in his database and over 1,900 responses (Musleah 53).

The myriad possibilities for three-dimensional holograph interview subjects with their potential for audience interaction are staggering. The holographic subjects will be invested with a technological immortality previously unfathomable except in the realm of science fiction.

Several decades ago viewers of the film *Superman II* were treated to holographs of Superman's deceased parents, exhorting him with their messages; no longer a cinematic fantasy, they are now a (virtual) reality. The organizers of the Holocaust project wanted to try to find a way to continue the educational tool of interactive survivor testimony after survivors are no longer alive. By preserving visual and auditory representations with the capacity to answer spontaneous interrogative queries, the production of holographs offers media version of (virtual) immortality. As futuristic as these auto/biographical forms may seem, James Olney's observation still rings true: "is not every autobiography the unique tale, uniquely told, of a unique life?" (47) In reflecting on the life narrative, author Ngugi wa Thiong'o remarked, "Every person has a book in them. Your story is different from my story" (Thiong'o "A Family Affair." Florida Atlantic University John D. MacArthur Campus, Jupiter. 30 January 2015. Reading.).

Modern digital media such as the film, videotape and the Internet, not to mention the ubiquitous cell phone, have transposed the autobiographical experience to images on a screen, rather than words on a page. The formerly written "I" of the narration becomes a visible persona, sometimes the actual narrator as in a life story interview, or an actor in a film adaption of an autobiographical life story. Like translation, film adaptation is a form of interpretation, converting a first person autobiographical account into a third-person cinematic rendition. Even with narrative first-person voiceovers, a third person story line dominates the viewer's perception. In "Leaves of Grass," Whitman observes, "This is no book,/Who touches this touches a man" (Eakin 222). To paraphrase, "Who sees this sees the person."

With respect to these heritage auto/biographies, three "I's" and one more "Eye" are intrinsic to the process: the present self "I" who is narrating, the textual "I" of the narrative, and the past self "I" on which the narrative is based. To this mix is added the "Eye" (and ear) of the video camera, a recording witness to the articulation of memory. Where am "I, the interviewer" in the process? I act as an assistant to the narrating "I's," to help them to follow the thread of their life story to self-discovery. Occasionally, I may offer a suggestion for a word that they are unsuccessfully trying to articulate, but I am exceedingly careful not to put (my) words in their mouths.

These individual life narratives are situated within the context of a larger reference, the family narrative. In turn, the family narrative informs and continues the greater saga of the Jewish people, presented in the narrative of the Bible. During the long diaspora, the Biblical narratives were regularly referenced by the exiles in the public reading of the weekly Torah portion. Over the course of a year, the entire first five books would be covered, as well as assorted excerpts of the rest of the canon. Other opportunities included the retelling the triumphant story of the Book of Exodus on Passover; the Jewish journey from slavery to freedom. For the celebration of the holiday of Purim, the victorious account of the book of Esther would be read aloud to the congregation, including the performative act of making noise at the sound of the name of the arch villain, Haman. For an oppressed, downtrodden population, celebrating past Jewish triumphs provided the rare opportunity of empowerment, if only by proxy in reliving events long past. These stories of victory presented tragic events located within the continuum of an ascending narrative, enabling the listeners to transpose feelings of defeat into feelings of hope, or empowerment.

The significance of the multigenerational Jewish family narrative supports the importance of accessing the diasporic details for past generations and generations to come. Psychologist Marshall Duke explains: "Psychologists have found that every family has a unifying narrative, and those narratives take one of three shapes" (Feiler 3). The ascending narrative relates a "rags to riches" story; the descending narrative goes from riches to rags. It is the oscillating narrative, the one with both ups and downs, which is the most inspiring. Throughout the long exile, the memory of the oscillating narrative was never lost, providing an important element of hope and inspiration.

Thanks to the miracle of 21st century technology, the ease with which a contemporary narrative can be produced and disseminated allows implementation of Steven Spielberg's exhortation in his Harvard Commencement Address. Spielberg advised the Harvard University graduating class of 2016 to "get the stories of your parents and grandparents" (Spielberg web). If those parents/grandparents are Jewish, a diasporic oscillating extended family narrative is more than likely. Modern psychological theory casts new light on old tradition.

Chapter 11
Conclusion

In order to supply the necessary background information to the life narratives, I begin with a chapter analysis of the concept of Jewish diaspora from several standpoints: linguistic, religious, historical, literary, liturgical, philosophical, theoretical, and political. It presents its subject in great detail in order to situate the five auto/biographical narratives along the historical continuum of an exilic experience spanning over four millennia.

To summarize, the chapter on diaspora presented several dichotomies on the Jewish diaspora in particular. Biblical excerpts demonstrate diaspora's retributive aspect(s), as divine punishment for transgressing holy law. Etymological studies reinforce the displacement aspect of diaspora, the scattering, as well as the potential for ultimate seeding and growth. Additional commentary, from 16th century Kabbalistic sources including Rabbi Isaac Luria, interprets diaspora to be a divine means of spreading holiness throughout the world; therefore, a good thing.

Within the liturgy, passages are cited which mentioned far-flung Jewish communities, demonstrating the Jewish diasporic precursor of Anderson's "imagined communities," i.e., non-interactive geographic enclaves located far from one another, linked together by performative prayer and ritual.

The Zionist movement of the late nineteenth and early twentieth centuries (re)offers the centrist model of diaspora, encouraging Jews living in exile to return to the land from which they had been expelled two thousand years before. Motivation was not religious in origin; rather, the goal was to shed the restrictions and anti-Semitic treatment imposed on Jews by the governing powers of the lands in which they lived as second-class citizens.

In the wake of two world wars and the Holocaust, with its loss of—a conservative estimate—six million Jews, the (re)establishment of the Jewish state of Israel in 1948 afforded diasporic Jews the right of return. At the time, some host countries did not allow their Jews to exercise this option, while some Jews voluntarily decided not to make *Aliyah*/immigrate to Israel. Voluntary reasons for remaining were vast and varied: economic, political, religious, social, and cultural, to name just a few, which persist to the present day.

The (non)movement to stay in exile engendered a wave of 20th and 21st century commentary. Alan Wolfe's book *At Home in Exile* supports the efficacy of living in diaspora for Jews and the world in which they live, pushing back against the attitude of "negative diaspora" reserved for those Israeli Jews who choose to emigrate, or leave the state of Israel. Included in the diaspora chapter discussion is the essay by Daniel and Jonathan Boyarin, which forefronts the concept that diaspora was the Jewish people's greatest world contribution.

The chapter ends with a discussion of diaspora *vis-à-vis* transnationalism, including Dufoix's models of diaspora/transnationalism and their relevance to 21st century multinational populations.

A close examination of *Megillat*/Book of Esther explores diasporic synergies with Robin Cohen's common features of diaspora. Briefly, feature #1, dispersal from an original homeland, often traumatically is demonstrated by the destruction of the First Temple and the Babylonian exile which brought the Jewish people eventually under Persian rule. Feature #3 "a collective memory and myth about the homeland," is shown by the familial nomenclature with which the principals are identified, including Haman, whose ancestor was an adversary of King Saul. The development of a return movement to the homeland, feature #5, is evidence by details in the Book of Ezra, written in the same time frame. A sense of empathy and co-responsibility, feature #8, is forefronted by Esther's request to have the people fast for/with her prior to risking her life by appearing unsolicited before the king.

Feature #9, "the possibility of a distinctive, creative enriching life in host countries with a tolerance for pluralism" would seem to preclude feature #7, "a troubled relationship with host societies," but unfortunately it does not. Though Mordecai held a highly respected governmental position, he was still vulnerable to the anti-Semitic actions of another government minister. Occupying a liminal space does not automatically erase the Self/Other dichotomy, as has occurred so many times during so many loci of Jewish diaspora, and continues to occur to this day.

As noted in the Esther chapter, 3rd person format for auto/biography is unusual, but not unheard of. Esther recognized the potential of auto/biography as self-help manual long before Harvard professor Tal Ben Shahar. She went before the *Sanhedrin*/Elders, the editorial board of the Biblical canon, insisting that the account be included as a referential text, should these importance lessons of personal experience be needed during a subsequent diaspora. The (co) author of this Ur-Auto/Biography proved to be prescient; as four hundred years later, a two-thousand year Roman diaspora would dwarf the Babylonian exile.

Lord Sacks regards Megillat Esther as "that paradigm of Diaspora life" (*To Heal a Fractured World* 155). Though the work is a paradigm, the behavior of the principals Esther and Mordecai demonstrate two opposite stances: keeping one's Jewish identity under wraps (Esther) and publicly identifying as Jewish (Mordecai). The obvious lesson is the necessity to adapt to varying circumstances in exile, but, at the risk of stating the obvious, another lesson is the importance of maintaining Jewish identity. Esther continued to have a close, if covert, connection with her relative Mordecai. Midrashic legend (*Megillah 13a*) has it that she continued to secretly observe the Jewish Sabbath by having seven different maids, one for each day of the week. The weekday maids always saw her working, and the Sabbath maid always saw her resting. She had found a way to retain her Jewish identity privately, unbeknownst to those with whom she was in close daily contact (Scherman, *Artscroll Youth Megillah* 14).

As detailed in the chapter, medieval sages laud Esther's rhetorical technique. Modern radical feminist rhetoric author Susan Zaeske also sings Esther's praises, as did female 19th century abolitionists who cited Esther as a source of inspiration for publicly speaking truth to power. In 2016, Israeli Prime Minister Benyamin Netanyahu opportunistically referenced *Megillat Esther* in his speech before the United States Congress. Until a few years ago, the tomb of Esther and Mordecai was designated as an Iranian historical site; Esther was the wife of one Persian king and the mother of another. Her universal appeal transcends the boundaries of culture and gender to this day. She is the only woman who called a fast, established a holiday and wrote a book of the Biblical canon—a genuine proto-feminist.

The five narrative chapters explore synergies with Cohen's common features of diaspora, as well as analogies to the "Esther moment." In conversation with each other, the narratives offer unusual insights into diaspora, particularly in the two dyad Baghdadi narratives of Isaac Jacob and Zmira Mozorosky. A closer examination of their stories reveals significant findings. Not every diasporic Jew connects as strongly with his/her Jewish roots as the people in the narratives, but the five varied narratives illustrate that it is not an isolated phenomenon.

Isaac Jacob (b. 1931) and Zmira Mozorosky (b. 1943) made *aliyah* to Israel within the span of a few years; Isaac in 1949 and Zmira in 1951. Though both could claim Baghdadi ancestry, the family dynamic was different: members of Isaac's family had been living outside of Bagdad for several decades; Zmira's family had been living uninterruptedly in their Baghdad home for several generations of the 2500-year Jewish sojourn. As they both relate separately, the families began life in Israel in tents, and then in tin huts. (Isaac was drafted into the army as he came off the ship, so he did not live steadily with his family for two years.)

Isaac's family managed to remain together, subsequently building a family home and replicating a closely connected family life. Zmira's family had a different experience. The first of her siblings who had arrived earlier wound up on secular *kibbutzim*/communal settlements without any access to an Iraqi community or place of religious worship. Zmira explains this arrangement as a deliberate attempt by the Ashkenazi-run Israeli government to assimilate Iraqi Jews into secular Israelis. As mentioned in the chapter, this attitude is a Jewish variation of what Edward Said described as "Orientalism," the negative attitude with which Western eyes view those of the East. Zmira felt marginalized by the lack of respect for her family's time honored traditions; she mentions that she was only able to "patch the path" by leaving Israel for an extended stay in the United States.

A commonality in the immigration of Isaac and Zmira to Israel is reflected in the beginning part of Cohen's first feature of diaspora: "Dispersal from an original homeland, often traumatically" (Cohen 17). Technically, the diaspora from Judea to Iraq is the first dispersal, but because of the 2500-year duration of the sojourn, the forced expulsion of Zmira's family from Iraq felt like an original diaspora. In Isaac's case, his family had not been forced to leave Iraq; they voluntarily participated in the expansion of the Iraqi Sassoon family business empire. They lived comfortably in India and then Shanghai, where they had been posted, in the bosom of family and friends, continuing to faithfully worship, preserving their age-old Iraqi Jewish traditions. Ironically, the immigration to Israel marks a great departure from their Jewish ways of life, as has been elaborated on in the individual narratives.

When Zmira shared her story of rupture and displacement, she was entering into the area of what John Beverly has termed "testimonio, to testify, to bear truthful witness" (Beverly 3). The story of the Mizrachi Jews, the Jews of the East, bears all the earmarks of subalternity. An organization, *Sephardic Voices,* sponsors programs for synagogues and other cultural groups featuring the collected narrative presentation of Babylonian Jews, in an effort to preserve memories of a culture that was all but obliterated by its traumatic 20th century expulsion. The "Sephardic" in *Sephardic Voices* refers to the culture of the Jewish population originating in post-Inquisition 15th century Spain, but the organization has expanded to include the equally, if not more, marginalized Jews descended from those Jews who remained in lands since the Babylonian Exile 2500 years before; they never were a part of the Spanish/Portuguese Jewish population.

Over fifty years were to pass before Isaac was to (re)visit Shanghai, the city of his birth/youth. The post-war years had brought the insular Communist Revolution, making a return trip difficult for the prior "stateless resident." He was able to find the street on which the multi-home complex had stood, but it had been made into a park. Though few landmarks remain from the pre-war era, Isaac still expressed satisfaction and closure it gave him to make the pilgrimage with his son.

Bagdad, the city of her birth and early years, still remains off-limits to Zmira. She uses 21st century map technology to take a "virtual" tour. Her family's large (former) home has been made into a community hospital. She would very much like to make a pilgrimage to her old neighborhood, if and when travel to the region is ever permitted for an Israeli-Jewish-American citizen.

In contrast, the voluntary diasporic dispersals of narrative subjects Rochel Berman and Jay Lauwick are motivated by wanting to be with their respective spouses. Rochel has gone back to her original Jewish community in Winnipeg to visit and present her study guide; it is no longer a Yiddish-speaking bubble. Jay Lauwick had intermittent contact with members of his French family in the years between his arrival in New York and his seventieth birthday. The year before she passed away, Jay's late wife presciently arranged a *reunion*/70th birthday in Paris, which reconnected him to family and friends. He visited annually for the next decade or so, eventually taking up permanent residence in France for the last few years of his life. Maybe one can go home again.

Within the narrative of Sibyl Silver, the diasporic dispersed subjects are represented by the one-hundred-eighteen Holocaust Torahs. They were displaced from communities most of whose members were murdered by the Nazis, all but eliminating any chance for rebuilding a lost world; post-war attempts of many Eastern European Jews met with a hostile political and social climate. The surviving Torahs act as a link between the vanished Jewish population and several thousand years of Jewish tradition. In restoring them and putting them to the use for which they were intended, Sibyl is reviving the rich Torah world from which they came. To be in the presence of these Torahs is to bear witness for the ones who are no longer here, assuring that they (and their Torahs) are not forgotten, a form of tribute and remembrance.

Last, but not least/*aharon, aharon haviv*, the research concludes with an historical overview of the auto/biographic format through the ages to the present day. From Biblical third person accounts, slave narratives, and "classic" auto/biographies, the chapter goes into detailed treatment of the genre, including printed format, vlogs, blogs, Facebook as well as the newest hi-tech edition, the interactive holograph. The discussion includes an examination of the narrative aspect of autobiography, including current challenges to its fundamentality.

When the 1960s media guru Marshal McLuhan famously proclaimed, "The Medium is the Message," he could well have been speaking of 21st century autobiography. From blogs to holograms, the medium is holding out the possibility of producing an experiential auto/biographic for the reader/viewer. A filmic representation draws the audience into the movie; an escape into a virtual reality. The newly minted interactive humanoid holograph makes participants out of spectators.

A common thread between older and newer forms of auto/biographical production lies in the profoundly human motivation to capture and preserve life experience, otherwise inevitably ephemeral and fleeting. The concept brings to mind an observation by the duke of Kalisz, Boleslaw the Pious, who authored a thirteenth-century charter of privileges accorded to Polish Jews. The charter opens, "The deeds of man when unconfirmed by the voices of witnesses or by written documents, are bound to pass swiftly away and disappear from memory" (Luckert x). Current visual/sound media technology now holds out the promise of immortal witnessing for each of our life stories; their interpretation will be the gauntlet taken up by future generations.

In the age of globalism, technology and world politics intersect to provide the diasporic option to live in many worlds, physical, social and spiritual. No longer bound by geographic limitations of transportation and distance, in the span of a few months, a diasporic subject can choose to divide time between residences in different loci, as does Zmira Mozorosky.

This "virtual" liminal space situates a citizenship of transnationalism, a viable contemporary alternative to prior binary options. The choice to live literally in two worlds has become increasingly popular for career professionals in the Jewish diaspora. Families are able to settle in Israel while the physician or entrepreneur continues to earn a livelihood in the United States by working part time on site and part time off site from Israel. Modern modes of transportation have reduced travel time; the Inter-

net has virtually erased distances of time and space with its capacity for instant communication.

Several other populations displaced through politi-
cal/religious upheaval share synergies with the Jewish diasporic
model; it remains to be seen if their journey takes a tribal or
transnational turn, from particularism to universalism. It should
be said that not every diasporic subject, Jewish or otherwise, is
motivated or positioned to retain strong ties with the root culture;
the choice to assimilate, if it is an option, is often the most compelling one. Whatever a diasporic subject chooses to do (or not)
is certain to furnish life story narratives which should be recorded and shared for generations to come.

In researching on Jewish diasporic life narratives, I have
gleaned many precious lessons: the long documented history of
the Jewish diaspora, the resilience of the Jewish people, the inspiration of Jewish survival against all odds, Esther's protofemi-
nist example, and the resource of Jewish tradition which speaks
to each successive generation anew, as well as the world at large.
Am Yisrael Chai!

Intersectionality

Intersectionality is a strong component of this work; areas of
intersectionality include postcolonial theory/diasporic Jewish
history, prior diasporic history/current life narrative, ur-
auto/biography of Esther with contemporary life narratives, the
genres auto/biography and biography, as well as auto/biography
and 21st century technology. Though the theme of intersectionality weaves its way through the prior chapters, a more focused
treatment is presented here.

Postcolonial Theory/Diasporic Jewish History

Through the readings for a class in postcolonial theory came
the realization that the events of the Jewish diaspora were inclu-
sive of several, if not all of the features of the "colonial encoun-

ter: trade, plunder, negotiation, warfare, genocide, enslavement and rebellions" (Loomba 8). By utilizing the prism of Robin Cohen's nine features of diaspora, synergies in the life narratives were forefronted, in both a contemporary and earlier historical context, creating a continuum of the Jewish diasporic experience.

Auto/biography, Biography and 21st Century Technology

As discussed in Chapter 10, "The Message in the Medium, over three decades ago," Timothy Dow Adams originally created the term "auto/biography" to reference both genres; the IABA, International Auto/Biography Association, utilizes the bifurcation in its organization title as well as in its ongoing journal, a/b: Auto/Biography Studies.

The format of an auto/biographical interview, which describes the genre of the five life narratives, is best described with a slash, because the interviews encompass elements of both autobiography and biography. They are the words of the interviewees reflecting on their personal life details, with the facilitation provided by the interviewer in the form of a pre-interview questionnaire and prompts during the interview itself. The interview is a hybrid form of autobiography and biography; hence the usage of a form of the word auto/biography in the title. Chapter 10s discussion of autobiographical theory goes into more detail referencing the elision of the two genres.

Enter 21st century technology. No longer solely the provenance of print, autobiographical production entered the media of film/video camera, radio, television and the Internet. The interviews would not have happened without a technology which made it possible to record a visual record easily and economically in a home milieu, rather than a professional photography studio. Viewing was simplified by making the interviews accessible to the committee with a private YouTube link distributed via email. Interviewees were given copies of their interviews on thumb drives for accessible viewing on their home computers.

They have the option to share their interviews on family web sites, blogs, etc., all courtesy of the ubiquitous Internet; a virtual world of possibilities.

Appendix A
Isaac Jacob Interview
December 2014

Hello. I'm Elaine Mendelow of Heritage Biography International with a dear friend, Isaac Jacob, who had a special birthday a few years ago. For his birthday my husband and I took him to dinner because his family was in Israel and I also gave him an outline of my heritage biography. It took a few years and a kind, loving persistent daughter-in-law, Beverly Jacob, so we can tell one of the most fascinating Jewish American stories I've ever heard. They don't call us the wandering Jews for nothing. If this is the beginning of the 21st century we would love to do your life story. I can be reached at heritagebiography.com. If this is later, we bring you greetings from the past.

EM: Let's start out by asking your full name.

IJ: It's Isaac. My middle name is Rachamim, which my father gave me. And my last name is Jacob without the "s."

EM: And the "Isaac" is spelled "Isaac," the Sephardic way, with two "a's."

IJ: That's correct.

EM: Do you have a nickname?

IJ: They used to call me "Ike" in school.

EM: And your Jewish name?

IJ: Yitzchak.

EM: What was your father's name?

IJ: It was Ezra. His middle name was Shaya, Isaiah.

EM: When was he born?

IJ: He was born August 27, 1876 and passed away January 1 1955. January 1, 1955. How did he pass away?

IJ: He had had a stroke and half his body was paralyzed. We tried the best we could—it was not easy he got bed sores— we had to move him around there was nobody around we had to work took turns a very difficult time

EM: What are some of your memories of him?

IJ: Well, he was a very strict man; he adhered very strictly to Jewish laws and things like that and he got very annoyed if we went against him.

EM: And talking again about your father, where was he born?

IJ: He was born in Baghdad, Iraq. It was Mesopotamia. When he was approximately 15 years old, he moved to India, Bombay, India. Now it's Mumbai. He lived there for fifteen years.

EM: What made him move from Bagdad to Bombay?

IJ: Iraq was under the Ottoman, the Turkish Empire, and they wanted to conscript all young people into the army probably at 16, so he had to leave. His brother left before him, and his father had passed away I don't know when in Bagdad, and his mother was ṣtill alive, and they all moved to Bombay and then to Shanghai. The brother moved there first and then he told his brother, told him to come.

EM: Was there a business connection?

IJ: They had a potential job at ED Sassoon company. They were very, very wealthy Jewish-Bagdadian Jews who came there in the 1850s and establish very big businesses, actually importing opium and exporting piece . . . goods, like cotton goods, a tremendous job.

EM: Yes, the Sassoons came during the Opium Wars to Shanghai. We'll get to that. As you said, the mother went to Bombay. And then did the mother come to Shanghai?

IJ: She was raised by my great-aunt, Hababi. My mother's name was Sophie and her maiden name was Reuben.

EM: What about your mother's date of birth?

IJ: August 8, 1892. She passed away in 1969 in America. My mother was born in Bombay, India. They came from Iraq also, but they moved there early. They came to Shanghai when she was 18 years old.

EM: Your parents met in Shanghai. They were married at the synagogue in Shanghai.

IJ: Here's the wedding picture of my mother and father in 1911. She was 19 and your father was 35. There was a sixteen year age difference. Picture of Parents (Isaac points out his father's spats and waxed moustache.)

IJ: They had eight children.

EM: You do have some early pictures of your mother.

IJ: (Shows pictures of mother with her two brothers and a sister.)

EM: This was taken in Bombay. Did your parents know each other in Bombay?

EM: Names of brothers?

IJ: Reuben Reuben. I never knew the brother; he died very young. My aunt is Flora.

IJ: My mother, my mother's sister Flora, my Uncle Jacob, my father's brother and my great aunt, Hababba, her father's sister and my sister Hilda and my sister Lisa.

EM: So H and L were the first two children. They were followed by four boys and one girl. We'll talk about them later. Let's show one before you were born.

IJ: (Showing picture.) This is in the 20s.This is at a dedication of a sefer Torah, and my older brothers are in this picture. This is my aunt Flora and there's my father with a sefer Torah and there's my mother.

EM: What are some of your memories of your mother?

IJ: She was the kindest person, very, very kind. She tried to help everyone, against my father's wishes.

EM: It happened when the Jews from WWII came.

IJ: We were not in the same areas as the refugees that came, the refugees from Europe and all the other refugees that came. They had houses where they could find houses. Then with the instigation of the Germans, who came to the Japanese authorities, they tried to convince the Japanese authorities that all these refugees who had escaped—they wanted to annihilate them. The Japanese authorities refused. They compromised. They said they would intern them in the ghettos. They didn't say Jews, they said all who came between 1937-9 would have to move into this ghetto and this was, it was a very dilapidated place. It was near the Japanese occupation section part of China, where these people had to go the housing was impossible, ten family cramped into one house, dysentery typhoid, all kinds of diseases. There was one person, one Japanese official in charge of giving the visas to exit the area. He was a very nasty person. They had a hard time trying to get out, to do business

EM: Did your family have to move?

IJ: No, we did not have to move, we were established but as Iraqi citizens we were considered by the Japanese as semi-enemies because Iraq had severed diplomatic relations w/Japan, so we would be considered enemies.

EM: This would be a good time to show your passport.

IJ: We were considered stateless in Shanghai. The Chinese didn't know what a Jew was; they said they were foreigners. We were actually stateless in Shanghai so when the Japanese came they—

EM: I was reading in one of the articles you gave me that the Japanese thought the Jews were very smart and also they thought that they controlled Congress, so they didn't want to irritate Congress.

IJ: (Shows passport) We had to pay a lot of money to get this passport. We went to the agent in the British Embassy in charge of giving passports. We bribed the people there. It doesn't say Jew.

EM: It's also in Arabic, because it's an Iraqi passport and Iraq is an Arab country. Here's the picture of you when you were—

IJ: Sixteen. I look like twelve.

EM: You had been through a lot by then.

IJ: We had a Jewish school and a synagogue which formed a compound. This is a B

IJ: A counsel came in 1949 from Israel to Shanghai and he issued visas.

IJ: (Picking up another paper.) This was my birth certificate. This was issued in Shanghai. The person who signed it was my sister's husband's grandfather.

EM: You can see the names . . . 6 Yang Terrace, born at home. How many children?

IJ: Four brothers and three sisters and only one [brother] is still alive.

EM: Your father had two bros, Jacob and Charlie, younger than your father

IJ: Charlie was in Shanghai. He passed away before we left, during the J occ.

EM: Let's show the picture of you when you were two years old. (Shows picture.)You're adorable.

EM: Now let's show the picture of your son Marty at two years old. Definitely a resemblance.

EM: What is your earliest memory? Your earliest memory, which you wrote down, you remember you were sick w/pneumonia.

IJ: There were a lot of doctors, my mother kept calling them, they said there was no hope, and my mother was frantic. So she didn't give up and she finally called a doctor from Germany, not a Jewish doctor. He said, "I'll try and save your son." . . . When he came to visit me, all the relatives came to visit and everybody was crying.

EM: So the doctor tried something radical [for those times].

IJ: There was some kind of patch. [mustard plaster] You heat it up on the stove to make it soft. When it's hot, you stick on your chest and back. That's what I remember. They had a steam kettle on the stove to make breathing easier in the kettle w/eucalyptus oil so I could breathe. It's amazing I got better.

EM: Ironic that a German doctor saved you.

IJ: Yes we knew a lot of Germans. One of our tenants was German, very nice.

EM: You also mentioned that you lived in Shanghai until 1949 and that you went to one school from kindergarten to graduation. What language was the school?

IJ: It was in English, because it was sort of a British school. They had two exams, there was 6th form and six upper. In 6th form, they had an exam not from the school, from Cambridge University, in England. You went to an auditorium. You went to a special auditorium, they opened a package, a special

EM: So in some way, you're a Cambridge University graduate.

IJ: Yes, that was the sixth grade and then another exam from Cambridge in Six Upper. That was like matriculation.

EM: That sounds almost like college.

IJ: Well, not really. They didn't have trigonometry.

EM: What did your parents speak at home?

IJ: My father and mother when they lived in Bombay, when they wanted to say something in secret. Where we didn't understand a word. My father spoke to me in Arabic, and I answered in English mostly, sometimes in Arabic.

EM: Do you still understand Arabic?

IJ: Sure.

EM: What about Chinese?

IJ: Well, we didn't write Chinese but we had to learn Chinese we had two or three servants, one for each kid. We had a person sometimes cooking for us, a man. We had to speak to them in Chinese because they didn't know a word of English.

EM: So you just picked it up.

IJ: Well you had to pick it up because you had to go to the store.

EM: Did you have any motor vehicles?

IJ: My brothers had cars, but in the Second World War, from 1941 to 1945 you couldn't get any gas. I went to school opposite a military camp, occupied by US soldiers before 1941, the Marines there, a big base. They knew that the war was coming, so they left. I don't know exactly when they left, but the Japanese Army took it over. My school was right across the street from this base. I used to watch from my window of the school. The way they trained was amazing. They used a wooden rifle, the same size and weight of a rifle.

EM: We have you as a young man in Israel, just short of eighteen. You got to Israel, you can tell us about the train trip all sealed off—

IJ: From China, we landed in SF and took a train to NY. It took 412 to five days. It was a sealed train; the windows were not open more than an inch or inch and a half. The FBI agents, many, many FBI agents in the cars to make sure that nobody gets off the train. They used to count at night to make sure that everyone was there. One day my brother was fed up with sitting on the chair to sleep, so he decided to find a place where he could sleep horizontally, so he went to the baggage car on top of the baggage and to sleep. The agents came at night, and realized one person was missing. They asked us who it was, and I said my brother was sleeping in the baggage car. They were very angry. We got to New York and we went on a small boat to Ellis Island, we were there for four or five days, the immigration center. We were grateful to be there because we hadn't had any kosher food for a very long time, and the Jewish Agency brought us kosher food. So we were very appreciative of that kosher food after five days. We went from Ellis Island on a ship from NY to Italy. We landed on the west coast of Italy, a city called Tradi. We stayed in Italy for 2-3 weeks they were processing us to see if we had any illnesses, contagious diseases just to make sure there was nobody sick going to Israel. My father had eye problems, glaucoma, so my father had to get treated for glaucoma and my brother stayed behind with him. We went from Italy to Israel landed in Haifa, Haifa port. The authorities came on board and they found I was almost 18 they said we need everybody in the army you're going to be in the army right away, so, they separated me from my family and took me to an army base.

EM: What year was this?

IJ: This was in 1949, the beginning of April and I was going to be 18 in July.

EM: There is a picture of you in a French cap in the other part of the video.

IJ: Yes, French caps. The back of the cap had a flap to prevent the sun from hitting your neck.

EM: Sounds like the hats worn by the French Foreign Legion.

IJ: (laughing) Yes, they copied it. A similar cap to the French Foreign Legion, they copied it.

EM: You got to Israel in 1949 and left for the United States in 1962. What did you do during those thirteen years in Israel? What type of work did you do?

IJ: In the beginning I was two years in the army, so I didn't do anything except serve in the army. Then I came out and there were no jobs to get, so I found different kinds of labor that I could earn some money, like picking oranges from the trees, making boxes for the oranges, picking vegetables, different odd jobs just to make a slight living.

EM: What were your brothers doing? Did they meet women and marry? Were they applying for visas?

IJ: Not yet. This was '49. My brothers started to apply for visas maybe five years later. My one brother met an immigrant from Egypt, from a Greek background and in 1951 he married her. So in1951 that brother who married that Egyptian woman started to build with 39 other people who didn't know anything about a brick or a log or anything like that, they volunteered to build houses in a town called Hadera; the construction should have taken two, three months to finish; very small houses, two small rooms with a small kitchen and a small bathroom, very tiny. It took so long because they didn't know what they were doing, so they had to learn on the job.

EM: So your family lived near each other in these houses?

IJ: No. In the meantime, my family lived in a tent, in a very, very hot American army tent, which is green, it absorbs all the heat. It was very stifling, no air conditioning. Then we got upgraded to a hut made out of wood paneling, a little better, but not the comfort of a solid brick house, that's when my brother was working to finish the house, then the family moved to this house it was like an upgrade a very small house. We had pullout beds to accommodate the whole family. It was very, very tight.

EM: How about food?

IJ: We had what was called a markolet, like a grocery store. In the beginning, for two years we didn't have electricity, so we had to cook on a kerosene stove. It was very hard, just one stove to cook everything.

EM: Especially since you had come from such a different life in China, life of luxury.

IJ: Very very difficult times to accommodate us, to let us be happy.

EM: Was there enough food to eat?

IJ: Yes, there was somewhat enough. Meat was very scarce. We had chicken. Vegetables were pretty well supplied. Sugar was very scarce; we couldn't get sugar, you know, things like that. They had to import it. They tried not to import a lot of stuff in Israel 'cause they didn't have money to do that.

EM: So, there you were, going along in Israel, and then you went to America. What made you emigrate?

IJ: Well, my brothers applied for visas to America. It took quite a few years, I forget exactly how long, but I didn't make an effort to apply for it, so, maybe I was lazy, or whatever. So one by one, my three brothers who were in Israel, they left for America. My mother and my sister— she had a job, my sister had a job in Tel Aviv and she rented an apartment there, and she looked after my mother and then somebody from China, an acquaintance of my mother's, they were friends, she came to Israel and she said, "You know my son. I'd like to make a shidduch with your daughter." Somehow it worked out okay. So then they got married and he went back to America and she got a visa to go to America with my mother, because mother and daughter is a priority, you know.

EM: And your father had passed away?

IJ: Yes, in 1955.

EM: So he was in Israel for six years. Then this all happened after. Then your mother went with her daughter to America, and you were the last one in Israel?

IJ: Yes, I was the last one in Israel, and I was lonely, you know all my family is in America. Luckily, the visa for a mother to a son was very good, so she applied for me as a mother and so I got the visa very fast, in just six months.

EM: You went to America in—let's say the date again.

IJ: 1962. I still had to have a sponsor—so my brother had to sign an affidavit—to see how much money he's making, how much money he has in the bank, so they really make sure that you're not a dependent on the government.

EM: Right, there were a lot of requirements.

IJ: Right. I had to take x-rays, to make sure I didn't have diseases.

EM: What did you do for your work when you got to America?

IJ: Well, I got a job like as a carpenter, one of the jobs. Another job was in construction in New York City.

EM: Did you work for your brothers at all, in the course of this time?

IJ: Well, in Israel before we left, my brothers were experts on radio repair, radios. In H, where we lived we lived in the outskirts of Hadera. In the main city, we opened a radio store for repairs of radios. . I studied by myself, I had a book, when I was in the army, I was reading over things so I would be also an expert on radios.

EM: There's a fancy word for you: it's "autodidact." It's somebody who teaches themselves.

IJ: Right. There was no opportunity to go to college. (because) I never went to college. I just finished high school in Shanghai.

IJ: We opened this radio store—the red tape is so. . . . They used to come to the store and check all the radios checked for the excise tax, a red tag, and if it didn't have a red tag, they would confiscate the radio. For instance, there was no tape recorder at that time; we had a wire recorder. That was the first kind of recorder that came out in the fifties. The recording is made on a very thin steel wire. We didn't have tape recorders, a wire recorder . . . the tape is made . . . we had that from Shanghai and they said where is the excise tax? We don't have it; we got it from Shanghai. Well, we'll have to confiscate it.

EM: A lot of bureaucracy

IJ: That's what killed everything, my outlook on Israel.

EM: The red tape was very off putting. So you were not unhappy to leave Israel because of *parnassah*. Was there anything you looked back on and missed?

IJ: We had a lot of friends, we used to go to picnics, outings we went to the Kinneret. That brought back memories.

EM: So you missed the camaraderie.

EM: You moved to the New York City area.

IJ: Brooklyn.

EM: So there were a lot of observant Jews.

IJ: I had an apartment.

EM: What kind of synagogue did you wind up going to?

IJ: Sephardic synagogue, Syrian Jews from Syria.

EM: Comfortable.

IJ: Yes, very comfortable. That's how my brother met his wife. Somebody from the shule invited him for dinner one Friday night. This person had six daughters. He got to know one of the daughters and he finally married her.

EM: And she was from the Syrian family, so it was okay with the Syrians.

IJ: Years and years ago, a cousin from my father's older brother. The oldest son was going out with a woman, a religious Jewish woman from Russia. The father was very angry. How could you do that? I love her. The father said, if you marry her, nobody's going to come to the wedding, he was like a commander, so he forbade my father and my uncle, my younger uncle, from going to the wedding, almost like marrying a goy.

EM: So there you were—when and how did you meet your wife?

IJ: One of the sisters of my brother's wife was a counselor in a Jewish camp, and my wife was there with her and they were friendly. So she asked me, "Do you want to meet this girl?" So I said "yes, sure." So she went to Joan, and she said my brother-in-law is from China. . . . She was in a PhD program, so a lot of people came from China, Japan a lot of foreigners, so she was used to seeing foreigners. So I called her up and we went on a date.

EM: Was it love at first sight?

IJ: It was pretty much so. I was concerned for the height, and she was small [EM: petite]

IJ: We got married three years later. I was 35 and she was six years younger.

EM: I noticed you got married on April 3rd. We got married on April 3, 1966. Everybody came. It was amazing.

IJ: And Marty was born just before Pesach.

EM: Yes, everything happens before Pesach. Speaking of Marty, I have a wonderful picture of Joan and Marty

IJ: Mt. Sinai Hospital in NY, April 2nd.

EM: We have another picture of Marty, grown up Doctor Marty and his beautiful wife Beverly. And here's a picture of Isaac with Marty, Beverly and Isaac's three grandsons, whose names are—

EM: So that's the family. You do have another son named Simcha. He was born in 1972 and he's married.

IJ: Yes, and he has two children—the boy is five-and-a-half and the girl is three.

EM: And their names are—

IJ: Avi and Yaffa. Joan's Hebrew name was Yaffa. She is named after Joan.

EM: And the name of your daughter-in-law?

IJ: Yoni.

EM: And your daughter-in-law is a physician.

IJ: Yes, she's a doctor.

IJ: He's a rabbi. He passed his *smicha* in YU [Yeshiva University], in rabbinical school. Also my daughter-in-law she came to America after she was working as a doctor, from Australia, and she wanted to advance her Jewish studies. So she signed up at Stern College, they have a course Advanced Talmudic studies for women for two years. She got a degree like a rabbi. So she got an advanced degree.

EM: We do have to talk about a sad thing, the fact that Joan did not live to see her kids grow up.

IJ: She died of breast cancer that had metastasized.

IJ: Yes, she passed away when the kids were fourteen and eleven. She died of breast cancer which had metastasized.

EM: So you were basically a single father for a while, raising the boys and that couldn't have been easy.

IJ: No, you know, with having a job, and raising them and doing the housework.

EM: You were Mr. Mom!

IJ: Not only that, I had to volunteer because I had subsidized tuition from the Yeshiva, so they asked me, I had to volunteer for Bingo classes.

EM: Would you say—Have you encountered any anti-Semitism in your public or personal life? All the way back.

IJ: Well, in China, when we lived in China, the Chinese really didn't know what a Jew was, he was a foreigner. Then when the Japanese occupied China between 1941-45, the European Jews came to China, and they started to know what a Jew was. There was never really anti-Semitism there.

EM: What about the United States?

IJ: I didn't feel it that much. Just recently there's more anti-Semitism than previously.

EM: Has your outlook or the way you practice religion changed in the course of your life?

IJ: No.

EM: Did you ever find it challenging? Did you ever say, "Oh, this is so hard?"

IJ: Of course it's challenging, because looking for a job, saying you're not going to work on Shabbat, you're not going to work on the holidays. For instance, I worked in a place and somebody came, there was a salesman, and he said, "I can give you a better job, because I'm going to be a supervisor in this new plant." Great. He told me what my salary was and I was looking forward to getting a bigger salary. So he invited me for an interview and I went to the interview. He liked what I was saying. I did repairs for the machinery, the quip, photo equipment, the printing things, some. So he said, "The biggest day is Saturday when we do all the repairs." "Uh, oh," I said, "I don't work on Saturdays." So he said, "Sorry, I can't hire you.

EM: So it was a given in your life. It wasn't like you ever said, "Well, I'll do this one job . . . and your brothers too stayed observant.

IJ: Well, A couple of my brothers went out.

EM: What kept you from doing out?

IJ: Well, getting married and having children. I spoke to Joan, and she said, "If you don't raise them as Jews, they'll marry out. I didn't have the money to send them to Yeshiva, so they were subsidized.

EM: Was she from an observant family?

IJ: Not really. She was the only child of the family and they were not observant. She went to the B'nei Akiva and the Young Israel because she had friends there and she became very observant.

EM: She was more observant, and she was fine with you being observant because that's how she wanted to be.

EM: Can you just recount any religious celebrations or family holiday rituals from your childhood? I know that you had written down about Passover.

IJ: Well the way that we celebrate the Passover. Before we
      said the *Manishtana* the young kids, the Israelites when
      they left Egypt they tied it on their back, and before Man-
      ishtana, we went out. We knocked on the door. My father
      said, "Who's there?" and we said "*Israelim*." Where did
      you come from? *Mitzrayim*. We came inside and then we
      said the *Manishtana*.

EM: What about now?

IJ: I try to do it with the kids.

EM: What role does Israel play in your life? You mentioned
      there's a grandson studying in Bar Ilan . . . . . . Does he
      have a plan to settle in Israel?

IJ: He did have a plan to settle in Israel, but

EM: Do you have any family left in Israel?

IJ: My brother's relatives. I was very friendly with one
      cousin.

EM: In the Jacobs family, did any descendants of those siblings
      wind up in Israel?

IJ: My aunt, my father's brother.

IJ: I have a niece in Ranana. We go to her house in Israel.

EM: No descendants of your mother?

EM: What about Sukkot? You said your mother would buy
      about fifteen chickens and . . .

IJ: Yes, fifteen or twenty chickens.

IJ: He wasn't a rabbi per se, but a very learned person, but he
      would come and do the kaporah for each person.

EM: And slaughter the chickens?

EM: There was a Chanukah dish that your mother made, some-
      thing called kachi?

IJ: Yes, Kachi. Not very healthy. [Sounds delicious!]Dough
      that was spread very thin and coated with butter and then
      deep fried in oil.

EM: The oil, the whole thing with Chanukah and oil. Was it
      sweet?

IJ: Well, we had to put sugar on top, and it was very crispy, all the thin dough with the oil is very, very tasty.

EM: Where did this dish originate, kachi?

IJ: It originated in Iraq, in Bagdad.

EM: When you went to Israel, did she still make it? Did she ever make it . . . ?

IJ: No, we never had it again. For Chanukah, my father used to buy wax, raw wax and he used to make his own candles to supply the community. It was a slow process, because you had a wick and you would pour the wax and then it would dry and then you would pour some more and it would dry to pour.

EM: Of course he made kosher candles.

IJ: Yes, of course.

EM: What happened when you went to Israel?

IJ: No, we didn't do anything like that. We bought candles.

EM: Now I'd like to talk about your pilgrimage a few years ago, back to China. Tell us about that.

IJ: Yes, anyway, I'm very close to my grandson in Israel. We get along very well, not as much as my other two grandsons here, so I asked him if he wanted to come to China with me, it turned out that he had school and couldn't come, so Marty said I'll come with you. I said okay (laughter) . . . so we took a trip to China, and there was a big group. We stayed in different hotels, we were in Beijing, we toured Tiananmen Square where all the people were slaughtered there, where all the students were killed. There's no sign of anything. You can't talk about it at all. If you talk about it and they hear you, you get arrested.

EM: You were told that, not to talk about it, not to say anything.

IJ: Yes, not to mention anything.

EM: So let me ask you about Shanghai.

IJ: So we went to Shanghai, and we didn't have so much kosher food there. We went with a rabbi he had his own pots and pans in different hotels, and he would bring, make soup. It wasn't very satisfying.

EM: Roughing it. They would bring some challah from Israel Somebody brought a bottle of wine, so we had that for Shabbat.

EM: What did you see in Shanghai that was left—Did anything look like it did from your childhood?

IJ: The first thing I tried was to look at my house, where I had lived for seventeen, eighteen years. We went to the area there, and we were looking, and it started to rain we were going in that area, I knew it was in that area and we were walking around and I couldn't find anything, I couldn't find it, we were walking around and I couldn't find anything. Then we went to Chabad, there was a Sephardic Chabad, we had dinner there, it was very great, the first meal we had and it was a real good meal. A couple of people who were serving were a Jewish guy and his wife, they were serving, they were working for the Chabad. We ate there two nights in this Chabad, and Marty got very friendly with the guy. So Marty said, "Maybe we should go out for a beer together." So we left the group, the group left, or whatever, they went back to the hotel and we stayed with this couple. They said they used to call her, "Hey, could you bring something," not very polite, the people from the tour. This guy was very angry. He said, "You know, she has two servants working for her. We're helping out, and they treated her like garbage."

EM: Did you see anything from your childhood? The high school or the synagogue?

IJ: Yes, so we couldn't find the house. So this woman said, "I'll find it for you." She ordered the Uber to come and took us to this area, and she speaks Chinese, obviously.

EM: You don't speak Chinese anymore?

IJ: They don't understand when I'm speaking, because I
       spoke the Shanghai dialect, which nobody speaks any
       more. Only in S they used to speak this. The government
       changed it to Mandarin. So they didn't understand what I
       was saying.

IJ: So [this woman is there in the Uber]

IJ: So she went to the corner, almost where I lived and there
       was a forty-story Four Seasons Hotel there near where I
       lived. So she went to the guards in the hotel and she spoke
       to them in Chinese and she said to them that they had a
       house where seven houses were attached and she explained
       to them. They said, "Oh we remember that. It was knocked
       down and they built a garden in the area."

EM: What about your school?

IJ: Yes, so we decided not to continue with the tour for one
       day. We hired actually a tour guide to take us where WE
       wanted to go. So we went to the school. And everything
       besides the school that I went to from kindergarten to
       twelfth grade was still standing there and the shule that I
       went to was still standing there. We tried to go into the
       shule, and they said "You can't go." So the guide she
       spoke to them. She said, "He was here," so they said,
       "Okay, you can go walk outside, you can't go inside." So
       we went to the shule. That's where Hillary Clinton went
       when she went to China, she visited the shule.

EM: What is it now? Is it a synagogue?

IJ: They said they made it into a museum, a museum for the
       past Jewish life. Chabad uses it once a year for Rosh
       Hashanah and Yom Kippur; they allow them to come and
       use it.

EM: So you found the school. Is it still a school?

IJ: No, it's a government business. I was telling Marty and the
       group that we went with, the private [tour] that my class-
       room when I was a student there was overlooking the

street and across the street previously was an American Marine barracks. So when the Japanese took over Shanghai, they had their army base there in this place. And I used to watch from the window how the Japanese used to train, with bayonets, make believe bayonets, made of wood. They really tried all out to kill the other guy. They had masks, like real fighting.

EM: So it was hard to pay attention to your studies, with this going on out the window. There was no competition.

IJ: (Laughing heartily) And now there's a Starbucks café in that area.

EM: So now it's a Starbucks café. Was there any moment where you stood and you said, "Yes, I feel I'm back."

IJ: Well, some areas. In other words, there's an area called the "Bund." The B is an industrial place where very, very big buildings were built, huge, huge solid stone buildings. One of the buildings was built, was a hotel, by the Sassoon family, the Sassoon was a Sephardic banking family.

EM: Wasn't that the family that got your family their occupation in India, and sent them to Shanghai?

IJ: Right so, they were very wealthy. So they built this hotel on the Bund, it's a unique kind of building, many, many rooms, a unique structure.

EM: And that was there when you lived there? And it's still there?

IJ: Yes. They changed the name, they made it the Peace Hotel they called it now. Also the Bund which was founded in Shanghai, a Hong Kong and Shanghai banking company. There was HSBC, you know, HSBC was founded in Shanghai, and the building is still there.

EM: Was there any person you saw in Shanghai who was the descendent of a servant you had known?

IJ: No. But, on this private tour, she took us to a Confucius Temple; Confucius is one of [the gurus, the main people]. I saw a janitor who was sweeping the floor and I asked him in Chinese, I thought that maybe he might know, and it turned that he understood me, and we were conversing. He understood what I was saying, and he was laughing his head off, because he couldn't believe a foreigner could speak [Chinese].

EM: Was he someone of your age, did he remember Shanghai before WWII?

IJ: NO, I didn't speak to him about it.

EM: Your English is because you went to British school in Shanghai, and we talked about this, at home your parents used Iraqi Arabic.

IJ: My father used to speak to me in Ladino Arabic, because he was not so good in English, and I used to answer in English, because I was not so good in Ladino Arabic.

EM And you went to school in English. Did you speak it with your siblings?

IJ: Yes, we spoke English with each other. And I had a private tutor teaching me the prayers and things like that.

EM:

IJ: Well, I was forced to learn Hebrew because I was with other people who didn't speak English.

EM: So now, let's get to the part about words of wisdom. I know you did this before and I have wonderful notes, but talk a little about your philosophy of life—in terms of if you could communicate with the generations to come, a hundred or two hundred years down the road, what life lesson would you tell them that you have found helpful in meeting life's challenges?

IJ: Well, The main thing is to stay with the family, to communicate, not fight with family, get angry; just be cordial with your family and family is the most important thing to think about.

EM: Family first.

IJ: Right.

EM: What other advice, that being a primary, is there another philosophy or some advice that you drew on during the hard times?

IJ: Uh, Just to be very strong and think of the future. You see, you know time will be better, like they say in Israel, *y'hiye tov*, it will be good.

EM: It will get better, things will be better, it will get good. Now this is the part—[you should live] to 120—do you have any special requests to your family? Are you planning to be buried in America? Did you make arrangements to be buried in Israel?

IJ: Yes, we spoke about that. My wife and my mother and my brothers are all buried in Staten Island, New York. So whether to be buried in Israel, who knows who is going to be in Israel? So I left it up to Marty and Beverly to decide. I gave them all the information from the cemetery. The cemetery that my father is buried [in Israel] is full, so it makes sense [to be buried in America] he's the only person I have there.

EM: Now [just to backtrack] we didn't talk about this [in this part of the interview] but it's very humorous—where did you go for your honeymoon with Joan?

IJ: We went to Florida! (Laughter)

EM: From the tri-city area you went to Florida. So Joan did not come [when you moved to Florida]—you moved to Florida when? That's what I wanted to get to.

IJ: I moved with Marty sixteen years ago, 2001.

EM: Okay, Marty and Beverly moved and you moved with them. Where was your other son at the time?

IJ: He was in New York. He was living with two other bachelors in Queens, New York.

EM: And you moved here. Anything else you'd like to say?

IJ: No, that's about it, you know?

EM: I think we've covered everything. And your hobbies are travel, you do a little handyman [work]. Now we could just end with that tiny little thing, it was so interesting; just recently for Passover——they say, "April in Paris," but this was "Passover in Venice!" Do you want to end with that beautiful little story you told me? First of all, in Venice you want to tell about——you took the Jewish tour.

IJ: We got to Venice and didn't know what to expect. We got by plane to Venice, and we came out of customs, and then there was somebody giving [gestures holding up a sign] us a name, Jacob. They said, "Come, we'll take you to the hotel." So they helped us with the luggage and they put us in a small boat. I didn't expect this right away, but, you know, that we'll go on a small boat. So from the airport we had to walk about ten minutes to the boat. And it took 45 minutes to go to the hotel—the boat landed, docked at the hotel, and everything is in water. The hotel was built about 610 years ago, a beautiful building, all statues, like a museum, huge. The dining room where we were going to eat accommodated 450 people, huge, very, very big.

We signed up for tours of Venice itself—we went to the Jewish Quarter, the Ashkenaz shules, they were very close to each other and they danced outside the shule. The thing was that they have guards now on each shule in case there's trouble.

EM: Now you told me a very interesting thing you learned in Venice about the toast, "L'Chaim."

IJ: Oh, yes, so we went to the king's palace. There was like a walkway where you could see—like lattice. The family of the prisoners would wait outside where they were going to be executed.

EM: This was a long time ago?

IJ: Five hundred years ago. And they were saying that The reason why people say "L'Chaim" now is at that time before the prisoners were executed, they would give them an alcoholic drink [to calm them down]. So that's how "L'Chaim" arrived, to life now, not to death. The prisoner would call out, they couldn't see him but they would hear his voice,

EM: And these were Jewish prisoners?

IJ: There were all kinds of prisoners, Jewish prisoners, too.

EM: L'chaim—who knew? I'm going to come over to here [to where Isaac is sitting] It's been a wonderful, wonderful experience. And there are going to be more photographs following—Beverly's going to send them and they will be on this tape, different things that you want. . . . As I said, if this is sometime early in the 21st century from Heritage Biography International.com, we bring you greetings from the past. Be well.

Appendix B
Zmira Mozorosky Interview
December 3, 2017

EM: Hello. I'm Elaine Mendelow, and this is a neighbor, friend and now an interviewee for my dissertation, "From Gutenberg to Google: Jewish Diasporas." I would like to introduce Zmira Mozorosky. She is Iraqi by birth, she married an Ashkenazi; that's why she has an Ashkenazi last name. Today is December 3, 2017, and if it's early in the 21st century and you want to contact me, you can contact me at elainemendelow@yahoo.com or emendelo (without the w) at emendelo@fau.edu and if it's further on in the 21st century, we bring you greetings from the past. And now, I'm going to move over and start the interview.

EM: All right, what is your name?

ZM: My name is Zmira Mozorosky, but my original name was Samira, a typical Arabic name, spelled with a samech like Sam, and it was very convenient when we wanted a Hebrew name, I just basically opened the kle, the samech, and made it a Z, and my name became a Hebrew name.

EM: And Zmira means "song." Does Samira mean "song"?

ZM: No, Samira means more shachoret, like in Shir Ha Shirim, dark, but beautiful.

ZM: No, but I just want to mention what—on the spot—made me want to change my name, because I did have a Hebrew name, and I still have a Hebrew name, but my Hebrew name was problematic. My name is Simcha and Simcha—by everything we had to adjust to the Ashkenazim, and we had to blend, so Simcha by them is a man, even though the format of the word is female, and we [Iraqi Jews] have a name for happiness for a man, is Sassoon, so we have Sassoon and Simcha for a girl. So, I go into this group of people, in the kitchen, not in a kibbutz, but a dormitory because I didn't want to stay in the Mabara, so this man, everybody is calling, "Simcha, Simcha," and my second day there, and I'm saying, this fat man, with this hat, a cook, Simcha, and I am Simcha? MmMm. [No.] Zmira, just like my cousin—she was Samira and she changed it to Zmira—I'm on the spot Zmira. People came to me and said, "Simcha," and I didn't answer. I said, "I'm not Simcha, I'm Zmira." I didn't answer. People said to me, "Didn't you say your name is Simcha?" I said, "Who me? I'm Zmira." So, that's how I got to Zmira.

EM: So interesting. What I want to ask you is, do you know who you were named after?

ZM: Simcha, yes. Samira is just like you give normal names, the real name is named after my mother's mother.

EM: And where and when were you born?

ZM: Actually, I was born in the house, in Bagdad, like all my other three siblings before me, and the midwife, just like in Egypt, they used to come to the house. The midwife used to say, "If everybody call me, I finish the coffee, I have time, but when Rachel (my mother) calls, I have to drop the coffee and run," because she called her at the last minute! So I was born in Bagdad.

EM: In Bagdad, Iraq.

ZM: Yes.

EM: And your date of birth?

ZM: I was born in 1943, and in order to find my real date, I had to do big research, because by them nothing is exact. It's before the Farhud, three years after the Farhud, and it's always there's a milestone and this. But because my aunt had a Sheva Brachot, and she remembered that in the last day of her Sheva Brachot that she knows when, she said they told her that her sister was having a baby, and I was the baby, and also there was another story that a different aunt from my father's side, she had the boy, and poor mom, my mom, had the girl, and he went to order the thing for the Brit, and somebody saw him, so he said my mother had a boy, and she said, "I'm going crazy," my mother told her, she went to visit her, and she said, "I had the girl, why are you going crazy?" So she said, "Because I saw him there, ordering the thing" and my father got into trouble. So that's how I established my real date.

EM: Which was?

ZM: Zion Nissan, April 12, 1943.

EM: What was your father's name and what was your maiden name?

ZM: So my father's name was Tzalach, and that means success—Arabic and Hebrew are very similar—*matzliach, hatzlacha.* We had a nickname, and we had the real name. The real name was Fetaya, a very well known Rabbinical family, he is very known, he wrote a book called Rachot Misaprot, or Rahot Misaprim, is more correct, but we had the name "Khalif," what we went by, that is because my grandfather, in the Ottoman time, before the British came, and he was very close to the Sultan, and in fact he used to play for him an instrument, the Sultan invited him for all the parties, because he used to put what "rap" or something, what do you call it—put words into music—

EM: Rap?

ZM: Yes, rap, and that's why we got the name Kalif, but my brother, alav ha shalom, when he became hozer b'tshuvah, very religious, and his wife they went to Columbia from Tasia Arit and he used to work in the air force industry after the army, and he just went straight to Fetaya, and everything had to change. However my sister and I were still Khalif, until we got married, and then we inherited different names.

EM: Right. And Fetayah in English would be Fedaya?

ZM: Fedayah? I don't even know what is the meaning of Fetaya; it would be if you said it. There is however a descendent of the family, she is a professor at Beer Sheva University, and she changed it to "Pedaya," with a "P" and "*Daled*" because it sounds better in Hebrew.

EM: So, you were born in Bagdad, and you spent your early childhood there. I know you have many memories and we will go deeply into them at another point, but can you just think back to the oldest relative and describe them?

ZM: First of all, I was known by my parents and everybody around me that I had a great memory. They would say . . . "How does she remember?" And I want to say that we did not speak Arabic in Israel, and I don't know how the word comes out. So I remember many holidays, but I will describe my grandfather.

EM: Speaking of language, let's mention now that the language that you and your family spoke to one another is now called—in academic circles—Judeo-Arabic, a dialect of Arabic with many Jewish/Hebrew words, like the counterpart to the Ashkenazic Yiddish, which is German, with a lot of Jewish/Hebrew words.

ZM: Yeah, like I came to America and was talking to non-Jews and using the word schlepping, thinking it's an English word.

EM: It is now.

ZM: If the Iraqi Arab, they supply us the milk, or the thing that we needed from the market, but it's not in the dictionary.

EM: So now let's go back to what you remember about your grandfather.

ZM: So now I'll start from the end what I remember about my grandfather. We were in Israel and we had everything in a small apartment and we had a closet with many, many shelves, and my mother would send me, let's say she's doing the laundry and somebody needs something, so she'd say, "Go to the closet, on the right hand side, the second shelf, there is something and bring it." And I would come and say, "I didn't find it." And she would say, "How is it possible you didn't find it? Your grandfather used to send me to that cider [cedar] closet, cedar wood, all from here to there, full of all kinds of jars and medicine, and that medicine, everything was herbs and whatever. And she used to be his helper. He was a healer and she was his right hand. She always went there and got whatever he would say, you know, "Second shelf, in the fourth row, and go from the back counter, one, two, and the third one bring it," and she would come with exactly what he needed. And my father, he used to get a different job. My father was a master of all trades. He was an electrician, carpenter, everything. If he was in our time, and we would use, let's say, a Black and Decker, my mother would say, "He created such tools, because there was nothing in our time, so whenever he needed tools, he would just get." So he used to get different jobs from my father. He would draw on a piece of paper which kind of plywood he would need. Basically, my grandfather Shuah he was a healer according to Rambam. He knew the Rambam way of healing and that is basically what he did.

EM: Did he live to go to Israel?

ZM: I just want to say one thing about the healing and then I'm going to tell you about the amazing way he ended in Yerushalayim.

So what I remember, those fights that were going on between stranger people. All the sweets we love to eat;

lakum and *melavas*, coated almonds and whatever. So I don't understand why they fight it. First of all, he didn't take any money, and they wanted to kiss his hand. And he would pull his hand [away], even that he didn't want to do. And that was the struggle I grew up to understand; he didn't even want a piece of honor or thanks—God gave me this, this power, and I'm just doing what I'm supposed to and really, we always used to get trays of the best types of candy and things, you know, what you would see at a wedding. So we lost everything in Iraq, we had a beautiful big home, twenty-eight rooms. So my grandmother—they wanted to sell the house—my grandmother said, "I'm not going from the house, you will take me dead"—so she died, we already registered, we were all ready to go on the airplane and she was buried in Bagdad. My grandfather merited to go with us and he was in the tent with us, he said a lot of wise words to my mother, and he said to her, "The house is gone, the wealth is gone, just watch your mind, keep it safe." The tent fell on him during the storm, and he said, "Rachel, why did you cover me with a blanket?" So my father ran to him, and he lived after that, and when he died, there was a big, big storm, I found out after that—December 30 something, it was written down. Nobody was going to Yerushalayim, but there was a truck, a worker car, a truck, a lorry kind of thing. Some workers who were going to Yerushalayim anyway, so they went with the body and my father, and he got buried in Givat Shaul. You could count the steps from the kever of the Chida, Rabbi Chaim David Azulai, and now Rav Eliyahu is buried in the same place, and according to this, I know how to find my Saba's grave which I'll show you later on.

EM: Now we're going to fast forward a drop—you had to leave Iraq—everyone had to leave—

ZM: We didn't have to leave, but there was a big pressure from Ben Gurion, from Israel to get more Jews to fill the number to leave—they needed more Jews, from Yemen. What happened is, in those places, they waited for Mashiach; they really believed they were going to return. Even though they never meant for us to continue the tradition; on the contrary, they planned to create a new nation they wanted a new nation, like all nations—

EM: Secular?

ZM: Yes, secular. Secular is not a word that an Iraq Jew knew—where is that animal? Where is that mifletzet? They didn't understand. In fact, they were so excited to go back to Israel, especially my mother. My mother was very active. There was a lot of activity in her house. If they had been caught, my mother would not have been alive. They were so excited, they were the Zionist party, but sincere. "Hashivenu l'Zion; what we daven in shul every Shemoneh Esrei, not necessarily in a kibbutzim, in shorts, serving pigs on the wagon. They got rid of the pigs, only when Tnuvah [a cheese company] was not accepting their cow milk, and then they were forced to get rid of the pigs. But actually, I was served pigs, I wasn't served, because I didn't eat it, because my sister, when the wagon came, she stepped on my foot and she said, "Ask for eggs." I didn't know what, so, okay, I'll ask for eggs, 'cause she didn't want me to discover that. So my mother sent three of her children, her daughters, to Israel ahead, because God forbid they would close the Aliyah, at least we will join the family and go to Israel. So my father, who was in Israel already, as teenagers, they came on donkeys through Syria. My father said, "I was in this place," because the train came there and you could see from the train. Here they send them in advance. My father didn't want to come that way. He said, "We'll go to Turkey." An Iraqi Jew who goes to Turkey can bring all the wealth, or to Persia, the Shah was good to the Jews. My mother said no, we'll be stuck there, and she'll never materialize her wish to come to Israel. So meantime, they put all my sisters in kibbutzim, and my third sister, when my mother came, after she was crying on the foot of the airplane, and the nurse came to her and she said to her, "Why are you crying?" My mother spoke Arabic, many Iraqis [Jews] spoke Arabic, but with a heavy accent, with a "kuf" they said "tzah," there's no tzaddik for the Sepharadim, so she said, "Ha Anayim Bocho, ha libab samayach," which means," The eyes are crying, but the heart is happy." She went down, she kissed the ground, she really believed that they were sacrificing for a reason.

EM: Was there anything that happened in Iraq? I know you said that your mother was a Zionist and she probably could have been arrested and killed for what she was doing—

ZM: And all her friends.

EM: And all the friends. But was there any special event, something that happened, that finally your family went, "Okay, that's it, we're all going."

ZM: Okay, so first of all, my mother was the driving force behind it—she was really not rational—and she was just emotional and that's what she wanted. But after the Farhud, 1941, when Amin Al Husseini [leader of the MUFTI] was chased—they realized in Yerushalayim that he was not a peacemaker, like the British was paying money, you know, in *The Farhud* from Edwin Black—

EM: Let's just say that the *Farhud* is a word in Arabic, like a "pogrom."

ZM: Farhud means hefker, Farhud mean like when somebody is taking too much of something—"What is it, Farhud?"— wait a minute, there is account, you can't just—; it's not hefker. Farhud is when you can do whatever you want—

there is no police, no account and if you kill somebody, if you stole, Farhud means—really, the closest word that I could think of in Hebrew, not in English, is hefker, like it doesn't belong; like you could do whatever you want.

EM: That was what the pogrom was, the same thing they took, they killed.

ZM: So the Farhud was because Amin Al Husseini, connected with Germany, the ironic thing I always say, he was Semitic, just like the Jews, if not more, and he goes to Hitler, who wanted pure blood, and he worked with him, so, when it pays, it's okay, you could overlook it! But when he was running over from the British, because he was wanted by the British, he went to Turkey, he went to Baghdad, and he actually created—I think the ruler was Rashid Ali, I'm not sure, because there were some rulers that loved the Jews, there was one that killed himself, and there is a statue with a pistol to his chest, they made it for him, because he was asked to do things against the Jews, he had no choice, he had to either listen to the government or to hurt the Jews—so he chose to commit suicide. But I think it was Rashid Ali, in the time of Amin Al Husseini that I think who created the groups, just like in [Germany], youngsters, marching with uniform and whatever, and after that, that built up to the Farhud. And suddenly there was nobody there, there was no British, there was no this, no police, so what I wanted to say back, when my mother came to Israel, and she was so excited—

EM: Ten years after the Farhud—

ZM: So here's what happened. You asked me what. So, at some point the government got together because—there was another thing: there was a bomb dropped in synagogue, in Bagdad. The Iraqi Muslim, the government, said, "It's not us, it's your people." And for a long time, two Knesset members were labeled that they did it. One of them was

Shamul Lev, the other one Ben Porat. And they were, they came to Israel and they were sent to Iraq. They dropped the bomb, I don't know on what holiday, I don't know what many people died there, I don't know if somebody died, I don't remember what happened, but the Muslims swore it's not them. What happened after that, people started—it did what it's supposed to do, and by the way, something like this happened in Egypt, but they were caught, and it broke the government for many, many—

EM: And it was done in Egypt by—

ZM: There was an argument whether it was Levi Eshkol who gave them the command, or was it Ben Gurion, and Ben Gurion said it was not him, and it broke the government, and now it started a new party; it's called Ha Parasha, when you say Ha Parasha, the issue, they mean the Parasha which was in Egypt, and they were caught, and they wanted to make like the British did it, but anyway, things like this did happen. So, it did what it did, and Jews did not feel anymore safe. And when you see somebody who is so established, suddenly packing and leaving, and this one is missing, so the government of Iraq said like this: "Whoever wants to go to Filestine (Palestine) has to register. By the way, we were called "traitor" by then. And then, whenever you registered, you basically give up your passport and citizenship. One Shabbat, when the registration was like, exhausted, was like, slowed down, they closed the registration. One Shabbat, my uncle comes home and says like that to my mother, "Do you know this table? It's not yours. Do you know this silver spoon? It's not yours." She says, "What are you talking about?" The news came, already, on Shabbat, they did it on Shabbat because the Iraqis knew very well Jewish people would not desecrate Shabbat. So, one Shabbat, they put a stamp on every business, the houses didn't belong to us. We heard after we left, that it turned into a local hospital, that's how big it was. Anything in the house, nobody wanted to buy anything, because it's theirs anyway. I would like some time to describe or find some house like that, I didn't find yet, I found something similar in Or Yehuda that described a little bit what a house in Iraq was, in the museum. Anyway, my mother comes to Israel after this, after going through such—devastation. Some people committed suicide. In a matter of 3-4 hours—they had a tent—who lives in a tent? No running water. Some people committed that because they couldn't handle it. No language, nothing. And then it was a whole different thing. My mother was the eshyet chail who took everything upon herself; she knew that she did it to my father, and there is a whole story, really the adjustment was terrible, my father never adjusted; he was a man of creation and doing. All his business was with the British, English sterling, that's what he got for rewarding. He couldn't supply them enough of what he was doing, you know. A different side, my mother's brother-in-law had a big, like department store for those things, and he used to bring it there, and he had an aunt working for him because she was a designer and she used to do the hand work, whatever. Anyway, he made a whole factory from table lamp from scratch. He used to do everything, from beginning, like designing from scratch. From really just material that God created, basically from nothing, just what he created. And now, not a language, he's not going to get a job. It was really terrible. I think the biggest sacrifice was my father. My mother somehow adjusted because she had to be the driving force to solve a problem, so she was busy emotionally—my father—he was the leader that everybody took advice from him. He gave loan to everybody.

But I think the most disappointing thing from my family, and also it had something to do with me, and maybe that's why I ended in America, is when she went to see where the children are, that's the first thing, she sent them, three girls, and each one they put in different place. . . . one in Kfar Menachem, Shomer Natzayir, the other one is Gal On, Shomer Ha Tsayir, the oldest one is in Ein Carmel near Haifa, the other one is in the South, and the other one is near Haifa and Carmel, and, uh, the one in Gal On is the younger one, and she went to see her first and she leaves her group there, my sister, she runs to my mother to catch her in a place where they don't hear what she's saying, and she says, "Ima, al tagid sheh yesh Elohim," please don't say there is God." You don't know my mother. What do you think she did?

EM: She said it.

ZM: She said, "Weh weh layham." There is an expression like, the worst thing you could say, like, what a disaster!" She runs to them and says, "Yesh Elohim! Yesh Elohim!" (There is a god.) That's my mother.

EM: So, you were young, and I'm fast forwarding—there's a huge amount of details we're not going to do today—and you were able to start school even though you had a year in Iraq, in Bagdad, you were able to start with the other children at the beginning.

ZM: In second grade.

EM: In second grade, but it was like the beginning. They were able to catch you up. So basically, you had an education, a childhood education, like an Israeli child, with your Hebrew.

ZM: Not. Not really. Anybody was a teacher, not qualified people. If there was any qualified teacher like my sister's friend, my mother's friend which she learned and graduat-

ed in Levanon, the American University in Beirut, so she
was an English teacher, but not necessarily ours.

EM: What I meant was, you weren't learning in Arabic, you
were learning in Hebrew—

ZM: Nothing was recognized in our culture, something we had
to forget quickly and blend,

EM: Assimilate to Israeli.

ZM: Not assimilate, only the thing that counts. First of all, I
wanted to go to kibbutz also, the summer I went to kibbutz
and after going a few years in the school, the Mabara, not
just like a tent, but like some kind of a hut, the outside
made of metal, like a *blech.*

EM: Tin huts.

ZM: Sometimes they used to put water on top, like a sprinkle,
but inside it was, to make it smooth it was sheets of asbestos. We didn't know what asbestos was, but I know exactly
what asbestos is, because that's what I remember. And we
learned in the shat and I was till fourth grade I went to the
kibbutz to visit my sister Dori in Kfar Menachem. I loved
it. I went on the tractor to the grove, the apples, and we
picked apples, and I learned how to swim in a beautiful
pool—we don't have this in the Mabara—there is new
clothes, there is nice shoes, a beautiful life. I went to the
meetings there, that when they had activities, and the
mitapelet, the one in charge said, "Okay, we have a group
for you," so after this, I was sure after this visit, I am gonna be just like them in the kibbutz.

EM: And how old were you?

ZM: I was twelve, just about twelve, because to do the other
thing, the compromise that my mother had, I had to be
twelve. So it was just almost at twelve and she [the coun-
selor] said okay, at the end of the summer, when I go back,
she will come to my mother, and she will convince her,
and I know that she just will tell her that she has a great

place for me, but by then my mother knew what's going on as far as the education, they stripped them from all education, some of them came back, some of them still there—

EM: The Jewish education. The religious education. None.

ZM: Yes, right. They taught them to sleep with boys and girls, it's okay to wear not tsnius clothes, Shabbat is like just another day. When they used to take off on Tuesday, they say, "Tuesday I have Shabbat." That's how they said. Shabbat is just another day.

EM: They ate whatever they wanted.

ZM: They systematically wanted a new kind of a Jew, a country just like everybody else, and still it's going on, the Smolanim, and that's what they wanted to do. So anyway, my mother, the mitapelet came after that. My mother went to sleep in the bed. She said, "Say I'm sick," because there's no way she's gonna let me go to a kibbutz. So my father said to her, "Listen, she came all the way from Matzmia"—that's very far to come—with busses, and this, you know, so he said to her, "Out of respect, just come in. So my mother got out. You know with my mother, she's like sharp—she knows what she wants, she says it very clear, and she doesn't coat it with any sugar, she just lets you understand where she's standing.

EM: She gets right to the truth.

ZM: Yes. She did a lot of things in her life. Like one rabbi said, "If you were born a boy, you would have been a great rabbi." She has picture with Begin, and with Bennie Begin, and with Sharon, anyway, this woman came—and I learned how to swim with Kfar Menachem—Kfar Menachem was already in my heart—this is a kibbutz. So she said to her, "Listen. First of all, you are very welcome in our house, really, don't misunderstand me, but I know why you came. Let me just make one thing clear before you start talking. After that, you can tell me whatever you want. So here's what I'm telling you. You take one more daughter of mine to Shomer HaTzair and I'm gonna sit shiva." You know, they sit shiva when you die.

EM: She will be dead to me.

ZM: Don't forget, Iraq was the first diaspora, when they lost Bet HaMigdash, Yerushalayim and Yermiyahu.

EM: And Esther and Mordecai.

ZM: No. That's Persia. Many people make this mistake.

EM: Oh, sorry. It's the Babylonian Empire.

ZM: Yes, it's Iraq, Bagdad, Avraham Avinu, it's Ur Kasdim, it is Abu Talmud Bavli, it is the dynasty of David HaMelech, Rosh Galuta, and all this, all this was, although the Persian did take over afterward.

EM: Yes, that's what happened. It was one empire.

ZM: But we were the "*Al naharot Bavel, sham yahshavnu v'gam bachanu*/When they asked us to sing the song of the field, they cut their thumbs, and they say it as a bracha which you say on Shabbat, Shir Hama'alot, but really there's a weekday [song] to say before you say the bracha, "*Al naharot Bavel, sham yashavnu v'gam bachanu,b'zochranu b'Zion*—so since then, they live in this place. How many Sifrei Torah was written, how many Rabbonim came out, the culture. The holidays were really holidays—what I remember from Pesach, Sukkot, and all this, nobody in our time, my children or grandchildren, they don't experience that. There's no way they could experience how we lived with my Saba and everything, before Pesach and achanot. So to them, to go to Kibbutz and everything gets wiped, who has the right to do that? You know, many times the Israelis talk about *k'fia datit*, like you force the religion on them, but you really did a *k'fia datit* in the worst way, to your parents, first of all you left the tradition, and you broke their heart, and now you take people who are not even prepared to understand what you're doing, and really *kufim Aleichem*, to be like without all this wealth, like the tradition/wealth that they came with. Who gives you this right? Who has a right to do that?

EM: So after your mother refused to send you to the kibbutz, you stayed with her?

ZM: I rebelled! I would not go to school. I am not going to the hut, the tent; I am in a place where it's better. I deserve better, no? I felt it, I came from Iraq, I remember, I remember the clothes, I remember the *chagim*—this place we have nothing. And all I see is a depressed father who doesn't have work, my sister went to work in a factory, okay, because to bring money, actually she's unbelievable, one of my sisters, the one who said "Don't say *Yesh Elohim*." She left the kibbutz after that, and with my mother, they went and they worked in a factory and my sister married an accountant in that office. But from their money, from going different shifts, one time in the morning until two, and one time two until ten, and that's how they bought the house, a little house, but all the money my father did bring, and all the money he had other people bring, because he was creative, pro-active, all kinds of things, in the heel, in the wood, there is a story about that, but our money was gone, and that's how they bought the house.

EM: And where was the little house?

ZM: That was, after we came for *shav aliyah*, then we went to Ein Shemer, that's where all the story of the Yemenite and you know, the issue that now they want to open the records, and then I went to where we live now, no then we went to Herzelia, then, that's where I was actually when— then we bought a house which is after Ramat Gan, which many Iraqis, which they call it in fact they call it Ramat Gan between Petach Tikva and Tel Aviv, they call it "Ramat Ha Iraqim," like in New York, there's in Brooklyn, there's "Odessa on the Sea," and you know who lives there, all Russians. So this was "Ramat Ha Iraqi, a little bit after that, it was called Tel Giborim, or B'nei Brak, we belonged to the municipality of B'nei Brak, we were like almost next to Pa Descat, which is known as a very bad place, you know, mostly Sephardi Iraqim, kids who went out of the derech, and whatever, crime. And they all came from homes like me, I'm not saying everybody was high, but even the middle class was comfortable, or was educated, or Torah keeping, or with mitzvot, so everything went, so they didn't give them good chinuch, but meantime, that's what happened, and, then I left, and from this house I went to—my mother said, "Don't worry, I'll get you to a kibbutz. I'll take you somewhere. You're not gonna stay." So she went to the best, where the children, there was a quota, from the children from Alyiah HaNor, some go to Shomer HaTzair, some go to Achdut Avodah, some go to Bet Ta'ar, some go to Chevrut. Everybody had a certain amount of children they took, and the person there, in charge, he said—she wanted to put me in Cherut Yonah Jabotinsky, which is in Be'er Yaacov, it's dormitory, and you work and you learn, and then after that you go to the high school, to the army, and whatever. So the man told her, "What are you doing? They're gonna grow up, they're gonna kill each other, because she's [her sister] gonna be Shomer HaTzair." I'm gonna be Cherut, and this happened. It took me a long time to get along with the sister; I went to visit her, and the mitapelet was the one, you know, that actually wanted to come and take me to her kibbutz. I had such a hard time getting along with her. I would talk about Torah, because I came here, and I went to Yeshiva University, and I became totally—I took a detour—I know that my grandfather and all what they did—it was not the stories, it's a real thing—and I made a detour, and I went back exactly, patching the path, going straight to the path of my mother, grandmother, saba, and all of this, and I feel I'm connected to Avraham Avinu through them. So, I did just a detour. But her! Like anytime we talk about philosophy, we talk about healing, we talk about this, and then I would bring something that Hazal said, she can't—like, wait a minute, don't take me there. She knew it. The guy said, "what are you doing," but she said, "Listen. She understands, but she doesn't want to put another child in your way of thinking." So that was another era for me—I was, I excelled in my learning, in fact I skipped one grade, and it was some experience, you know. Then there was another issue when we finished, and I went a different way, and I ended coming to United States, on my own, like I invented it almost.

EM: I want to get to that. So you were educated, and you did well in your education, you were fluent in written Hebrew—

ZM: Except in Yiddish. That was the reason—one of the reasons why I decided, look—if I came from the dormitory, Yonah Jabotinsky, and therefore I have a gap in English, and therefore I'm not gonna graduate, and there was issues there, peer pressure, whatever, somebody knew English and whatever and they were friends and I said you know what, I'll show them—I decided I'll show them I'm gonna speak English better than any of them.

EM: You do.

ZM: You're right.

EM: So, you left for America in—

ZM: 1962. March 25, 1962. I remember.

EM: So you were nineteen years old. You said your birthday was in April.

ZM: And my official birthday was August 5th. I made it up.

EM: You were not even nineteen yet; you were eighteen, almost nineteen.

ZM: Yes, it's true, because now I'm remembering something, and you're right, because I was going every day to the mailbox. After I agreed to come to America, I had to have release from the army. And, yes, I was eighteen, because that's when either you go to the army or get a release.

EM: Right. So, what I want you to hone in and then we're gonna pause and do the pictures and then we're gonna to go into philosophy of living in Israel, being out of Israel, doing all that. Now I know we've skipped a lot, we've skipped a lot of gorgeous details which we are going to do, mirtz HaShem, in a book. I will talk about at the end. But, what I want you to talk about particularly is your feeling in Israel, not a good feeling, because of being Sephardic, feeling second class and how this shaped your—it pushed you to leave.

ZM: Elaine, that was a secret. That was a secret nobody knew what you said. I didn't let anybody know. I, it—it was a fact. I will prove it to you. What name I took—I'm not Kalif anymore, and I'm not Ftaya. What [does] "Mozorosky" sound like to you?

EM: It sounds Russian.

ZM: Not Sephardi. Not Iraqi, not Moroccan. What do you think people do near me?

EM: They say things.

ZM: They open—if I tell you a story. The thing is, I feel so Israeli, I feel the feeling of my mother.

ZM: Like when somebody I talked to, she's a friend, and she's great, she helped me so much now, now to go to the Alon Shvut, Alon Technach, and she tells me every time what's going, and one time I expressed something that was on the news about the Ministry of Education, something somebody was fighting for now, let's make up for it, let's make justice, whatever, they had the power to do it, and they were criticizing what I said, I don't know what she said, ah, there is something, a meeting, about Sephardi Jews, whatever, yeah, [she said] we need to know about it too, and then I started to tell her, [she said] we have to know something, we know, we don't know enough, and then I said to her, "You don't know nothing." That's what I said to her, and I'm a guest, but she's a good friend, and I start talking, and she said to me, "Okay, Zmira, now we accept you," and I said, "Excuse me, I accept you, this is Eretz avotenu, what are you talking about? That's my mother's answer. I feel so Israeli—I feel pity for people who came from a certain place, they were not as open like the Bagdadian, they went to India, they went to China, they went to this, and there are people all over the world, like if somebody had eight boys, eight children, and it happened, and they lived in Japan, or they lived in China, in the British Empire, they sent a child to England, and one in Switzerland, and one in India, and one everywhere—they were Empire, they didn't have to do any paperwork—do you understand how they grew up? All our house was full of China, of food, of things that come from India. What did they know of in Europe? They couldn't even talk loud, because next door is the cardboard wall, and you were afraid from the goyim, and you were suppressed by the goyim, and feel afraid and whatever. The Enlightenment—they want to be like goyim. We want to be like goyim? The goy [would] shake my hand from my father and make a business for half a million dollars, nothing signed, he would say, "I trust you, you are *ibnes Sabbat.*" You know what *ibnes Sabbat* means?

EM: Like *Shomer Shabbat.*

ZM: Right. They are the "son of Shabbat," like ibn, that means—

EM: Oh, son of, like *ben.*

ZM: Yes, you are *ot bei.*

EM: Like Bar Mitzvah.

ZM: Yes, so the goyim had respect for us. So which Jew want to be a Muslim? Which Jew want to be an Arab? So we— and also they [the Jews] had very key positions in Bagdad. I remember that one time that somebody said not only that the treasurer of Bagdad was a Jew, but they insisted that he would be a Jew. I mean, I [haven't] researched this, this is something I heard, I mean, they were in schools, they were in the government, they were in the banks, they were trans- lator—I had an uncle who had seven languages—he was a translator, Turgeman, he was from the Turkish time. By the way, he spoke also Farsi. So remember when we were trying to figure out—Hebrew for sure, Arabic for sure, English, because of written English, French—

EM: Judeo-Arabic.

ZM: Well, I take it as Arabic, Persian and Turkish. And he was a translator in the government. So, they [Ashkenazim] come from a place where, like a box, and they finally with all the Enlightenment and losing children, and hating each other, the Jew against the secular, and the—we didn't know what it means to hate a Jew, we didn't know a dif- ferent Jew. We had Rabbonim that they wouldn't eat in weddings, in nobody's house. You know what they would say? "I eat only the cooking of my wife." But not the Cha- sidic, this Chasidut, this [other] Chasidut, there is more the Rabbinical, and more the other, but we did not have hate for another Jew. We didn't know that. So, coming from there, bringing this to Israel and not necessarily the people who kept tradition—on the contrary, the people who did not kept (sic) tradition—they were close to Christianity, they were willing to wipe the name of Hebrew—coming, making, capturing the land, and we are now, they think, we are just like Arab. They don't speak our language, they don't know our mentality—we are very close to Avraham Avinu—Avraham Avinu put matzelet, he put the food on the floor, and I assure you, he gave them a beautiful Hachnasset Orchim. Yes, we did not have all the forks that's written in the books, and we did not learn from the German all the perfectness—

EM: It wasn't Western. That's the difference.

ZM: But is it better? Is it necessarily better? Different. So when something is different, you cancel it like it's not existing?

EM: Terrible. Okay, so for this purpose, for this interview, we've got you finished with your high school, explaining that in your heart, even though you didn't share it and make people upset, you were very kind, very kind.

ZM: Not upset, I didn't want to lose, because if they will know I'm Iraqi, I'll get maybe second treatment.

EM: You did what you had to do to succeed, to survive, and you decided you would go to the United States in order to perfect your English. Now I want to ask you, when you left for the United States, did you feel you were going for a short period of time, or did you feel you were leaving Israel to settle in the United States?

ZM: I felt I was in a crisis, and I have to find a way out of the crisis.

EM: But you thought of yourself as an Israeli.

ZM: Of course, of course. I'll come back and I'll tell them, I was in America, and America for me, it was Hollywood, what we see in the movies, and I was so depressed when I came, I was crying for a whole week, when I finally came on the boat, and I know what was waiting for me. But the thing is—and I felt—there was another issue. To be part of ten children, eight children, a family of ten, you get only part of the pie, and I felt I cannot—you know, I saw my sister going to work in a factory, I worked in a factory, and

I thought my father was satisfied with that, I thought, I'm just gonna earn some money, so I said, "I'll fix my father." What did I do? You know, there is—tsniut is something very, very—it's a value that they keep, and, you know, a girl doesn't come late at night, doesn't sleep over, dressing, whatever, so what did I do? I said, "I don't want to work in a factory. If my father is satisfied with that, if this is gonna be my life, because I saw what happened to my sister, actually she got a better job in the factory, they let her go work in the office, and then she got married, to whom she got married. I wanted something to know who am I. I knew that HaShem gave me more than what men would allow me to have, you know? And I said—and I looked at the sun and I said, "Wait a minute. The sun is over there, God created the sun, the ray[s] go all over, so whatever God gives me, I'm allowed to take it and I won't allow men to interfere with that, how much sun am I getting?" And that's what I meant in my mind, and I decided I'm not gonna be part of a pie, I'm not gonna be part of ethnic, I'm gonna be—me. I know I should have said Simcha, but I want to be Zmira, and that's basically what I thought. I didn't know what, I thought I'll come back and I'll show them, I'm speaking English, you know a little better than me, but it doesn't matter, I'm not behind. And I couldn't stand being behind and not using what I have. So that's the force that—

EM: So I'm gonna fast forward this a little, for now, you got to America, here you are, this beautiful girl, and you told me many different things, teaching and dancing, etc., and you met your husband Tuvia Mozorovsky—

ZM: It's Mozorosky, without the v. I used to say as a dance teacher, I have three circles in my name.

EM: No "v". I'm sorry. And so you met him and you married. And what you told me, which I'm fast forwarding, which is so amazing is, he was an American born in Walla Walla, Washington, and when he married you, I don't know if he was religious before he met you—

ZM: Well he went—a rabbi by the name of Telenski, a rabbi from Portland, Oregon, told him, listen, you're going to college, why don't you go to Yeshiva University? And they sent him to Yeshiva University. That is the key to how I met him. How? He went to Yeshiva University for one year, and then his father got sick, he went back to Portland, Oregon. However, when he came back, a year later, not as a student, and that's when he became religious, actually, when he went back, had his own pot, I gave him a very lot of credit for his own dishes, suddenly he's at home, and nobody was religious there. They were Americans that came over for a few generations. Okay, so there was another person there that he was a friend with, that they were there in Yeshiva University, that friend, he was a Sephardi friend, his name was Chaim Azuwan, he was a teacher. By then I became a teacher, by then, in a short time, I became a teacher, and I worked myself, like it was *yaretbalgab*, I didn't go out with boys, I didn't date, I didn't go to parties, I didn't do anything except studying. I said, "I want my teacher diploma," and they gave me credit for the fact that Hebrew is my mother tongue, and I was very much in demand because all the yeshivot want ivrit b'ivrit then. I finished with tsainut, cum laude, in all in literature, in Tanach, They turned me—I asked a question and they answered me—because there were teachers and I was their pet because they felt they're really putting in me, and I was absorbing.

EM: And what is the name of the institution you got the degree from?

ZM: It was TIW of Yeshiva University, stands for Teacher Institute for Women.

EM: And then this ultimately became absorbed into Stern College.

ZM: Yah, well, today Stern College produced teachers, and they don't need that Institute, it became like, Rabbi Fiverson was heading it, zichron l'vracha, and many, many teachers came, like all the yeshivot, they were all full with teachers that came from TIW. After that, I did my BA when I was a little older, but the thing is, then I started teaching in Hillel, which is called today Hafter, and the reason it's called Hafter is a combination of Hallai, Hillel, another yeshiva, and there was another yeshiva in Five Towns a little further, there is another yeshiva, they got together, and they made one big yeshiva, Hafter. And there was a teacher named Chaim Azuwan, he went to Yeshiva University and his brother David Azuwan, and Tuvia, who became my husband, he said, "What about this school? There's no young teachers there?" So Chaim said, "No," because Chaim wanted to go out with me, and he did go with me once, you know, and David said, "Hey, what about this Zmira?" 'cause he met me, his older brother. And he said "Nah," so he comes to me, it was erev Pesach, we had to pack from school, it's in Hillel, and he said to me, "I don't know, there is this ugly guy, he wants to go out with you, can I give him your number?" I said, "I'm packing, my ride to go to Crown Heights is leaving in a minute," and I said, "Give him." Since he got my number, till we actually got engaged, he did not let me breathe. Pesach was in between, and I told him I have already plan from before, so my lipur came to me, I don't know if I told you from before, I was already renting her place with my sister. Basically, he [Tuvia] wanted what he wanted, and that's the way he was, he wants what he wants and he gets it. So and then I married him, because different calculation, I didn't look for him, he looked for me, and then it ended, but I have wonderful grandchildren, let me tell you.

EM: And you're divorced. The irony here is that this American—you married in '66—and this American wound up—you had four children—

ZM: We made Aliyah also.

EM: Right. You're in America, and in what year did you make Aliyah?

ZM: So we went in 1967 for a visit where people did not even come back from the war, there were some people, I saw them coming back from the war, that everybody was like drunk from all the victory and Yerushalayim and whatever, so, then, but after that we made Aliyah in 1970.

EM: In 1970. And so he fell in love with Israel?

ZM: No, it's not that. When he proposed, he proposed, he never said directly, "Listen, I can't promise you that I am going to live in Israel right away, and that's how he proposed. So he did go to Israel.

EM: Did you want to go back when you had your children?

ZM: One child, I have. I had in Englewood Hospital one daughter born and then I had all the three in Israel, one is in Kiryah, Asafu Rufeh, one is in Rechovot—each one of my children is born in a different hospital.

EM: So were you the one originally who wanted to go back to Israel?

ZM: I never thought I'm staying, but I met him, and he understood that somehow he had to blend to that, I was always with Israelis, Pesach, on vacation, or went to Washington, D.C., it was all with Israelis, he see[s] me only with Israelis.

EM: So you went to Israel and you had three more children, so that was 1970, and you stayed from 1970 to—

ZM: From 1970 till '78.

EM: Till '78. And what made you come back to America?

ZM: I didn't come back. I stayed there and he came for six months without me. He wanted to continue, he said he—I got him a job in Tazia Virit, which is the American Embassy, he was a librarian, an advanced librarian. He was telling me about the microfiche, and all this and this before it was—it was still books on the shelf, okay? So after that, he left that, and worked for Tasia Averit, after that he worked for Bar Ilan, like, when somebody, like I talked to her, he was a librarian in Bar Ian, he was basically an information specialist. People didn't have their own computer then, so he knew how to narrow the search, and give them whatever they want, whether it's in the library or in the Tasia Averit, you know, the airplane industry in Israel, it's like—

EM: The aerospace industry.

ZM: Yes, the aerospace industry. You know, it's like when I used to come to Israel, in the beginning, not after we kept coming, he used to come through the field and he would take me from the foot of the airplane. So, he worked in the Tasia, that was my brother, actually, he worked just in the Tasia as a librarian. And then he [Tuvia M.] changed, he worked in Ashdot, and then he worked in Bar-Ilan. At some point, he said, "I need to go. Here there is nothing for me." So he went back [to the US] and I was still there [in Israel], and finally I was offered the real job I wanted in teaching, in the right school, whatever, and she couldn't believe that I'm turning it down because I said, because I don't know where I'm going, six months I'm telling him come back, and he's telling me to come, so my sister was here [in the US] at the time, she got married, and so we came for the wedding, and I came, and it was like a letdown for me, we had a penthouse in Israel, just built, modern kitchen, American kitchen, whatever, I did not have enough time to enjoy it, and, actually I sold it later on, when we were divorced, so I actually went and I sold the house, and from this I actually [was] with the children alone after that.

EM: In Israel.

ZM: No, in America. I went from America. I came back in the end for the wedding, and after the wedding I was very depressed, I go to the closet, I had a closet, I would open it, I pick up the shelf, and the mixer is already connected to the electricity, I make my cake, I wipe it, I put it down. [In America] I go to the closet, but I don't have anything. And then a job came about, I was a resident manager of the first group home of organizers called Bet Israel.

EM: These are assisted livings for people with challenges.

ZM: And I was doing everything, I was a coordinator. My boss, he was just busy opening other homes, I was doing everything, and that's when I did my BA from Adelphi University, but it was run by a man, very creative, his name is Dr. Milyan, that's his name. He took a place in Manhattan, that was Jewish offices there. We learned only on Sundays, putting the program and the amount of days Adelphi University required. The only thing, he fitted to the Jewish calendar, so I remember, it was so convenient, Tsom Esther, we didn't have to go, even though it's Sunday. But we went Sunday in the morning, till the evening. I did this a whole year, I got a lot of credit from TI, I had credit for my languages, and I had actually very little to complete in order to get my BA.

EM: So we also should add two of your sisters did come to America, so it isn't like you were the only, only one—you did have some family in America.

ZM: I was the pioneer.

EM: You were the pioneer. But you did have some family, when you had your children, you had your family. So, you came back and you got your degree, and you had a successful career—I'm fast forwarding cause I know where I'm going—and then you are divorced at some point in America?

ZM: Uh, see, when he came back, I was very concerned about the children, and they had a very hard time adjusting, because we went to Brooklyn.

EM: And they had been to Israel.

ZM: My son, in second grade, they knew Mishnayot by heart, and here, maybe sixth grade they could do that. He went to Yeshiva in Brooklyn, and he doesn't know English, he doesn't know Yiddish, so he must be stupid—in the eyes of the children, whatever. The Rebbe was not creative, and my son knew what he is, [in Israel] he had a wonderful teacher that was a musician, he used to play in weddings, and he used to leap on one foot, I don't know if it was his or not, one foot, but every time he used to play for them music, he used to love this teacher, he had for first grade, and then for second grade, and he comes here, there's nothing of that, and he treated him like he was stupid, so what, a small child—you should see what he is today. This Rebbe, my son, I'm just going ahead, he's in Hatzalah, and, he went from school to school—

EM: He's the youngest?

ZM: No, no. So because didn't know, he's misbehaving, he went from school to school, Torat Emes, whatever, but one school he had a Rebbe, and that Rebbe, years later, my son is in Hatzalah, he's many years.

EM: And what is his profession?

ZM: My son, he's in business. And for a long time he was working for the city, by the way, his children, everybody know him, he's thirty-nine, and so one time he was saving no other than his Rebbe of many years ago, on top of him, and he opens his eyes finally and he says to him, "If I would have been shown, I would never have believed it."

He became a very good friend to him. And he didn't learn—at his wedding, he had so many *Ribbono* at [his wedding]not because he was an ilui, but because he was in so many Yeshivas, when he learned, did biology, not easy stuff—when he wanted to learn, he knew how to learn. He had it, but they were not equipped to understand him.

EM: So, you have *kinahora* four children, and how many are in America and how many are in Israel?

ZM: So because I ended [up] coming here, and staying here, at some point my husband wanted to go back, and that would have been exactly the time that they have to do a Regent's, Bagrut, and it's not like today that they have things in English, and they give them a break—they had to do hard things, and they would have been nothing, because they didn't learn here, to be prepared, and I wouldn't break them one more time. But they did go to seminars. His children, all of them went to Yeshivot there and they all, you know—

EM: So you have two in Israel—

ZM: No, I don't have two in Israel. I ended with all of them here, and one went to seminary and came back, and another one also did it and my son never went to Israel to learn, and he got married the first one, but my daughter, the youngest one, was going out and she never wanted to go out with somebody out of town, not California, definitely not Israel, because she became American soon after she came here, and she didn't want to go out with somebody who wanted to make Aliyah, but, she met her husband, in a wedding, in sheva brachot different places, about three times, and he said to her, the last time he met her in America, he said, "Don't move. I'm parking my car, and I'm coming back." And I always educated them more religious. So it wasn't exactly—but her brother was very much for it. So he didn't tell her that—actually his name is

Philip—at least what I heard—he went to study, and went to study second year, and then he made Aliyah, and at this point, he came just for the wedding! So when she cared for him, then he said to her, "But only in Israel." But he made it so easy for her, because he just made Aliyah with Nefesh b'Nefesh, and he did everything for her. Now she is my joy for one reason—not that I love her more than [the] other children, but I have grandchildren that are singing the same songs, the same education, the same—things that I could talk to them that I grew up with—they are so Israeli. They speak English, so she lives in Modi'in—

EM: And you're leaving for there in two days—

ZM: Yes, Chanukah I'll be there.

EM: So what is the role now that Israel plays in your life, Israel and America? Would you consider yourself—you live in both worlds happily? What do you consider yourself now and where do you think you want—where do you see yourself in five years?

ZM: Do you know what happens when you answer on one foot, a question on one foot? I live here [America] on one foot, I'll always live on one foot. You know many Israelis do that. They stay here, but they never consider it. So when is it actually I'm going there? Actually now I'm trying very hard to come to visit here, not to come to visit there, to live there. But, you know, the damage was done. I came here. The children are here. The grandchildren are here. You know, like I have to be—like I remember, when we went to America, when I went to America, the neighbors were talking, how lucky my mother, whatever. And she said, "You know what? I wish America on whoever is jealous of me with America. When I go there, my heart is in Israel, when I go in Israel, my heart is in America." Cause her children are scattered all over. Now I feel it.

EM: The same. But you feel Israeli.

ZM: Of course.

EM: And you're living somewhere else, but you don't feel—

ZM: What do you call me? You don't call me Israeli?

EM: I call you transnational. I call you both. You're of both worlds. Your heart is Israeli, but you have bits and pieces here. You have an education, you have a career here, but you're not—

ZM: Typical Israeli.

EM: No. You're not typical Israeli, you're not typical Iraqi, you're very special, but you have a life that transcends. It's a life in both places. Your heart is in the east, as Rabbi Yehuda HaLevi said, "I am in the West, but my heart is in the East." So, because of the grandchildren you probably will always bounce between the countries.

ZM: I don't know, Yehuda Ha Levi did not have the choice to be, and after that he did get to Israel, but it's not like that. I feel I'm Israeli, I am in Israel. The explanation I gave my-self, the resolution I made myself, that, you know what it is, it's wider than that. A person—and me, I'm talking about me—but still it's every person—has to act wherever he is right now—that's where God put him in. So what is my best me, right here, with my capability? So, if I'm here, like my mother said, when she's there, she'll wor-ry—I don't do that. Wherever I am, I say that, how can I maximize, because I'm not gonna be here, I know I'm gonna go, and there, I'm gonna come back. So wherever there, I go to all kind of lectures, and I go to museums, and I get involved with regular people, not hotels and things like that, but, you know, live. When I come here, I know I'm gonna prepare to go back, so I know basically my head is there, my feeling is there, but I don't dislike especially being in Florida, it's really nice and warm, I suffer from the cold, so it really keeps me very happy, you know, I go out, and it's the home of HaShem, the trees, the sky.

EM: It's the whole world, HaShem made the whole world.

ZM: But you see it. When you live in a castle, with walls, and pictures and frames, and beautiful mahogany, and all this, this doesn't mean anything to me. I would live here more than indoors, and that's what I like. I enjoy nature, I see, I walk in the morning, that's my first prayer, is the walk. Just to look what HaShem created, and how lucky I am to be here and enjoy it. And it's a philosophy that I developed for myself, I almost was like they say, *hava b'miuto*, minimize the evil.

EM: Look on the bright side?

ZM: Yeah, look on the bright side.

EM: Glass half full?

ZM: Yeah, I don't know why. That bad thing happened to me [living outside of Israel.] I want to tell you, I'm convinced almost 100 percent, almost 90 percent, I would not be back traditional, understanding Tanach, understanding Torah, connected—my mother used to say she has the first cordless telephone, before everybody had a phone, [talking to] *Ribbono Shel Olam*. My mother used to talk to *HaKadosh Baruchu* straight, connected. So I got this back. In Israel I would have had the peer pressure. [not to be observant] How do I know it? Because when I got married and I became religious and my husband is religious, that's the time I didn't want to go back to my own friends, to my own circle. And you know Uri Zoar, who was like Steven Hill of America, Mission Impossible, so Uri Zoar was like this or greater, and when he came out, to say he's religious, he picked up the yarmulke in his hand, he said—he spoke in Queens on the way to California, he landed and they took him for the evening—and he said, "Look, this kippah, how much does it weigh? What, a few grams? If I tell you, it weighed a ton when I first have to put it on my head." That to tell my friend, wait a minute, 'cause they view and they

try to say religion is primitive, old fashioned, and what
happened? Uri Zoar said, "Till a certain age, I didn't see a
real page in the Tanach" so the freshness of seeing the opposite of the opposite is what made him cling to it and
want it even more. So I had the same fear—I'll go back to
my friends and they're gonna make fun of me that I'm religious, because they used to make fun of the religious
there, and that's how we grew up.

EM: And let's end this piece of the interview by asking—you
have said—any words of wisdom. If you had to say—like
you said, "Look on the bright side,"—I know I'm making
you do it *al regel achat* [on one foot] if you had some
words of wisdom thinking way [ahead] to your grandchildren, your great grandchildren, think a hundred years from
now, what would you want to say to those—God willing—
descendants sitting in front of this interview?

ZM: First of all, what you think it is, it isn't. You know, I saw,
somebody showed me a cartoon, where somebody in a
coffin—it wasn't a Jewish thing—it was, "So now you
have an eternity to think in the box." (Laughter) So it
means, if you are alive, think out of the box. Don't let
people impose on your beliefs. Find for yourself. And you
always have more strength than you think you do. Just
connect to the source of the strengths—meh anyeh vo esri,
HaShem could do it all. Ezri m'et HaShem. That comes
from my mother, not from learning, and not from Shiurim,
and not from Psukim. You are always—whoever created
the body, he could renew the body. So always you could
use the brain, and for my children I used to say, something
else. Today almost everything is acceptable, especially if
there's a group of this and a group of that, so you belong
to a group, so you are something acceptable. So I said,
"Listen. If you're going with a group, and you are with a
group, you know everybody's going, that's fine. But just

do one test—you know when you sit on the river and you see a school of fish going, and another school of fish going, but then, you don't know—are they dead, are they alive? You know sometimes maybe they were poisoned, and they go over the water? But then sometimes you see a fish that's jumping against the stream. If you are with a group, stop for a minute, and ask yourself: If I was not surrounded by all these people, and this one wasn't doing this, and this friend wasn't doing that, if they were not going, I am alone, would I do what I'm doing right now? If the answer is yes, go ahead, lead. Don't even go behind, just go. But if the answer is no, don't follow. Don't force yourself to do something just because somebody else is doing it.

EM: That is very good advice. I'm going to move over a little bit, and I'm going to thank you, Zmira. So wonderful. What we're going to do now is I'm going to turn it over to Zmira to just sit next to her pictures and go through a few of them and tell what they are.

At the end of the video, Zmira shows pictures of the gravestone of her grandfather who is buried in Jerusalem, and his picture from the time of the Ottoman Empire, red/burgundy fez and all. She mentioned he was a healer. She showed descendants of Yehuda Fetaya, a relative. She also showed Internet pictures of the tents of the new immigrants, the huts which followed, a plane landing with the new immigrants, and a picture of the story of the landing in Yedidot Aharonot.

She mentioned that she has no regrets, wonderful children, wonderful grandchildren, they all keep Shabbat.

Zmira and I are planning a future collaboration on a more detailed written format of her autobiography.

Appendix C
Rochel & George Berman Interview
January 15, 2018 MLK Day

Introduction: Good morning. My name is Elaine Mendelow and I am here with an esteemed community member, Rochel Berman, and we—it is Martin Luther King Day, January 15, 2018, and we are here—I am privileged to be here to interview Rochel for my dissertation, "From Gutenberg to Google," on Jewish diasporic biographies. Now, if this is the early part of the 21st century, after this dissertation, I'm going back to my business, heritagebiographyinternational.com, and you can reach me and I will be happy to help you tell your life story. And if this is further along in time, we bid you greetings from the past. And now, we're going to start the interview:

EM: So, Rochel, can you start please with your name and where you were born.

RB: My name is Rochel Udovitch Berman, but that's not on my birth certificate. My birth certificate is Ruth Roselyn Udovitch, but I was named for some kind of *Tanta Rochel*, and here I am, "Tanta Rochel." And since I grew up in a Yiddish-speaking home, that's the name.

EM: That's what you were called.

RB: That's right. And I chose to carry it through my life—oh my God!" (Laughter)

EM: And you were born when and where?

RB: I was born February 14, 1936 in Winnipeg, Manitoba, and it was forty degrees below zero, the day I was born, and my mother told me that it was so cold in the hospital they had to get extra heaters. Now nobody here knows about the cold in Winnipeg. I mean, we used to have to plug our cars in at night so that they wouldn't freeze over. It's cold.

EM: What were your parents' names and their ethnic origins?

RB: Both my parents are from Russia. My mother's name is, was Minnie. And my father's name—I have to give you the way he would have said it—"Benyamin Eliyahu ha Cohen—Udovitch.

EM: You're a *bas Kohenet.*

RB: I am indeed.

EM: So what about growing up in that Yiddish environment— what kind of personal and professional impact did it have on you?

RB: Oh, well, first of all, it was a total environment. We lived just around the corner from the Yiddish day school that I went to, and it was like a seamless place, being at home and going to school, and my mother was in the *Mutterfahrein*—I haven't used that word in a thousand years— that's like the Sisterhood. The teachers were all our friends, and Yiddish was my primary language, and this is what I spoke at home.

EM: You spoke it at home, and in school did you have both Yiddish and English?

RB: Yes, there was a half a day of Jewish studies, and a half a day of general studies.

EM: So the Jewish studies were conducted in Yiddish?

RB: In Yiddish, absolutely, absolutely.

EM: As far as your further education, after you were finished with those Yiddish day schools?

RB: I went to public school, for, like, middle school and high school, and then I went to the University of Manitoba where I got my—both my degrees, actually.

EM: And your degrees are in?

RB: I got a BA at the University of Manitoba, and it was a BSW, only one year of graduate work, but it was a bona fide degree, because that was all they offered. I subsequently got a master's in social work at Hunter College in New York.

EM: So that would bring us up to love and marriage—when did you meet your husband George?

RB: I met my husband when I left Winnipeg and I moved to New Haven. My brother was a graduate student at Yale, and there weren't any women at Yale—there were [women] in the graduate programs, but there weren't any women in the undergraduate program, it was a male—it seemed a good place to get a husband, right? (Laughter) I'm telling you like it was, and I don't think I was there for three days, when my brother introduced me—it wasn't a direct introduction—a classmate of his, he was in Near Eastern Studies, had a roommate who was looking to learn Hebrew. (The story varies; it's apocryphal, depending on who tells it.) Anyhow, I didn't know much Hebrew; I knew more Yiddish, but I did teach in the Hebrew School, I knew enough of the *aleph-bet,* you know, I was one lesson ahead of the kids. So, I did teach him how to read. So he introduced me to George, and, uh, that was it. (Laughter) It was love at first sight for me, and not for him.

EM: So how long after you met did you marry?

RB: It wasn't long, maybe about a year, a year and a half, something like that. I had my own apartment in New Haven, in walking distance from my brother's house. My brother was a graduate student at the time, and I had a job at the New Haven Jewish Community Center, and I didn't have a car, so I took the bus every day to work and that was it.

EM: New Haven must have seemed warm in temperature.

RB: Yes, it was, but it was very humid, and you should see what it did to my hair. Now I'm happy it's curly, but I wasn't happy then.

EM: Well, obviously you still achieved your goal.

RB: I achieved my goal.

EM: So then, and married. George graduated, and so you found yourself living in—

RB: Springfield, Massachusetts.

EM: And you were there for a long time, a short time?

RB: Like about a year. We moved a lot.

EM: His field was—

RB: He was a chemical engineer, and then he decided to go back to school for an MBA, so we moved to New York.

EM: And that was the beginning of his MBA career.

RB: Right. Right.

EM: While in New York, you pursued your career.

RB: Yes. I worked at several long-term-care facilities.

EM: And in the course of that time?

RB: Actually, he got his degree, his MBA, and then we moved to Woodbury, New Jersey, and then I think to Richmond, Virginia, and then we moved back to New York.

EM: And in the course of that time your family arrived?

RB: One child. We had Josh.

EM: And he was born in—?

RB: He was born in Richmond, Virginia, no, he was born in actually Woodbury—I can't remember.

EM: And how old is Josh?

RB: Fifty-three!

EM: Unbelievable, considering you're only fifty-five!

RB: That's right. Yah. (Laughter)

EM: And you have another son, Jonathan.

RB: Fifty.

EM: And the boys grew up in New York?

RB: Yes. A little bit in Richmond, Virginia. Jonathan was still saying "Yes, Ma'am" when we left.

EM: We'll talk a little later about Josh in another context because Josh now lives in Israel.

RB: For more than thirty years.

EM: We'll be talking about Josh in the context of your career. Shall we jump right in to the subject which has become your Jewish spark, your anchor, your *raison d'être,* your *cause celebre,* all those good things—of *Chevra Kadisha?* First of all, let's explain what Chevra Kadisha means.

RB: Chevra Kadisha, the literal translation, is the holy society, but it's known more conversationally as the Burial Society, the Jewish Burial Society.

EM: And what does the Burial Society do?

RB: The Burial Society prepares the deceased for burial. This involves washing, purifying and dressing the deceased while there are simultaneous prayers said from Psalms and Isaiah, and so on. And the whole Gestalt is really like a splendid opera·in which the libretto and the music create perfect harmony. Let me give you a good example. (Picks up a paper)

RM: Let me show you, like for example, as we dress the deceased in white shrouds, we recite this passage: "My soul shall be joyful in my God, for He has clothed me with the garments of salvation. He has covered me with the robe of righteousness as a bridegroom puts on priestly glory, and as a bride adorns herself with jewels." Is that not exceptional?

EM: It certainly is exceptional. Can I ask you, how did it happen that you became involved with Chevra Kadisha—where did that come from?

RB: When my father died in 1985, he predeceased my mother, so that was my first experience with death. I was living in New York, my brother was in Princeton and he had already arrived in Winnipeg, and he was there when my father died. He called me immediately, and when I came, I arrived in the hospital—they hadn't—I guess he had asked them not to remove him from the room until I arrived, and

I remember walking into the room, and he was lying very stiff, and everything was very neat, they didn't cover his face yet, and the clothes were perfectly neat, and that wasn't my father. (Laughter) My father was the messiest person—he kept everything, every envelope, every book, every—everything.

EM: He was an archivist.

RB: Oh, yes. Anyhow, I walked over to the bed, and I put my arms on his shoulders, and I kissed his head, and I noticed that it was getting cold, and I never had that experience, of embracing my father and his not being warm. And then they took him out of the room, and I remember I went out and did I cry! You know, here I was in a strange environment, and I felt so bereft. Anyway, the next morning he had a graveside funeral, and when you live to ninety-five, there aren't many people around who are gonna come, the children live far away, so their friends aren't gonna come. Anyhow, we had a graveside funeral, and I kept thinking, where did they take him? What happened to him from the time I saw him till now? I didn't have a clue, so where did I go to with my head? I went to—I knew there was a Chevra Kadisha, and I knew the Chevra Kadisha had tended to him, but what was my idea of a Chevra Kadisha? A Chevra Kadisha were asocial, tiny little gnomes, who came out only in the dark of the night—well, that didn't bring me any comfort at all. I didn't know a single person who had been in Chevra Kadisha. Anyway, so, when I came back to New York, our shule had the beginnings of a Chevra Kadisha, and they needed more women, so I signed up so I would find out. And from the very beginning, it was very clear to me that this is something I could do and that I should do. First of all, a *tahara* is very organized. There's a beginning, a middle, and an end, there's these prayers, this kind of thing, I had been trained, you know, I got trained first before I went, and actually it wasn't one *tahara*, it was two, back to back, which was hard, but anyway, I was so emotionally elevated when I was finished, because, when the medical profession can do no more, and all the lines and all the drips and tubes are pulled out, we can do this one last thing. That is so elevating. You know, George was in the Chevra before I was, and he was invited by some Westchester Jewish cable group to talk about this—he was invited by the rabbi, and when the rabbi asked him, "How did you feel at the end," he said, "There are just no words to describe how I feel," and he too I guess used the word elevated, and I nearly dropped off the chair! You know, you're supposed to be revolted, sad, and it was hard. I went into it wondering what it was all about, you know, but from the beginning, it, it—

EM: It spoke to you.

RB: Absolutely, and you know what? I think in all the years that I did *taharas* in Westchester, there might have been one or two times when I had to say no, and I hated to say no, and when I'd get the call, I'd be so glad. There was two other women I would do it with, early in the morning, cause we had our own business at the time, so I had discretionary time. What a start to the day! What a start to the day!

EM: Amazing.

RB: And the two women I did it with, are like, you know, so close to me. Here he comes. [Husband George walks into the house.]

EM: Now what I wanted to ask you is, going from this experience, why and how did you decide to write the book, *Dignity Beyond Death?*

RB: Well, I had begun to do some talking about it, to school groups.

EM: You appeared on *Religion and Ethics.*

RB: Not till after I started the book. I'm trying to think—I had been invited by a Women's Tefillah Group to—this is just an anecdote—to do a presentation on *tahara,* and it was—they met on a Shabbat—of course it was a Women's Tefillah Group—at the Riverdale Jewish Center. And I stayed with a friend of mine in Riverdale so I wouldn't have to walk all the way from Westchester, and I brought a set of *Tachrichim* as a show-and-tell, so I delivered the *Tachrichim* the night before to the synagogue, indicating that this was for my presentation. So the ladies came early, cause they were setting up the *Kiddush*, they didn't notice what was written on the box, they opened it up, and they said, "Oh, Rochel brought her own tablecloths." And it was the shrouds.

EM: Well, they got their education, right? So, moving along, the book evolved.

RB: The book. I remember before we moved here, my son called and he said, "Mom, you'd better get yourself a project, or you're gonna be in real trouble when you get there." And then, do you know there are all kinds of people who had this idea, you move to Florida and you play Mahjong, and I don't know what else you do, cards and whatever, and, I remember saying to my boss—I was working at the American Society for Yad Vashem—and he says, "What are you going to do there?"—no, that wasn't my boss; my boss disappeared when I left him, I just disappeared from the world, but his son did ask me, and I said, "Maybe I'll write a book." I had no idea about a book, at all. I had been writing.

EM: Yes, I was going to say, you are an author, I knew you, long, long before I ever knew you, I read your article in Hadassah Magazine, so you were an author. You had written and been published. You had the talent. You had the ability.

RB: Right. Yes, I had written some stuff. Yes, in the years that I worked at the Hebrew Home—I just went through a whole bunch of old stuff—that was a very productive time in terms of publishing. Every year I would do some creative project that I would then write about and present at a conference and get published. So that was practically every year that I had worked there and that was like almost two decades.

EM: Right. So you had authorship.

RB: Oh, yeah. So that writing a book wasn't totally off the walls.

EM: Yes, it was in the path. And what made you decide to write this one?

RB: Well, I'm telling you, it's weird. I was unpacking stuff, and I remember unpacking the Wedgwood.

[Husband George comes into the room]

EM: Hello, George. Good to see you. We wouldn't mind if you came up and we said hello to you next to your lovely wife—This is George Berman, the other half of the Berman team, and this is the gentleman who Rochel met all those years ago at Yale, and we told the story already—

RB: Yeah, his is a slightly version.

EM: Of course. We should say here that George has been a collaborator on many aspects of your project.

RB: Yes. Absolutely.

EM: So, when you speak for the Berman team, we're including George in the project, because it was a team effort.

RB: Absolutely.   ·

EM: And your name is on—

RB: And my book is dedicated to George.

EM: And you did write a book with George about Eli—

RB: Wiesel.

EM: And also the other Eli, Eli—

RB: Zborowski. Forget about Elie Wiesel

EM: I'm so glad that we got to see you in person.

GB: In person.

EM: Thank you so much, George. And don't worry about any-thing, it's fine. We're not putting it on national TV—it's okay.

RB: Not yet. Okay, so where were we?

EM: We were—the motivation. You decided you would write a book.

RB: So I was unpacking this Wedgwood, and I dropped some-thing, and it broke in little pieces. And I decided, hmm, I'm sorry this broke, but maybe I will save it, and it'll serve as the shards when I die, to cover [the eyes of the de-ceased] And that was the beginning.

EM: Shards are used to cover the eyes.

RB: Yah. The eyes, the heart. Several places.

EM: Do you still have the Wedgwood?

RB: No, I didn't keep it, because it doesn't really qualify. It has to be pottery, and that wasn't.

EM: So you decided that this would be ‘a good subject for the book.

RB: I decided to write the book.

EM: And it was the shards.

RB: The shards. Right. Because I knew that people didn't know about this, and anybody who didn't know who finds out is fascinated, so that's when I started to write the book. And then I decided that the way to tell this story, to make it pal-atable, I remember. I remember when I told somebody here I was writing a book, she said to me, "Let's face it, it'll never be a best seller." (She has said that to me twice.) It hasn't been a best seller, but it's been highly acclaimed, and I won several prizes. So much for that.

EM: Do you have a copy right here? Thank you. I would love us to hold it up.

RB: [Getting the book from the other room] This one doesn't have the seal that I won the Koret, but it's all right.

EB: Well, we'll talk about that. Don't worry. So this is the book, *Dignity Beyond Death: The Jewish Preparation for Burial,* and this—

RB: This is—we had debated—what should go on the cover, and I don't know, I have a friend who is an architect, and who has, you know, design sense, and I sent her that picture. And she says, "There's nothing better. Use it." Now, what is this? This is a shin knot. See? It signifies God [EM: Shaddai] yes, and it is the signature knot that's used in fastening the shrouds. It's not used every place, but in the important places.

EM: Very, very interesting. Now, you did win the Koret International Book Award.

RB: I did.

EM: And when did that happen?

RB: 2006.

EM: And that of course is on different copies, the seal of it, subsequent copies. Did this change the reception of the book or the trajectory of the publicity?

RB: Yes it did, yes it did. I got a lot of publicity, and then it spiked the sales for a little while. But the nice part of that is that—First of all, the Koret winners are like highly acclaimed Jewish authors, like Philip Roth, Samuel Heilman, and Cynthia Ozick so I felt in good company. Then the *pièce de resistance* is that one of my competitors for this was Debra Lipstadt.

EM: Wow.

RB: And I won out over her. Now I don't see myself—in my own way, I've made my contribution.

EM: It's important. It has an importance.

RB: Yes. And then, the absolute frosting, candy, whatever you want to call it, was, that I received the award from Theodore Bikel.

EM: Ah! Was it at a ceremony?

RB: There were two ceremonies, one in San Francisco and one in New York, and they flew me all over the place.

EM: Very exciting, and of course there are videos of this and whatever.

RB: Not that many—oh, we have pictures. We have a lot of pictures of the event.

EM: Did anyone get to join you from your family?

RB: In San Francisco, only George, and in New York, certainly Jonathan and Monica were there, and Josh happened to have been in the States, he was there, too.

EM: How wonderful. So that was 2006. Now this book has a life of its own, because the next wave was the project of the high school course.

RB: Not quite. There was a big, like—

EM: A gap?

RB: Yeah, like, a decade, almost a decade, in which I spoke all over the country. And it became clear, that people are fascinated by this and that nobody knows about it. And so, I decided early on this has to be taught in high schools if it's to be perpetuated. And I made one attempt here in which I was told it's too sad, it's too—they're not prepared, high school kids, and kids who are having emotional problems might commit suicide because of this—I mean, you can't believe what went on in that meeting. So, I gave up. What are you gonna do? And then I continued to speak at conferences and at synagogues, whatnot. And then along came Jonathan Kroll from the SAR Academy, where my kids went to school.

EM: And he's now principal of, we should say, Katz Yeshiva High School in Boca Raton.

RB: So I went to him and I tried again. Now I got a very different reception because he had come from the SAR Academy and he was in the same synagogue and in the same Chevra Kadisha as I was in, trained by the same person. Now is that all *bashert?*

EM: It's *hashkocha pratis* for sure.

RB: And how. Anyhow, he said, "Okay, let's do it." So I developed a whole curriculum and we launched it for the first time in 2014.

EM: And it met with success—great success. The Sun-Sentinel, the local paper—

RB: Yes, and the *New York Times.*

EM: Yes, the *New York Times.* And the high school course was entitled?

RB: It's titled "The Final Journey: How Judaism Dignifies the Passage."

EM: And "Jewish Teens Encounter Dignity Beyond Death"?

RB: That's the paper I wrote.

EM: And the reception has been stellar.

RB: You know, I would never have believed that it would have the response that it did. It so exceeded all our expectations. It had a profound effect on the kids spiritually, practically, philosophically, changed their relationship with Judaism, changed their relationship to life!

EM: Can I ask you—all these steps and protocol for the *tahara*—where does it come from in the commentaries and the writings of Judaism?

RB: Well, there's not too much about it—it's supposed to date back to the death of Moses on Zion Adar. The birth and death of Moses is on the same day. And since there wasn't a Chevra Kadisha, it is said that God performed that.

EM: And so all the different instructions are—it sounds as if it's almost a different tradition passed on—

RB: Now what we do now dates back to 15—I can't remember—15—

EM: Five hundred years or so.

RB: Right. To the Chevra Kadisha of Prague. They're the ones that formalized all the things that we do, and it's essentially what we do.

EM: So, going back a little, there's a study guide, and just for the record, it's available. Do you have a web site or anything like that?

RB: Yes, there's a web site. It's on the Yeshiva web site under "Academics," "Final Journey."

EM: Let's say someone reads about this and wants to access you and your study guide.

RB: It's all there. It's part of the Yeshiva web site. [Katz Yeshiva High School]

EM: So, would it be all right to give your email?

RB: Absolutely. It's rochelberman@bellsouth.net. You could go to the school, too, but they have other things to do; I have this to do. (laughs)

EM: Now, after you wrote *Dignity Beyond Death,* I know—because I went to one of your presentations at a local library—you wrote another book called—

RB: *Oceans Apart: A Guide to Maintaining Family Ties at a Distance* (holds up book)

EM: And you are personally so well acquainted with maintaining family ties at a distance because as we just barely mentioned—we're going to get more into it—your son Josh Berman lives in Israel.

RB: That's right. My son Josh made *Aliyah* right after he graduated from Princeton. And, you know, we've lived with this—by the time I wrote the book—for twenty-five years. He married an American girl—I always thought he'd marry an American girl and of course they would live here, cause what American girl wants to live there? But that's not the way it worked out. He married an American girl, the wedding was there, and all four children were born there.

EM: So you have *mishpocha,* close family in Israel, and what I wanted to just ask you, if you'd care to shed some light on it, Josh physically ended his diaspora by making *Aliyah.* Is there anything you can see, in your time, your upbringing with him that became the source of motivation? Could you trace it at all?

RB: Oh, yah, well, he went to yeshiva day schools, orthodox yeshiva day schools, where it, you know, Zionism and making *Aliyah* was the goal. And, with regard to the SAR Academy in Riverdale, all his teachers made *Aliyah.* The principals made *Aliyah.* So, you know—

EM: So he was motivated and had a lot of support.

RB: At RAMAZ similarly, and at RAMAZ, they encouraged kids to go to Israel for a year before they went to college. They were already accepted; then they got deferments. Now, this was a big shock to us. If you go to Israel, you're never gonna go to college. How can you do this! We were educated and all his friends were going, that kind of thing, but after a year all his friends came back, except he decided to stay another year. So we said you could stay another year, only if Princeton would offer you another deferment. And they did.

EM: And then he did come back—

RB: He did come back, to get his undergraduate degree in religion. He did it in three years because he had a lot of AP's, and then he went back immediately. And that's where he met Michal, and the rest is history.

EM: Now he did ultimately get a doctorate—

RB: Yes, at Bar Ilan.

EM: And is utterly fluent in English and Hebrew.

RB: Oh, yes, although his dissertation and everything he writes is in English. Although, you can tell that he's fluent in Hebrew, because—totally fluent. He went—we didn't go to the book launching in Israel, but he represented us. And he didn't know until he got there that they wanted him to speak in Hebrew. And he was a resounding success. He's fluent, and a phenomenal communicator, and amongst the best public speakers that there are, and a seminal thinker—what else can I tell you? I'm his mother. Thank God.

EM: So *Oceans Apart* focuses—just briefly in a nutshell—

RB: It's a guide to maintaining family ties at a distance, and it deals with a variety of issues. Probably the most important is how to grandparent at a distance, and how to deal with illness and death. That's a very big one.

EM: And also the role of technology. There's all sorts of suggestions.

RB: Yeah, technology, but you know, *a hin a her*—you can't hug a jpeg.

EM: And you have successfully bridged the gap.

RB: Well, we've certainly tried very hard, and I would say, "Yes, we have," because there's nothing any of them want more than to come visit. And if there's one piece of advice I can give is you have to be proactive. It doesn't happen all by itself. I remember somebody in the community with whom I'm friendly, has children in Israel, said to me, "You have to teach me how to talk to my grandchildren in Israel." Well, you know, you have to work at it.

EM: And I'm thinking they speak to you and converse in English, which is a wonderful incentive for them to strengthen their language skills.

RB: The second child you'd never know. His vocabulary is phenomenal.

EM: So the children in some way live in both languages, in both worlds.

RB: Oh, yah, well they speak English at home.

EM: So they have this language bond.

RB: Sure. And they live in Bet Shemesh, where a lot of English-speaking people live, not only Americans, but from South Africa, from Great Britain.

EM: So, I know that you have an interesting story, going back to your *Dignity Beyond Death,* a visit that you made to the Boca Raton Islamic Center.

RB: Yes, okay. So, that's been on my To-Do List for a decade or more, as long as I've been involved in Chevra Kadisha. Now, why has it been on my To-Do-List? Because my brother and my sister-in-law are Islamicists, now both Jewish of course, but [it's] their academic field. And so I have known for some time that the Islamic preparation for burial very much mirrors what we do, and I have always wanted to know more, but, you know, I didn't do it. Then one day this past summer I said, "I'm going to find out." So I went on their web site, and it seemed to be very open on having people come, so I made an appointment with the Imam, and I took George with me, because he too has been interested. So, we were greeted so warmly—it was phenomenal—and we began to talk about the burial practices, and, you know, I was just amazed that not only do they do things that are very similar, but the reason for doing them are the same. You know, the whole egalitarian aspect of it, the respect and dignity for the dead body, and keeping it covered, you know, the whole modesty idea, so we were just thrilled. Anyhow, there were two things that happened there. At one point we were sitting in a room facing their parking lot; I see that all kinds of men are arriving, some just in Western clothes, some in partly Islamic dress; he wore, what is it called? [EM: Djellaba.] Yes, that long thing, and a little yarmulke. He was just the sweetest, nicest person. Anyway, so he says, "I'm gonna have to excuse myself because it's time for our prayers. You know, they *daven* five times a day. And he said, "You are invited to join us," you know, to observe. So we went into the mosque—we had to take our shoes off, that's the only thing—and we sat at the back. And they prayed. They prayed mostly standing up, until finally they were down on the ground, and then as part of that—and the prayers are in Arabic—they call this young man up, and I didn't quite know why, and then he reads from the Koran, you know, chants from the Koran, and they all applaud—I can't remember quite, but I knew it was something festive. Well, as it turns out, it's a "mitzvah" to memorize the Koran, and this young man had just finished memorizing it, and it was like a *siyum*. And following his recitation, we went out and we had *baklava* and drinks, how do you like that! It was like a *siyum*. [EM: Sounds familiar.] Yeah, I didn't feel strange at all. And then also after the prayers, they came and they talked to us, and there was an Arab from Israel who wanted to speak Hebrew with us, though we don't speak Hebrew. It was really very nice. And then we continued our discussion, and I happened to tell him about what I was doing with developing the course. He says, "Oh! Now I'm learning from you." And I ended up sending him all of our material. He has a school on the campus that goes from first grade to twelfth grade and is analogous as far as I can tell to a yeshiva day school. Anyway, he wanted all our material so he could fashion a course for his teenagers.

EM: How wonderful! So it's radiating, this course is radiating. Now, it's almost a given, but what role would you say that Judaism has played in your life?

RB: Well, it's been the cornerstone, you know. It's what informs my moral compass. It informs what I do. It informs how I make decisions. Let me tell you something. I don't know if you know, but a couple of months ago we were robbed. [EM: I didn't know.] Yes. Weird. While we were home. It was one of the—it was written up in the Sun-Sentinel. They come, (gestures the outline across the forehead of a cap with a visor) they say they're from Florida Power and Light, and if they don't check our water immediately, we're gonna get poisoned. So I let them in. There were two guys, they're very professional beyond belief. They keep us busy, George was upstairs, they sent him down to help with the water, what water, there was no water, cleaned out all my jewelry and ran away. Anyway, there's another part of this story. My next door neighbor is president of the association, he has nothing else to do, he's forever wandering around, and he had seen them, and he knew that they were up to no good. And then he saw them coming to our house. And he says, "Oh, I should let them know. No I won't—I had a disagreement with George." Now, since then I have not dwelled on the robbers—they were making a living. Were they entitled to what they took? No. But they were making a living. He [the neighbor] that was a *chilul HaShem,* because he put our lives in danger. What did he know? What if George—George was lying down upstairs—could have refused to come down? He could have said, "I'm sleeping, leave me alone." [The robber] He'd- a knocked him out, and taken his goodies. Now, so I ask myself, "If the guy next door—he has a very bad heart; he could drop dead any time—if I saw he was in need, what would I do? There is no question—I don't have to think about it twice—I would do whatever had to be done to save his life. So, that's how it [Judaism] informs.

EM: Now would you say that your affiliation or observance— how would you describe it, and did it change in your life? For instance, did you start out *Shomer Shabbos*? How did it go?

RB: We came from a cultural Jewish home.

EM: Your childhood. Yiddish-speaking cultural.

RB: But as far as *Shomer Shabbos,* well, my mother would have wanted it, but my father didn't really. He said he didn't have to go to shule because God was in his heart, and stuff like that, but a tremendous sense of social justice and of equality, and that's *Tahara.* Everybody, you know—the thief. My neighbor, he should live till a hundred and twenty, would be entitled to a *Tahara* even though he put our lives in danger.

EM: Yes. So, you started out in a culturally Jewish home, now did your observance—these are general categories—did you become more observant as you—

RB: Well we became more observant. We had to make a decision when we got married, you know, what kind of home we would have. George comes from a totally assimilated home where Judaism didn't come up on the radar screen, ever! Well, I can tell you a very funny story about when it did, but in any case, so we decided we would keep a kosher home, and when we had children, we sent them to day schools, orthodox day schools.

EM: Are either of them orthodox?

RB: Well, Josh for sure. Josh has *smicha* from the Israeli in addition. He's always been *frum.* For Jonathan, it's on the back burner, we don't know yet.

EM: Right. He knows the drill, whenever he wants to access it.

RB: He knows the drill. He told me he's gonna have a *Tahara* as well.

EM: So this is how your outlook and practice of religion has changed—

RB: Has evolved.

EM: A work in progress. Now, have you ever encountered any anti-Semitism in your public and personal life?

RB: Oh, yeah. I mean, in Winnipeg. We lived in a—well, it was a mixed neighborhood, but there were Ukrainians, Ukrainian nationalists who hated us, Polish nationalists, and, oh yeah, oh yeah, lots.

EM: And then in your career in the New York area though you were able to—what I'm trying to get to was did you encounter any career blocks, was there ever a house you wanted to buy that you couldn't?

RB: No, nothing like that. We made sure that our houses, though, were bought by blacks.

EM: Well, there you are.

RB: That's exactly what happened.

EM: This question I'm very interested in hearing your answer: What do you see as the future of Judaism in America and Israel? Is there interplay in the future? Anywhere you want to jump in.

RB: You know, I see that Judaism has tremendous strength, and it will survive, wherever it is, in whatever form it is.

EM: And what do you think is the impact of the existence of the state of Israel on the survival [of Judaism] everywhere?

RB: It's the one thing that binds all the streams of Judaism, so. And then the fact that Israel has triumphed under such extraordinary adverse circumstances to be a respected democracy and economic success and every success. I mean, it's astounding. (laughing) And only the Jews could do it, I don't know if only the Jews could do it, but the Jews did do it.

EM: Now, do you have any special religious celebrations, memories, of family holidays, rituals, anything from your childhood that you would like to share?

RB: Oh, well, we celebrated Hanukkah in a very different kind of way. I mean, lit candles, but, I think the menorah my father hand made, and we didn't buy *dreidels*, they were made—my father was a tailor—they were made from spools of thread, and we wrote on them *nes, gadol, haya, sham.* I don't have one, unfortunately.

EM: Did you ever have a session where you made them with your grandchildren/children?

RB: No, no.

EM: There you go, that's a whole other project.

RB: And the Hanukkah gelt. We didn't get presents every day or anything like that. There was a little bag that we got at the Yiddish day school we went to, a drawstring bag, and we put money in it, a little bit of money and then I guess we gave it to *tsedakah.*

EM: Now, if you could, to many, many generations down the road to come, of your great-great-great-great-great-great grandchildren, what words of wisdom or philosophies of life that have carried you through, what would you share with them?

RB: Well, this is one of the reasons I feel so strongly about *Tahara.* Despite the fact that my father wasn't really a religious man, like quote, unquote [Orthodox], he taught us about a sense of justice and about egalitarianism, that you treat people humanely, no matter what. And it has nothing to do with money. (Laughs heartily) You know, we lived in a poor neighborhood with all kinds of people of various backgrounds, mixed marriages and whatnot. And there was a family, a Jewish family, that—we lived in the north end—who moved to the south end, the south end is where it was more affluent. And one day my father meets Mrs. Nieman, that was her name, in Eaton's which was the big department store, and she says to him, *"Yu woint nach haus auf Redwood Avenue?"* "You still live on Redwood Avenue, like incredulous, how could you possibly? And my father said to her, *"Auf Redwood Avenue woinen oich menschen."* "On Redwood Avenue, we're still human, you know, people still live there." It hasn't changed us. So that's what I carry with me, *Auf Redwood Avenue woinen oich menschen.*

EM: This is a beautiful philosophy, treat people humanely. Is there any advice you would give to some of your descendants who are going through a challenge? In addition to the whole corpus of Judaism, is there something that carries you through?

RB: You know, I can't really answer that; I would try to address them individually on what the challenge means to them before I would give any advice, so there isn't really [EM: a pat answer] an answer to that, nor would it be helpful to anybody.

EM: So, we've done all the things that we said we were going to do, and would you say in your life, there was any time that you could describe that ignited your Jewish spark—to tell you the truth, listening to you, it's almost like a pilot light that has been there, on forever.

RB: Yah, well for sure *Tahara*, because inherent in *Tahara* are the core values of Judaism, and I can't tell you how that egalitarian aspect has spoken to the kids, that every Jew gets treated the same. And I think that's really important.

EM: So I'm thinking that seeing the forest for the trees, that your message, if you could give one for the generations to come would be, "Look to Judaism."

RB: That's right.

EM: In other words, it covers everything, and I think that would be—I don't want to put words in your mouth—but it's "forest for the trees"—it will have what you need to get through.

RB: Right. Absolutely. And marry the right person.

EM: That, too! Now, I'm going to come and sit with you for a minute—

RB: Am I telling you my Martin Luther King story?

EM: That's what I wanted you to do. I was gonna come over, but tell it now. We're on Martin Luther King Day, so tell your story now.

RB: It's not about Martin Luther King Day specifically, it's about integration, but of course he championed. When we lived in Woodbury, New Jersey, it was in the 60s at the time of the civil rights movement, and Josh was about a year and a half, we had one child, we lived in this nice little apartment house, on the second floor overlooking a pond. I look out the window one day, and I see we're being picketed by some black people. So I wondered, what was going on, and I couldn't leave the house because the kid was napping or something, so I called the local NAACP, and they said that they had been trying to get a black couple into our development for a long time, and they're constantly being told there are no vacancies. So, I told George, and he said, "Let's invite the NAACP to our house, and all our neighbors—let them tell the story." Well, so, people came, our next door neighbors were outraged. They figured the NAACP paid our rent; we were plants. And we used to listen through the wall, what they were saying about us. And I kept Josh's carriage downstairs—we lived on the second floor—it was a walk-up—and they put garbage in the carriage. Anyway, it turned out that, as I said before, they had been turned off—turned away because there were no vacancies, and we knew that there was a lot of turnover. So, they petitioned and they got a hearing, and they asked if we would testify. Now I couldn't testify cause I was with the baby, but George did testify. The night before he testified, he went around and determined which houses were vacant. And then we already had a history of this one moved, the other one moved in, that kind of thing. He testified, and they won, and the couple were allowed to move in. Now this coincided with our decision to leave Woodbury, and move back to New York at that point, and we were evicted, we were evicted, but we had planned to move anyhow. We got a letter of eviction, can you imagine this? But anyway, the day we moved, they had our security, which they weren't giving back, and the NAACP felt a debt of gratitude, so they sent members, many of whom were not black—I remember we had a pastor from a church came to help us clean up—*he* cleaned the bathroom! Now, you know, talk about humanity. I'll never forget that. Anyhow, we moved without our security, but the NAACP got us the money back.

EM: And did a black family move into your apartment?

RB: We wanted it, but we had the prize apartment. They moved in, but not into our apartment. We couldn't maneuver that. Now, you have to think, here we are, we were members of an orthodox synagogue, our orthodox synagogue thought we were off the walls—"What are they doing?" And we have since told that story to Shabbos lunch people—they can't figure it out, either. But if you're a real Jew, you can figure it out, because it's our Judaism that sent us, and gave us the courage to do this.

EM: It's a beautiful way to end, that Judaism informs every aspect of life.

RB: Oh, yes.

EM: I want to come here (walks over to Rochel) and I want to thank you so much—it's an honor and a privilege to have interviewed you, and once again, if you need to get in touch with me, elainemendelow@yahoo.com, and as I said, if it's way, way down the road into other centuries, we bid you greetings from the past. Be well.

Photography Interval: Rochel shows a picture of her parents, mother-in-law Claire Cecile Blumenthal Berman, her books, *Dignity Beyond Death: The Jewish Preparation for Burial, A*

Life of Leadership: Eli Zborowski, and a flip-through of the study guide *The Final Journey.*

EM: Hi. We're here with George Berman, who was definitely part of the Berman team—his authorship is here, (pointing to book) Rochel and George Berman wrote this book about Eli Zborowski, the biography, but I would like to ask George, since I have the opportunity, a few questions. So, now we'll go just to the piece of the interview. Your very esteemed wife said when she was asked about words of wisdom and advice for people, she said it's important to marry the right person. And she told us how you met, and all those good things. So, evidentially you both married the right people.

GB: Yes.

EM: And you can see it in the success of all your projects, but what I would like to ask you is, would you say that there was a time in your life where your Jewish spark was ignited? You came from a more assimilated background than Rochel did—can you pinpoint a time when you ignited your Jewish spark?

GB: Well, when we were getting married, we discussed affiliations and so forth, and we agreed that we would go to a conservative synagogue, and our house would be totally kosher, acceptable to anybody, and it started there. And that's about as inspiration[al] as it got, so I went to shule, and began to see Judaism in a different light as [I was] brought up to see it.

EM: How would you say that Judaism has informed your life?

GB: Wow.

EM: In twenty-five words or less. I know we can't get into it deeply, but if you could take an overview.

GB: An overview. (pause) I think it's made me think much more deeply about a person's soul and how it evidences itself and what it means to have a soul.

EM: So you would say that it has informed your spiritual reflections and philosophies.

GB: Oh, yes. In fact more recently through Rochel's course, I would not say what I just said, what it means to have a soul and have a body. You are a soul.

EM: So you would say that her project—your project—I know you were the first one to go to the *Tahara*, and, as I said, you married the right person, you led each other into it and through it, and from that has come this amazing project. What would you say, if you could reflect on it, what would you say the role of Israel would play—I want to say it this way—the future of Judaism in America and Israel. Do you have any reflections or observations on this?

GB: Well in Israel it's very obvious, the future of Judaism. In America, I think that we're probably going to continue to see a lot of secularization. I don't foresee a rush to join synagogues, especially the orthodox synagogues.

EM: Would you ever live in Israel?

GB: I might—not really—I don't care for the thought.

EM: What is it that you like or dislike about life in Israel that would have you not choose it as a place to live?

GB: Well, it is a foreign country; it's a place where I don't speak the language, and where I don't know many people. My interests here are largely nature, getting out, getting out in the woods, but it's kinda late in life for me to affiliate with that kind of change in life, to assimilate.

EM: Speaking of this perspective at life, are there any words of wisdom or guidelines, if you could say something to the generations to come—is there any sort of credo or philosophy or something that you would pass on to the generations to come, if you could say something to them?

GB: (pause) I'm sorry, but it's just not coming up at all.

EM: That's okay. Is there any saying that you find you repeat over and over when you're in some sort of a challenging situation? Any sort of a little saying to proceed? There might not be.

GB: I'm not going to be a very good interview, I'm afraid.

EM: You're fine, you're just fine.

RB: What about victimhood?

GB: Yes, there's that. Eli [Zborowski] never considered himself a victim. That was a big factor in his success. He came to America without a penny, with a wife and a child. And he went out and he walked the streets, came across a box of umbrella heads, and they sell for nothing, a penny apiece or so. So he bought 'em. Then he looked up in the yellow pages where the manufacturers of umbrellas were, went down and he sold the umbrella heads. And that's where he got his start. It never occurred to him to take a job, because his father never did that. His father was always an independent as a businessman. And he just went on. He became a leader in the Jewish community and a major manufacturer, eventually as well.

EM: So, I think you're saying that—you're saying something about resilience.

GB: About resilience. More about independence, I think.

EM: So, is there anything you would like to say about working with your wife on these projects and maybe the role Judaism played in your joint efforts?

GB: Well, we work very well together. We each edit the other's writings, except this book where I participated in the writing, we're the *hiv* and the *her,* we carved out a section for me, and the rest of it I just contributed my comments.

EM: And you did contribute photographs in *Oceans Apart,* didn't you?

GB: I guess I did.

EM: Yes you did. And it's been a joint community effort and of course, and you have answered all these things—I did want to ask you one tiny question—did you encounter any anti-Semitism in your personal or professional life?

GB: No, I don't think so.

EM: Your wife told us the wonderful story about the NAACP and the apartment, and it's very appropriate for Martin Luther King Day.

GB: That is the one place where I did [encounter anti-Semitism].

RB: What about the anti-Semitism when you were a child?

GB: Well, we were talking about that.

EM: Yes, I would love to hear anything you remember.

GB: In that case, while I was working with Philip Morris, I overheard a conversation. There was a report about my participation in integrating the apartments, and someone said, "Why would a white man ever do that?" and somebody else said, "Well, George is no white man—he's a Jew." I rather liked being on that side of the fence.

EM: Absolutely. And of course it didn't do anything to jeopardize your professional career?

GB: No.

EB: And to end, what role would you say that Judaism has played in your life?

GB: It's basically organized my thinking about ethical issues.

EM: And would you say it played a role being Jewish? You might not have been orthodox or whatever, but how did being Jewish play a role in your life decisions is what I wanted to ask you.

GB: My life decisions.

EM: Well, for instance, choosing who you were going to marry. Did it have a role in that? (Rochel laughs heartily in the background.) Not that you didn't love each other, etc., etc., did you have a predisposition to marry a Jewish person? That's what I'm really trying to ask.

GB: I think I did.

EM: Was it something that your parents were insistent on?

GB: Yes. My parents weren't insistent—

EM: But they were encouraging.

GB: Yes.

EM: So we could say that this was a good guidance, because look what it engendered.

2018-01-14 23.57.05

GB: You know how I remember Rochel, how we came to be married is a story.

EM: Yes, she told it. Of course, it's different when the husband tells it.

EM: Did you want to say something about your secular background?

RB: Well, there's a perfect example. Horace [Mann High School.] And there was never any chaplain there—it was 95% Jewish. And when they hired a chaplain—George, go ahead.

GB: It was a gentile chaplain.

RB: Wasn't he Asian? George said to his mother, "Guess what? They hired a chaplain, and he's Asian." And she said, "Oh, what did you expect, George? That they would hire a rabbi?"

EM: So, just as the battery died, and I had asked you how Judaism had informed your life, and your Jewish progress, and your spiritual spark you said the most beautiful thing—I said, "Has the choice of a wife informed your Jewish pursuit?" and you said the most beautiful thing, I'd like you to say it again.

GB: I said that Rochel is my proof of God, my evidence of the existence of God, because when you look back and you see our events, so improbable, it had to be guided by something. (Rochel laughs in the background.) It certainly wasn't guided by me. It might have been guided somewhat by Rochel. But in the end—I don't want to come to the conclusion before I go through the information. I was taking my master's degree in chemical engineering. I was now at the stage where I was finished doing all my course work. I was now doing my experimental work. I was living in a dormitory, I was living in a graduate housing facility. My next-door-neighbor was orthodox, and I came by and I said to him one day, "You know, I'd like to learn to speak, I'd like to learn Hebrew." He said to me, "Well, I'd be pretty expensive." So I said, "Well, if that's the way it has to be, that's the way it has to be." "It doesn't have to be," he said. "I have a friend whose sister is coming into town, and she can teach you Hebrew. She'll do it for much less than I do." Well, the truth of the matter is, I never learned Hebrew.

RB: (interjecting) You never paid for it, either!

GB: It's been far more expensive than that in the end.

EM: Well worth it.

GB: But the fact is that I met Rochel, I liked her and I took her out, starting taking her out. It occurs to me only in reflection that she didn't come to New Haven because she liked her brother, because she wanted to be next to, near her brother. She came because he was at Yale, and she wanted to be at Yale, because she was at an age where she was looking for a husband, I think, she might have told me. [EM: Yes, she said it.] Well, a long time went by, she was being her wonderful self, but I wasn't ready to get married. She asked me, she called me one day and she said, "What's your plan to be ready to get married?" [I said] Five or six years. She said, "Well, my planning is ready for five or six months, so maybe we'd better break it off." I said all right, feeling this was too much of a difference, we both agreed. Well, it was at the time when hi-fi was just coming in, and I had put together a set for her, the parts—the amplifier and the radio. One day she called me and she said, "My hi-fi is broken, not working right." Like I was responsible for that. All right, I took the responsibility. I said, "I'll come down and fix it." I came down. The only problem was the cable was unplugged. It didn't occur to me who unplugged it. But, anyway, having said that, I started to leave, and I could not get out the door. It was like a post-hypnotic suggestion; you will be afraid to cross this door—I could not get out the door. I finally realized I could not imagine life without this woman. So I stepped back and said, "Will you marry me?" She said, "Sure." I said, "But you can't tell anybody." I don't know why I said that; it was so unexpected, I didn't want it to be revealed. Well, I was still there when the phone rang—it was a friend of her father's congratulating her. I don't know when she got away long enough to tell him, but anyway, we went on from there, and the feeling I have is that we were *bashert.* That's it. I didn't want to get married, but I didn't see any other way to spend my life with her, kinda thing. And since then, some other things have come about that made me feel it was so right. And I didn't anticipate them, I didn't analyze them as I normally would—very analytical of the whole process—that I have to say, when you see a sequence of things that happen, that wouldn't have happened without some guidance, you have to believe there was guidance.

EM: Divine providence. *Hashkocha Pratis.*

GB: Right.

EM: And it's very interesting, because her advice was, "Marry the right person," and you both have. And I thank you.

GB: Look at our kids—look at what they're both doing. And I say to myself, that's part of it.

EM: Fabulous. I thank you so much for sharing all of this with us. Is there anything you want to say—I didn't want to cut it off.

GM: So *bashert* or not, I love my wife very much.

EM: (to Rochel in the background) George just said he loves his wife very much, and I'm pretty sure she loves you, too.

GB: (looking towards Rochel) I think so.

EM: How about ending with you two standing together? (Rochel comes into the picture to stand by George, who is seated.) Yes, this is the typical Yiddish picture. (All laugh.) I'm so glad you came back, George. This has been an honor and a joy. Be well.

Appendix D
Jay Lauwick Interview
September 8, 2005

EM: We are going today to have Jay tell the story of his life. First of all, Jay, what is your name?

JL: My name is Jay Lauwick.

EM: Do you have a middle name?

JL: Yes, but I never use it. It was—It's "A," middle initial is A for Antoine, which is the middle name of every male in the Lauwick family.

EM: How interesting. Can you tell us what your name started out with—we're jumping ahead—when you were born in France? Your name wasn't J-A-Y—

JL: Oh, yes. I was born Gerard, and Leah didn't like it because it doesn't sound "American." She decided I should be "Jay," and I liked it. It's a short name, you can shout it, you know, it bears. And when I was naturalized, I chose to remain "Jay." Now "Jay" is my official name. But, in France, on my French passport, I'm Gerard.

EM: Do you have a Jewish name at all, a Hebrew name?

JL: Jonah.

EM: Okay. And do you know who you're named after?

JL: No. That does not—naming does not exist within France. Maybe it exists now, but I just learned about it when I arrived in this country.

EM: Were you named—I know Antoine you said is the name that your family—the Lauwick family name—were you Gerard, were you named for anyone in particular?

JL: No. The funny thing is that my mother wanted to call me "Alain," and her sister refused—had a fit, I understand. She wanted "Gerard." So my mother gave way and said, "Okay, let's call him Gerard, but—I was only five days old at that time. So for five days my first name was Alain, and afterward it moved to Gerard.

EM: It's funny. Now we're going to start on your family. What was your father's name?

JL: Emil.

EM: And what was his occupation?

JL: He was a director in a fabric company. His company was manufacturing, weaving things like sheets, all types of different work clothes, and things like that. They had a tinting plant, and my father was in charge of the sales, and managed the sales office.

EM: And where and when was he born?

JL: He was born in a small village in the north of France between—next to Roubaix. He was born in 1900.

EM: Yes, June 2, 1900, as you've written in your notes. (Not that I know.) And when did he pass away?

JL: He passed away on August 1981.

EM: Okay. And how—what was his cause of death?

JL: He had colorectal cancer.

EM: And what are some of your memories of him?

JL: A very quiet man, devoted to his family, to his children, but, without great emotion. He was not thick cold, but I don't remember a lot of warmth in his relationship with his children. He loved us, we loved him. He was not the authority figure in the family, my mother was.

EM: Did you know any of his family, your paternal grandparents?

JL: Yes, I knew his grandparents—his parents and his brothers and sisters who now are all dead, of course. They were living either in the north part of France, or in Rouen.

EM: And what were his parents' names, do you happen to know?

JL: My grandfather was also Emil, and his mother was Julie.

EM: And you don't happen to know her maiden name or anything?

JL: Her maiden name was DeCrain. She was, like my grandfather, they were both Flemish, living in France, but born in Flanders, Belgium, and I understand that during World War II, in 1915, I guess—

EM: World War I.

JL: World War I. They moved from the north of France to Rouen, where they settled in a tiny village, next to Rouen, which happened to be the place where the king of Belgium was also a refugee, and the Belgian government in exile was in that little village called Bon Secours.

EM: How fascinating. Now, working your way up, I think it's very interesting how your parents met.

JL: Okay.

EM: And oh, before we go further, let's make sure we say your mother's name.

JL: Okay, my mother's name's Margaret.

EM: And her maiden name was?

JL: Her maiden name is Becker. And her parents were—had a bakery in a tiny street in Lisle, and my father's parents had a grocery shop in the same street, across the street, and they knew each other for almost ever. And my mother stayed there in Lisle during the war, and my father moved, with his parents, he was 14-15, and they went to a place in Bon Secours, where, as I told you, the king of Belgium was there, and I remember myself, in the late 30s, 40s, probably, on the walls next to hotels or shops, there were still old writing in Flemish, because they were speaking Flemish in this area.

EM: My goodness. And your parents then met—your grandparents—no, your parents then met after the war.

JL: Yes, they knew each other, and they were married in 1929.

EM: And they settled in—

JL: They settled in Rouen. My father had a job there. And my
mother was a pianist in Lisle, and quite famous, I understand. And she was well-known in the industry. She played
for the president of the Republic at that time, and she gave
up everything when she was married, with children and
things like that, but up until I left the house when I was
nineteen, twenty, sometimes she was sitting down at the
piano and began to play, and everything stopped in the
house. You know, we had two, three stories of bedrooms,
and children—when my mother began to play the piano,
everybody met, sat down in the sitting room, and she was
playing, nobody said anything. That was really something.

EM: Now, did you ever visit that little street with the bakery—

JL: No. I don't think so, I don't remember.

EM: Not in your childhood.

JL: No. I don't remember. I've seen photographs of it—I have
not seen it, I've never been there.

EM: I was going to ask you, in your mother's family, do you
have any childhood memories of her family? I think you
did tell an interesting story of what happened in WWI with
her family. Why don't we go through that?

JL: Yes. My grandfather—both my grandfathers—my mother's father and my father's father were friends. They lived
next door to each other—

EM: And they were merchants—

JL: Yes, and they decided to escape the German invasion, because the Germans invaded this part of France, and they
moved to—they moved by sea from Dunkirk to Cherbourg
and they settled in Rouen, and uh, let me try to remember.

My mother's mother—my maternal grandmother died in 19—I think during the war, World War I.

EM: So during the war, you were saying that your mother's father and your father's father were friends and they escaped before the Germans came.

JL: Yes, they both escaped, settled in Rouen, and during that time in Lisle, north of France, my maternal grandmother died. I don't know exactly what happened, but she died in 1917 or 1918. And, her husband, who was in Rouen at that time, lost his mind. He was institutionalized, and he died in 1931, completely out of the world.

EM: And you said what happened was he came back and found she had died, and the shock of it—

JL: No, he was institutionalized in France, in the southern part of France, I don't know exactly where and it's after the war that my aunts brought him back, in the northern part of France, where he was also institutionalized. And my mother and her sisters were raised by the older sister.

EM: Did you know this older sister?

JL: Yes, yes I knew her. She died in 1950.

EM: Is she the one who insisted that you be named "Gerard?"

JL: No, this one was Claire. She was—she stayed single. There was another sister whose name was Mathilde, who want me to be Gerard. She was a nurse, and she died of leukemia in 1939, and I knew her. I remember her very well. She was sick. And another sister was Marise, and she was the "gung-ho" person in the family, and she was a fashion designer, she was involved in fashion, and she had a big atelier, with a lot of employees and that, she was very famous at that time.

EM: And what was her name? Her last name?

JL: Marise. Becker. She was not married. And she was—she died—I think she died in 1941. I remember her very well. At that time, she was driving a car, which was, absolutely, extra for a woman, you know. Then there was my mother, then there was another sister whose name was Eugenie, and Eugenie was a nun. And she was a very—very interesting person, very bright. She was very friendly with my mother. And the last sister was Elizabeth. Elizabeth, we called her Betsy, she was the baby, and I knew her very well. And she married very late, she was forty-five or fifty when she married, and she died probably in the late sixties or something like that.

Are there any cousins from your mother's family or any relatives—

JL: There are some, but I don't know them. I met—let me backtrack a little bit—during the war, World War II, it was not possible for political reasons to go from Rouen, Normandy to the north of France, which was included in the German influence. There was some kind of a boundary and you must—you had to carry some ausweiss, special authorization, German authorization, to go through. So, because of that, we were completely cut off. After the war, of course, when things began to be free, traveling was, we went to—we went to Lisle with my parents, and we met some of her family—I don't remember. I remember a cousin who was a pastry shop owner or something like that.

EM: In Lisle?

JL: It was in Roubaix, which is right next door. But, no I don't think there's a lot of family left.

EM: So, were there any brothers of your mother?

JL: No.

EM: All sisters.

JL: I understand and I know that later on that my mother had one brother who died very, very young, and I don't even know if she knew him. I don't know what happened.

EM: The reason I asked just because Becker isn't the name of these cousins because the sisters married, so they're all different names.

JL: And I don't know if it was Becker, I'm trying to remember the name, which I knew.

EM: Well, the thing is, somebody could go back to that little town and find it. Now, we talked about your mother—when was she born, when did she pass away?

JL: She was born in February 1905—

EM: A hundred years ago.

JL: Yeh. And she died in May 1997.

EM: And that was her cause of death, old age?

JL: Old age, natural causes, old age.

EM: So she lived till ninety-two.

JL: Ninety-two. Yeah. She was a very active person, she was running the show in the family, and her husband and herself, I think they were a very nice team, doing things together, good relationship with values, devoted to their children...

EM: Are you friendly with any relatives or children on your father's side?

JL: No. All the brothers and sisters—my father had one brother and he had one, two sisters.

EM: And their names were—

JL: Jacques was the brother, there was Louise, and there was Andre, and they are all dead now.

EM: And their children?

JL: Their children, who are married, I don't know them. I've lost track of all the family things, whatever they are, when I went to sea. I lost contact.

EM: Well, now with the internet, you'll be able to—

JL: Yes, but even so, even so.

EM: It's hard. All right, now we're going to get up to your family. We were just getting up to the point of your mother and father meeting, after the war, and you said they married in 1929, and they lived in Rouen and your family now. Let's talk about your brothers and sisters.

JL: Okay. First child was Francoise, born in 1930. She was married in 1950, I think, or 1951. Her married name is DiFrancesci.

EM: And you're still in contact with her.

JL: Yes. She lives north of Paris, not far from Paris, and she had five children, and I met them last time I was with her. Her husband is Ambroise, of Italian origin. They had and still have a building material business. In the building business you would say—

EM: Construction.

JL: Construction, selling almost everything like Home Depot, did not exist of course at that time, but they were like a construction material, of course, tool, gas, gasoline, brick and cement, and whatever. But also they had, they were also kind of an outlet store. It's a tiny village, next to, not far from Paris.

EM: And your next sister is—

JL: Then I come, I'm number two, then there is Brigitte, who was born in '35. She lives between Paris and a tiny, tiny village in southern Brittany, a tiny village where there are three houses.

EM: Wow. Now let's give your birthdate, because you were in between Francoise and Brigitte. And your birthdate is—

JL: Thirty-three, 1933, August 12th.

EM: And you even know the street you were born on.

JL: I was born in a street called Rue Richard le Noir, number six. I was born there, like my older sister, and like Brigitte, who was born there. We moved when Brigitte was three months old, and that's the first memory I have. I remember that day, my father moving. We moved from # 6 to # 7, on the same street, so it was just across the street, and I remember my father and a neighbor carrying pieces of furniture, and I remember Brigitte being a tiny, tiny baby in a crib. I remember that, the first memory.

EM: Your earliest memory. What I wanted to ask you is, do you see any physical resemblance in your children to any of these relatives?

JL: Uh, Stephan, my oldest son, is definitely my son, okay?

EM: I can vouch for that.

JL: And, if you look carefully you can find similarities with my father, okay? Severine, my first daughter, has the stature of my mother—tall, stronger, my mother was like that, and Severine and Yocheved [Jay's second daughter] are the same. They are tall, strong, I don't say bony, but—

EM: Yes, and they definitely look like sisters.

JL: Yes, and my mother was like that. So Francoise, my sister Francoise, is like that also. Brigitte, a little bit. And Ann, my third sister, who was born in 1940, is more on my side, more Lauwick than Becker. She's rather thin, dark hair, at least when she was young.

EM: Well this is all very interesting, and we're going to lead up now, we've got you born, we've got you moved at twenty months—how about telling us something about your earliest—your school experience—your first years at school. Did you have a little school that you walked to nearby?

JL: Yes, yes. I began my very first year was in a private school, next door, not far from the house, five minutes walking, where my sister went there, too, all of them. Then, I moved to a boys' school, a private boys' school, also next door, less than five minutes' walking distance, and then after, then I went to another private school for boys—it was junior high, I guess, like middle school, junior high. So I went in one of two different schools, in this area, and then I went to a technical school, south of Paris for one year. My parents had decided I would be an engineer—they had not really any idea of what it would be, but they wanted me to be an engineer. I didn't like that idea very much, it was not my choice, but I followed. And so I went back to Rouen in a technical college, too. Then I made my choice and opposed it—I say I want to go in the merchant marine, so, that's what happened.

EM: Now, before we go into the World War II part in France when you were just young and growing up, I would love you to tell the story that you started to tell to me, that hooked into the merchant marine, how your father had a collection of, was it National Geographic type magazines or books—you tell it, how you were up in your room, you looked at the books, you looked out at the seaport—how old were you when this—

JL: That began, that anecdote about books, happened in 1940—let's say 1945. I was twelve, and my father bought a collection of books—they were a very luxury at that time—leather bound, things like that—about different countries in the world—and of course, there were two books for the United States, and New York was in that book. And I remember reading that book about New York and being fascinated, absolutely fascinated. I knew everything in that book about New York. I knew everything— Manhattan, Fifth Avenue and Battery, everything. I was twelve, thirteen. At the same time, my bedroom was under the roof, on the three-story home that we had, a three-story house, and from my window I was able to see a huge panorama including the river and the seaport of Rouen. Rouen is inland, but it was a very active seaport with cargo ships coming in and out, and that was the beginning of my interest, yah.

EM: Now let's hone in on your World War II experience, which was unique to say the least.

JL: Okay, World War II experience.

EM: Where do you want to start, with the invasion of the Germans?

JL: Yes, I will try to keep it on a chronological order. In 1939, in the summer of 1939, we were in a tiny village, a tiny, tiny village; there were probably less than ten houses—eight miles, ten miles from Rouen. My mother had been sick the year before, and the doctor has said that she must not go to the seashore, she must go next to the forest, and that village was among the trees, among the forest, so we were there. 1939 September—war, and, as you know, nothing happened. My father began to—was working, and at the end of the summer we went back to Rouen, and my father was—it was in 1939—my father was—I think my father was a reservist, I'm not too sure of that, I don't remember. I know that he was too young during World War I, but after that he was probably involved in the military service, something like that, he was picked up in 1939 in an anti-aircraft battle, and he was assigned very close to the house in an anti-aircraft gunnery, whatever it was, he was a sergeant or something like that, and it lasted two weeks or three weeks, and he had three children, and his wife was— she was not pregnant yet, so he was selected as an affecte speciale, I don't know the name in English, but you keep your civilian status, you work in your job, you keep your family, you keep your place to live, but you are not in the army.

EM: It sounds like a military advisor.

JL: No, not really. It has nothing to do with the army, it's even not deferred, it's some kind of exoneration, okay? So he was an affecte special. Because of that, he was able to stay with his family, to stay [in] his job, it was fine. In 1940, when—on May 10, 1940, which was Leah's birthday, by the way, the Germans invaded France through the lower countries, and came. And that created a panic, and France, from one day to the other, found itself on the road, escaping, big exodus. And we were part of it. First, we went back to Montenis, that little village, and after a while, involved with everybody's panic, we escaped. And we escaped with my father's boss, who had a car, and took us. We had three kids at that time, and my parents, plus him, and we went. He was some kind of a wealthy man; he had a castle in Normandy someplace. We went there, and he took us—all the family. And we stayed in that castle for probably one week, I guess, and the Germans came, and we escaped further south, and we took a train, and so we had a lot of experience there. We lost all our luggage, in Rheims, we were bombed by the German planes, we went to Nantes. Anyhow, we ended up in a tiny town south between the Loire and Bordeaux, in LaRochurions. And we stayed there till September, I guess, 1940. And it is there that I met, I saw my first German. I thought he was an English soldier, green, instead of khaki. He was in a truck, and I remember, at the window, saying "Oh, Mom I've just seen an English, with a green uniform. My mother says, "No, he's German." That was my first experience. So at the end of the summer we moved back to Rouen and life was back to normal. My father was working, the bridge had been broken, and we were on a boat bridge to cross the river, and there was nothing special that happened. I was young, knowing nothing, not aware of anything—yes, the Germans were there, that's it. And the first thing that happened was on 18th of August, 1942, the first bombing operations by the US—the 8th US Air Force was bombing in Rouen, very first in the world, first operation. And we were—it was in August in summer, it was in Montenis, and I remember with my sisters, we were in the forest and we were looking at a plane, and we saw the bombs leaving the plane and pshhh, falling down, and that created a panic among the children. I was nine years old, my sister was twelve, the other one was nine, you know, it was a panic.

EM: Did you say one landed quite near?

JL: No, at that time, no. They aimed at a marching station, they missed it completely, and they went right into the middle of town, and they killed, among other people, they killed the woman who owned the pastry shop in our neighborhood. And that was the first victim that I knew, and I can still remember her. And that was the beginning of really—afterwards, there were more bombings and things like that, and afterwards we were looking at the planes coming,

EM: Now what I want you to get into is—there was a special circumstance in your family that made it very tenuous for you to be in or near the Germans—your mother, even though she didn't actively broadcast it, your mother was Jewish.

JL: Yes.

EM: And of course your father knew your mother was Jewish, and that made all of you candidates to be counted as Jewish, and—tell about that.

JL: We were—my mother was Jewish—

EM: By birth.

JL: By birth, but that was the only thing that happened. There was nothing Jewish in the house—

EM: Well you said one of her sisters became a nun.

JL: There was nothing. And that came because it was her choice, and thank God, it was her choice, but it was also family stories when she was young, okay? We knew that it was not a subject of conversation, we did not—almost never talk about it, and because of that we were—we didn't feel threatened. I went to private school[s], that were not religious, but Christian, definitely, and as far as anti-Semitism, that did not exist in my life at that time. I was—I was—knew about it later on, in 1944, something like that, [at] twelve years, and the war, the involvement in the war, became more important, after April 1944, when there was a big bombing of the city. And, at that time, the Allied forces were trying to destroy all communication, bridge, in order to prepare for D-day. On the 19th of April, they were aiming the bridge at the boat—there were three bridges[s] in Rouen, on the river, and they came with, I don't know how many planes in the middle of the night, and they let go of the bombs and everything fell, you know, it was—it was a mess. And I remember we were all huddled, bunched together in the kitchen, and the bombs were coming down, was noise, there was fire, we could see fire, we could see, smell the powder, the dust, the smoke— it was a big thing. No bomb reached our vicinity, our ar- ea—it was one mile away, you know. The following day, I went to school, and, of course, I had to go through the—

EM: The rubble?

JL: The rubble. And the fires, and the streetcars' wires down, you know, that stuff. And that was the last day of school. And I remember that school, in the playground, there was a cobblestone that came—nobody knew where, but thrown away by a bomb someplace, you know, and, anyhow, that was the last day of school, and we immediately moved back to Montenis, that was still at that little house, and we lived there for—until the end.

EM: Now there was a point where your family was hidden.

JL: Yes, that's much later. After April '44, my father was still working in Rouen, and he left in the morning on his bicy- cle, went down to the city, he worked there and came back at night. And bombing was—were more frequent. They always tried to destroy the bridges, and they came for one week. At night, it was the British—they flew at night—to bomb. During the daytime, it was the American Air Force, they bombed—it lasted at least one week—there were at least two bombings every day, and . . . there were a lot of victims, and Rouen was badly destroyed. And we were far from it. We were always trying to find out where the bombs were falling, trying to find out if my father was alive or not, and sometimes he was able to give a call to our neighbor—there was only one telephone in the village, and sometimes he was able to call and say, "I'm fine, please go and tell my family I'm fine." So, across the meadows, and the neighbors would call and say, "So, Mrs. Lauwick, your husband called and he's fine." Sometimes my father would come back, bicycle early, and say, "You know, I'm fine." "Oh, and we don't know," that type of thing. But, it was a scary, scary situation.

EM: Now, I remember you telling about the circumstances—well, first of all you were hidden, you were separated at some point.

JL: Later on.

EM: So, should we tell about the birth of your sister, how your father was prepared to deliver your mother?

JL: Oh, okay. So that was in July, 1944. The situation was bad. The Allied Forces had landed in Normandy. We saw all the German armies coming to reinforce their army in Normandy. We saw them coming back completely destroyed, you know? They were—anyhow—so we saw it was something serious, and my parents decided to split the family. And the three girls—Francoise, Brigitte—no, the two girls—Ann was born in '40, so she was three-and-a-half years old, so she stayed with us. Francoise and Brigitte went in a tiny village where a woman we knew was taking children, usually sick children, take them to the countryside, to give them better food, better air, and protection, and far from the bombing, and things like that. And, my sisters went there.

EM: What about [your brother] Patrice?

JL: Patrice was born afterward. I'm coming to Patrice. My
      mother was pregnant, of course, and, in order to protect
      ourself (sic) my father had dug, with a friend, had dug a
      shelter in the meadows, in the orchards, and there was a
      bench in that shelter—it was like a trench—we called it a
      trench. And my father had collected a lot of medications,
      and material, whatever, because he thought that maybe my
      mother will have to give birth there. It did not happen, but
      we had a lot of—we had a lot of bombings, a lot of bad
      things that happened. When my mother was ready to give
      birth, everything was arranged by my father. They took the
      milkman car, who had an Ausweiss. He picked up my
      mother, my father. They went to the German lines, I would
      say, and they showed a paper, they could go, and my father
      came back, a little bit later on, and he was stopped by the
      Germans, he was on his bicycle at that time, and, uh, he
      had an Ausweiss, but they didn't want to believe it, be-
      cause he was alone. So, he had to tell them, "Madame
      malade, kinchunch," [gestures a pregnant silhouette] and
      they remembered what happened, so they let him go. But
      we had—so my brother was born in a tiny clinic in a sub-
      urb of Rouen, and it was a bad thing, because it was—he
      was born on the 13th of August, and the Germans escaped
      on the 25th. So there were tank battles, bombings, guns, so
      it was a bad, bad situation.

EM: Now how much was all this hiding necessitated by the fact
      that your mother had Jewish ancestry?

JL: Nothing, nothing. Nothing.

EM: So it was just because you had to save yourselves—

JL: It was a matter of situation, because of safety. It had noth-
      ing to do with Jewishness or anything like that, no.

EM: That's quite a story. Well, then came after the war. I think
      you did mention the day of liberation?

JL: Ah, yes. The Liberation. Of course, there was a lull in the activities. The Germans were retreating, completely beaten up, they were preparing trench to fight, and things like that, but, nothing happened, and then one day my father came back and said, "Look over there," and there was a big pine tree, and there was a big flag, a French flag at the top of the tree, and that meant that we were liberated. And everybody was very happy, and the very first Allied soldiers I saw were two Scottish soldiers who were in a tiny little tank that were just moving around, you know, so, that was the first days.

EM: Now what was your—physically, your closest call in the war? In other words, was there a point where you or your family was near something that had been bombed, or you went by and realized that had you been there five minutes earlier, that would have been it?

JL: No, not really. Of course, there were—

EM: You said there was a time when you were in a field, I believe?

JL: Yes, yes, that was probably in July, I guess, 1944? I was in a field, not a field—I don't know how to call that—an "orcard, orchard?"

EM: Orchard.

JL: Okay, the house was a very, very old house, three rooms, two bedrooms and a kitchen, built in the 17th century, very old. And it was probably 1,000 feet from the road, and the road was a—it was not a dirt road, but close to it. And there was a lot of German traffic coming in and out on that road. On that day, I was on my way to the road, I don't remember, and a German truck loaded with food and stuff was attacked by a fighter, I don't remember which type of fighter it was, but I was in the line of fire. I was not shot at, because the truck was there, [gesturing] and I was a little bit further, but the noise of the gun was—I was terrified! I remember I fell on the ground, and—it was, I don't say close call, because the bullets were hitting the ground 200 feet from me or something like that—

EM: Close enough.

JL: But the noise, the noise, and the truck was destroyed, Germans were killed, I remember a German was in a dungaree, without shirt, just a jacket—he opened the jacket, and a bullet came through, completely through—he died a little bit later. Anyhow, that was a big thing.

EM: Yes, sounds like being in the middle of it.

JL: And sometimes we had the German patrols coming at night, waking everybody up, they were looking for paratroopers or anything, they were inspecting the house. That was a little bit scary, but not dangerous, really.

EM: Sounds like a huge adventure. Well, then after the war, you got to resume what was normal life.

JL: Yes, all the activities, and I remember at the end—it was in September, we moved back to Rouen, to go to back to school and things like that, and I remember, alone—I have never understood how my parents allowed me to do that—but I was alone on the river quay, that was the docks—covered with German equipment—trucks, tanks, all kind of things, and they had been completely destroyed by the planes, the Allied planes. Everything was completely destroyed, and I remember, looking out on—I was not interested at that time, but I could have taken all the arms and weapons I would have liked—the smell of dead corpse was impossible—I was twelve, I could not imagine that my parents let me do that, and I remember, I was alone! Almost nobody there, anyhow.

EM: Anyhow, so after the war, you resumed your education as you said, in the technical school—

JL: Yes.

EM: And then, what happened—you went to technical school, and then you decided you were going to go into—

JL: Yah. So I began to go into the Merchant Marine, okay? My parents were not very pleased at the beginning, but it didn't last, and finally they have been very supportive, and, as it was—so they decided, are you sure? So they tried to—they didn't try to discourage me, but they decided that I had to be sure, and the only way to be sure was to try. So, they find, my father find, by relation, a ship where I could be on board, during the summer of 1952. And, I went on board that ship, it was a Panamanian ship, and I boarded the ship in Rotterdam, all alone, I was eighteen, and I went aboard the ship, and I spent four months—we went on the Aegean, Turkey, Greece, North Africa—came back, and I liked it, so my parents said," Okay, fine. Now what do you want to do?" I said, "I want to see, I wanted to learn a little bit." The thing is, in order to graduate from the Merchant Marine Academy, you must go at sea for some times—thirty months, twenty months, depending, you know, on what you want to do. Then, you are allowed to go to classes. After class, you go back at sea for twenty, thirty, forty months, then you take another class. So, the idea was, to go at sea, to acquire some practical knowledge, then, go to school. But I wanted to go to school a little bit before in a private kind of private school for merchant marine studies in Brittany. I stayed there three months, just to have a rough idea. And afterward, the French Line took me as an apprentice, on board a ship, and that was the beginning.

EM: And you said you got your captain's license.

JL: Much later, because once again, you go at sea for thirty, forty months. Then, you go one year class, pass an exam, go back at sea, pass another exam, and so on and so forth.

So, I went for my last class, my last course of captain, in 1965.

EM: And now, we're up to the love-and-marriage chapter.

JL: (Smiling) Aha!

EM: Love and marriage. When and where did you meet your first wife? And what was her name?

JL: Colette. Colette was her first name. I met her in a hospital where we both volunteered for—in a children's hospital—where we both volunteered separately, for the library for children.

EM: And how old were you?

JL: I was nineteen, just before my first ship.

EM: Was it love at first sight?

JL: Not really. Interest, but not really love, I would say. And I met her probably in the middle of the school year when I was still at school. In the summer I left for my first ship, and, I was on, and we saw each other a couple of days—

EM: Here and there.

JL: Here and there. Yah. We wrote, and it was not really a courtship, but, uh, we stayed like that for a long time, and I met her in '52 and we were married in '59.

EM: So it was a while.

JL: It was a while, but I was at sea most of the time.

EM: And did she have a profession?

JL: She was a teacher. She was a nursery school teacher, and we were married in June, '59, and we settled in Le Havre, and as a teacher—she moved to LeHavre—job also, and as a teacher, in France, you're entitled to lodging facilities. Because of that, we had a nice apartment within the school. She was not teaching there, but, that's where we were living. It was nice, and she moved—we moved in another school in the suburbs where they built new houses, so we had a new apartment. And we stayed there many years.

EM: And you had a family.

JL: So Stephane was born in 1960, and at that time, I was in my first year in the Merchant Marine Academy in Le Havre. It was very good.

EM: And you had other children.

JL: So, then seventeen months later Olivier was born. And at that time I was at sea. I was in Cuba when he was born, and I met him the first time when he was three months old.

EM: And unfortunately—

JL: And unfortunately he died when he was seven. He had a brain tumor, and he died after surgery in '68.

EM: And then you had a daughter—

JL: Then we had Severigne, who came much later.

EM: In 1970.

JL: In 1970.

EM: Now can I ask out of curiosity—does Stephane have the middle name "Antoine?"

JL: No. He has middle name "Henri," which was his grandfather's, the maternal grandfather's name.

EM: What was his mother's maiden name? Colette's name?

JL: DeLepine.

EM: Okay, so you broke with tradition with Stephane.

JL: Yes. Yes.

EM: Has he given his son "Antoine?"

JL: I don't know. You know, it's an unspoken tradition. I mean, it just happened like that. My father, he was Emil Antoine, his father was also Emil Antoine. There are two Antoines in each family—it just happened like that, Antoine came, you know.

EM: Now, we talked about your married life—let's talk about your career and your career in the Merchant Marine also involves the fact that you were drafted—I don't want to miss that part, in October 1955.

JL: Yes, at that time, I was drafted like everybody; every young man was drafted in the military forces. As a professional merchant marine, I was drafted in the French Navy, and the draft at that time was for eighteen months, but, it was the end of the Indo-China War, and the beginning of the Algerian War, and instead of eighteen months, I was drafted for thirty.

EM: And also the Israel war, in 1957 with the Suez.

JL: Now that's something a little bit different. In 1956—let me try—yes, in 1956 I was on board a destroyer, and we were dispatched to Haifa, to provide fire for anti-aircraft fire power to protect the city, because the Israelis did not have anything. They didn't have the land power and the marine power. So we stayed there probably for two or three weeks, turning around in front of Haifa. Then, at the same time, there was the Suez Canal operation against the Egyptians, with the French and the British. And then we stayed for several weeks; my ship was an escort to aircraft carriers.

EM: And you said that was your closest call, the Suez War.

JL: Yes, there was—we were far at sea, you know, we saw airplanes, landing on the aircraft carriers not far from us, and so the planes—some were damaged—but for us, we were at war, it was a war mood, okay, but it was not really dangerous. It was—they had nothing against us.

EM: Okay, so you didn't have like a close call—

JL: No, nothing at all, no, nothing at all.

EM: And is there anything you would like to tell—we're jumping back to your family—something, any unusual circumstances, like you told Olivier was born when you were at sea—anything unusual about the birth of Stephane or Severine? Anything unusual?

JL: No, the birth of Stephane, I was present, I was there. I was not there in the room when he was born, I was not allowed to do that, for Severine same thing, I was there.

EM: But you saw them right away.

JL: And, yes.

EM: And of course, let's talk about your child with your second wife—before we—so, let's just say her name—

JL: Leah.

EM: You have another daughter named—

JL: Yocheved. Who was born on June 20, 1975.

EM: In?

JL: Paris.

EM: Paris—"Paree"—a Parisian child. Okay, before we get to anything more about Yocheved, let's go back—so, life went on, and you and your wife separated, whatever, and you continued, you had a job, where were you?

JL: At that time, I was on a passenger ship, and we were cruising in the West Indies, there was all those ships cruising, especially at that time; now it's a little bit more elaborate. You know, Sunday was Puerto Rico, Monday at sea—

EM: If it's Tuesday, we must be in Belgium—

JL: Exactly.

EM: And what was the name of the liner?

JL: DeGrasse.

EM: Okay. And the year was—

JL: It was—I met Leah in February '73.

EM: Okay, now I would love you to tell the story of your meeting, because it's such a special story.

JL: Okay. She board (sic) the ship on Sunday afternoon, on Monday we were at sea, and of course I was working, and I had my job to do, and things like that. On Tuesday we were in La Guairá, Venezuela, and she knew all those places because she had been traveling a lot, she was a travel agent, so, she had traveled all those places; so she was not interested to go ashore. The ship was alongside in La Guairá, and I was not on duty or anything like that, I remember, and I was in the swimming pool, with friends, with colleagues, and it was noon, time for lunch, and we left, and we saw that woman, who was on a chaise lounge, you know, next to the pool, and reading and sunning, and I was looking at her, and I say eh, that's a nice girl, you know, and that's it, there was nothing else. And in the evening, we sailed, and we were on our way to Grenada, and I was on—I think I was on—my watch was from eight to twelve. And around ten-thirty—it was night, and you know how it is on board ship—you have the chart room with light, you need light to do your job—and the bridge is up front, and there's a curtain; and it means that the bridge is completely dark, it must be dark to keep your sight available for outside. So I was in the chart room, and the door opened, and the captain's maître d' came. He said, "Mr. Lauwick, the Captain would like you to give a tour of the bridge to Mrs. Goldstein, there, and, came that lady that was at the pool. And I had the time to look at her, and she was lovely, all dressed up, very nice, she had dinner with the Captain, and, so, that's fine. So, we talk a little bit about all the things, the equipment, you know, the tour, you know, is very technical. And now, let's go to see the bridge. But the bridge, the bridge is completely dark, with no light. So I say, "You will be completely blind, so let me take your hand and guide you. And I know the place, but you don't. So, I took her hand, and I immediately felt that (makes the sound of a crash of a lightning bolt) that tension, you know that ah—

EM: That electric spark—

JL: Yah. Anyhow, so we went outside, it was completely dark, she was blind, I knew my way around, we were on the wings outside, eyesight adjusted, and we spent a good hour, talking, and it was just more than a normal tour. And she left. And before leaving, we made an appointment to meet on the following day in Grenada, at the pool, after lunch. Fine. And after lunch I met her. She was there, so, she say, "I would like to—I would like you to give me a tour of the ship." "Let's go!" So, we went all over the ship, and we went in the fo'c'sle, in the back, the kitchen—I introduced her to the chief cook, you know, and she was delighted, and so we went all over the place. And that was the beginning.

EM: And then you had an international courtship—

JL: Yes. It was international, because I was there. She came back—she flew back—the first time was in February. She flew back on the third of April and she flew back to a hotel in Puerto Rico, on a Sunday. We were there, it was Sunday, it was Puerto Rico. So, I knew that, of course, and I was—I had planned to be free, as I had my day free, so I jumped in a taxi, and at nine o'clock we met at the hotel.

EM: Very exciting.

JL: Very exciting.

EM: So you met in different ports, met in New York, did all this, and finally you decided that you were going to make it a permanent arrangement—

JL: Yah.

EM: And then you had to decide where to live.

JL: Yes. It took some times, and we met in France—I took some vacation with her, in France, in Paris, where did we go—the south, the Cote d'Azur, we went in the champagne area, renting a car, you know, going places, and that was fine. She had come several times in the West Indies when we were there. I was—I met her also in the North Cape—I was on a cruise in the North Cape, so I met her in—I met her in Bergen, and I met her also in Narvik. And in Narvik she finished the cruise, she finished the cruise with me—we went to the North Cape, I guess. And then, after a vacation I think we were coming back from vacation in the south of France, I called my—the office of the ship owner company. He said, "You are not going back to the liner, you are going back to France." It was a big promotion, a huge thing, but I refused it: "I don't want it, that ship's too big for me, my DeGrasse, that white ship that I loved, that I met her there, no way I couldn't do it. So we were on the run, between New York and Europe, and that was—I didn't like it at all.

EM: But at least when you got to New York, you got to see Leah.

JL: I was working all the time in France, but in New York my two days were off. So, as soon as I arrived in New York, she'd come and pick me up. She was living in Briarcliff which was one hour north of New York City, and I spent all the time there. And she sailed also—she took the ship to Southampton and flew back, or the other way around. And she took a cruise in Africa—we had—it was in Africa, I remember, and she was there also. And that created some problems, because if she was in my cabin, that was no problem, but if I was in hers—I had to tell the people where to reach me in case of emergency, like that. So only very few people knew.

EM: And then after a while you decided to get married—

JL: Yes, after a while we decided to be married

EM: Married in Switzerland, due to the mail.

JL: Yes. And when we went—the ship first went on a worldwide cruise, and I was on board for two parts. The first part was from New York around South America to Gaillard—and I met her there in Lima, in Peru, and we spent some time there, we went in the West Indies for a couple of days on vacation, New York, back to France, and I flew from Paris to Hong Kong to meet the ship at the move to

Hong Kong at that time. And I stayed on board between Hong Kong and Cannes; the ship arrived in France in Cannes. And I left the ship there, permanently, for no return. I met her there, and we had arranged—it had been a huge thing to do—because she moved—to rent a container on a ship, and the thing with two dogs.

EM: Very complicated, very involved.

JL: Very much indeed. On the fourth of April, 1974, I left the ship and we moved to Chateau-Neuf-de-Grasse, which is next to Grasse in the south of France, and we stayed until I had a job in Paris, and that was the following year. In between we were married, and there was a mail strike, and all the documents couldn't move from France, my birth place, birth town, to my place of living, of my home, and in order to do that we decided to be married in Switzerland. So, I collected the documents—my parents collected the documents necessary in Rouen. They took the car to Paris, I flew to Paris, took the documents from them, brought them to Geneva, flew back. And all that had to be sure, couldn't do it again. I remember we had to mail something. Leah had called me—telephone was working—she had called me from Switzerland, so in order to mail that paper, we drove to Italy and mailed that paper in Italy.

EM: Oh my gosh.

JL: Anyhow, we were married in December, in Switzerland, validated at the French consulate, and that was it. So, a week later, there was a move to—we moved to Paris, Yocheved was born, and Leah—it was a very difficult pregnancy, very, very difficult. The last four months, she was not allowed to leave her bed. So, a new apartment, a new job, a new baby to come, and it was a tiny apartment. I remember—incredible—the washing machine was in the bathroom, because it was ours—in France the washing machine is yours—but I had no space for the dryer in the house—so I put a board on top of the bathtub to put the dryer there, so the bathtub was covered.

EM: Oh my goodness. You'd have to take a bath under the dryer.

JL: And she was sick all the time, she was not well. And she had to go to the hospital. I was doing all the things, I began to be proficient in ironing.

EM: And thank God, Yocheved was born.

JL: Yocheved was born, on the 20th of June.

EM: A little premature.

JL: Yes, three weeks premature, but that didn't matter. It was okay, and the doctor did a fabulous job with her, with Leah.

EM: And then you lived in Paris—

JL: We lived in Paris until—from the hospital, Leah moved directly to a nice little house I had rented in Portois, which is a suburb, north suburb, and Yocheved stayed in hospital for two, three weeks before coming home, and she moved also in this place. And we stayed there until—until June '75.

EM: '76.

JL: No, '75.

EM: Oh, sorry.

JL: Leah one day told me, "I want to go back home. I want to move back home."

EM: When Yocheved was a year old.

JL: Not yet. She told me that—I think it was in September '75, just a bit later, because when Yocheved was three months old, Thanksgiving, Leah and Yocheved went to New York for Thanksgiving, and they stayed there a few weeks. And when she came back, she couldn't readjust, she say, "I want to go back home." I say, "Okay, let's go." So we sold everything we had. We sold the house—not the house, it was rented. We sold the car, we sold—we sold everything we could. We gave everything—we were very friendly with a next-door neighbor, who was a doorkeeper in Paris. She was

EM: A concierge?

JL: A concierge. She was a lovely old lady.

EM: The one who taught Leah French.

JL: Exactly. And slang. At that time, Leah was very good in French, and she was controlling slang very well. Anyhow, we left; we take the boat in Cherbourg, thirty-two pieces of luggage, a baby one year old, and two dogs. We arrived in New York on the 20[th]of June 1976, just on her first birthday. And we bought a house in Long Beach, New York, in Long Island, and, that's it.

EM: And life went on. And then you got a job in America, with—

JL: So I got a job first in Paris, just after leaving the ship. I was involved with a marine electronic company.

EM: Raytheon, was it?

JL: Raytheon. Yes. It was the national dealer for Raytheon. I was managing the Raytheon part of that company. And when I moved to United States, I had some contact, and I found a job, a similar type of job, and I got that for one year, I think. And after one year, a friend of mine, who was a captain, also a traffic manager for a French company in New York was killed in an accident, and his company offered me his job, usinore, and that was it. I took the job which was a very good job; I liked it, paying very much, a lot of travel, until 1987 when the company disappeared, for political reasons. And for several years I kept going on my own, all related to ship and steel. And finally in 1997 my mother-in-law was in Hollywood, Hallandale, died, and Leah decided to buy a house in Florida, and I retired—

go, and that's exactly what we did. In '97 I retired, and we moved, we bought this house, and we moved.

EM: And here you are. Sadly Leah passed away in 2000—

JL: Four. The 25th of April.

EM: Of a combination—the perfect storm of blood diseases.

JL: Yes, blood diseases. It was one thing after another.

EM: You went so many places—in your travels, in your profession with the merchant marine, and you know your captain private industry. What would you say your favorite—do you have a favorite place?

JL: You must know that being on board a ship, professionally, it's very nice, it can be glamorous. But, you don't have opportunity to see the country. You create some times available for some tourism, but it's very limited, because you are not there for tourism, you are there to work, on your ship, okay? It's a full-time job. So, it's not vacation, okay? So all the countries that I visited on board the ship, I had just had some ideas. I knew more when I traveled with Leah, for vacation, for pleasure. That was different. So, things being as they are, there is one—there are two countries that I liked, although I didn't know them very much in depth, but I went in enough places there to like them was Chile. I liked Chile, I have always liked Chile. I've been in many places, I didn't do very much, but whatever I knew was pleasing me a lot. And, having anything to do with Leah or Judaism or anything, Israel. I was very impressed by Israel when I was there; I was there twice in 1956. First time in May was some kind of courtesy visit with the French navy, to Israel, and we had some tourism, it was fine. The second time was during the war, several months later. But I was very impressed with the attitude of the people.

EM: Did they know you were Jewish? Did you have a special feeling because you said, "Oh, my goodness, this is my heritage."

JL: No, No. I had nothing at all. In fact, I was involved in Judaism only after arriving here. [United States] Even in France, almost nothing, barely. Leah was not involved with Judaism in France, not at all.

EM: Right. It's easy not to be. So your involvement with Judaism came later in this country, and—

JL: Oh, yes, absolutely. I have no formal Jewish education.

EM: Well you're doing great. But I think also from—if I can put words in your mouth—it's having a child, and then the child goes to Jewish day school, and then you start to get more involved—

JL: Yes.

EM: It kind of draws everyone in, and you become learned and aware.

JL: Yes, absolutely.

EM: Well, speaking of things like that, do you have a philosophy of life, or anything you would like to say, for posterity.

JL: No. I would say no, okay? I have nothing special philosophic, no. I'm not a philosopher.

EM: Would you say there's a guiding—

JL: But—I would say that you have to live your life in such a way that—First, you have to be happy. It's not always easy, let me tell you. If you live in New Orleans, your happiness and your philosophy of life probably has changed. [Hurricane Katrina had recently devastated the city.] You have to do the best with what you have. You have to be good, that's important, I guess. That's that. I hate people who are bad.

EM: So, be good, live your life and do the best with what you have. That's pretty good.

JL: And be good. Be good for yourself, be good for the people around you, love people. It's important.

EM: And can I ask you one more little question: what about your experience of living in two cultures? Your re-flections—

JL: You call that a little question, a small question?

EM: It's really not a small question, but I did want you to touch on what do you feel like now. Do you feel like a French-man who lives in America, or do you feel like an Ameri-can who has a background of, you know, who started his life in France? Where are you in that spectrum?

JL: I don't think I can answer that question straight-way. When I arrived here, I had—I was French, okay? But, I had a background, a professional background, that helped me a lot. I'd been changing horizons for twenty-five years on a constant basis, meeting different people constantly, every day; dealing with Japanese, Hispanic people, Ger-man people, going places, hot weather, cold weather, you know? So it means that even living in France at that time, you felt not really assimilated, because you don't live in your city. Yes, you spend two weeks, one month, three months, but you leave—and you go places, to see different countries, different people. So, when I arrived in this coun-try, I had that as a background, you know. I was not just. I did not have too many problems to adjust, for several rea-sons. First, the background that I'm talking about. Second, Leah, who was American. So it was easier for me to adjust because of her. She helped me.

EM: And what about the language? Did you know English be-fore you came?

JL: Yes, yes. I did, I did. I was not as fluent as I am now, I probably—I still have a terrible accent, but—

EM: It's very wonderful. A French accent in English is a "plus." It's an accent, not a handicap.

JL: Yes, you don't know—but too many people when you talk to them: (squinting) "What? What did you say? Can you say that again?" You know, all the time. That's one of the reasons why I cannot stand the telephone, because I have to repeat myself constantly. You know, I've been working for now—five years I guess—with an old person in Delray, and picking up their book, you know? The woman–she's fine, she's lovely. If I talk to her, I have to repeat at least twice, everything.

EM: I have news for you—everyone else has to repeat twice for her, too, I'll bet. She probably has a [hearing] problem— don't take it personally.

JL: And I will say another reason why I had adjusted myself easily: not only did Leah help me, but she insisted I was not allowed to make mistakes, or ignore. I was forced into it. This being said, I did not have major problems. I know the United States before—I've been—the first time I was in New York was in 1953, and I've been there many times in between, so it was not a shock.

EM: It's not like a war bride, who's never seen the country and comes over and—

JL: Absolutely. I was—I don't say I was familiar, but I knew enough; Manhattan, you know. I remember when I arrived, a friend had bought a car for us, and the car was parked some place. And he said, "Jay, take the car, take the kid, and bring the car." So, I had to walk maybe two miles to bring the car, but I knew the place—at the port. I'd been there many times. So, you know, I was not a "war bride," you know. I was not culture shocked. Now, I had to adjust. There are a lot of things that you don't know, buying a house, I have to do with lawyers, with repairing—I fixed this house—I bought the house for almost nothing, okay? But, there was a lot to be done. I spent seven years, all my weekends, fixing this house. I did everything, the windows, the walls, and what—anyway, so I had to learn that, because it's different in France. But, it was not a major problem. Now, was I a Frenchman living in America? No, I gave up France, maybe not easily, but Leah forced me to give up France. She couldn't cancel who I was, okay, but she didn't like it. So, because of that I had to tone down my French "ship," and I did it, I had no problem, I had accepted that. That was part of my agreement to settle here. In fact, I am much more French now that I'm alone. I have renewed so many contacts in France.

EM: Let's talk about three special contacts that I didn't mention: Stephane's children. Would you tell the names of your three beautiful French connections?

JL: (laughing) My French connections. Suzanne, she's my first. She will be fourteen soon, I'm sorry—she will be sixteen soon. Lucas is fourteen, fourteen and a half, soon, and Adele will be twelve soon. And they are lovely, lovely children.

EM: And they call you?

JL: Grandpapa d'Amerique.

EM: Grandpapa d'Amerique. And you know, Jay, I think this is a wonderful place, unless you have something else you need or want to say, because you said, "Make the best of what you have, and now, you never planned on losing Leah, she was several years younger than you, but here you are, and you have turned a new corner, renewed your French connections, kept your American roots, your American daughter, and are doing more. I know you're leaving for France, and may you have a long, long time to come of beautiful travels and experiences.

JL: I hope so. I'm already preparing, I leave in three weeks.

EM: To see la famille.

JL: To see la famille, meeting all my friends from thirty years, my reunion, non? It's a big thing.

EM: So I think the beautiful way to end this is to say to you, "Bon Voyage."

JL: Merci.

EM: Je vous en prie.

Appendix E
Sibyl Silver Interview
20 March 2016

EM: Good Morning. Today is Sunday, March 20, 2016 and it is my privilege to be here with Sibyl Silver to tell her special story. If this is the 21ˢᵗ century, early in the 21ˢᵗ century, you can contact us at Heritage Biography International dot com. [heritagebiographyinternational.com] We'd love to do your story. If this is much later on, we bid you greetings from the past. And now, to the interview.

EM: All right, Sibyl. Let's start at the top—what is your name?

SS: Sibyl Joan Silver.

EM: And do you know who you were named after?

SS: I was named after my grandfather's mother Sarah, and the "Joan" was just stuck in to give me a middle name.

EM: How nice. Do you have a Hebrew name?

SS: Sarah.

EM: And when were you born?

SS: August 2, 1939.

EM: Where were you born?

SS: Brooklyn New York.

EM: Do you remember any details of the hospital where you were born?

SS: Well, it's the same hospital that I gave birth to my son. I was born in Maimonides Hospital and so was he.

EM: It was a family tradition.

SS: Well, his sister wasn't born there—we didn't have enough time to get there.

EM: [laughing] Oh. We'll get to that. All right. Now you grew up in Brooklyn, and you grew up in the home of your mother's parents.

SS: That is correct.

EM: So let's just say your father's name.

SS: His name is either Isaac or Irving. It probably was Isaac, but then they tried to make it more American, so it's Irving.

EM: So he had Russian roots.

SS: Yes, his parents were from Russia.

EM: And your maiden name?

SS: Geller.

EM: When you think of your childhood and what childhood is today? And your grandchildren's childhoods, what stands out as the greatest difference?

SS: We are not as connected verbally as we were then. Today everything is Facebook, Twitter, Google. It just seems that beautiful times are not spent as family anymore. More time is spent away doing other things. We've become a very insular kind of people, which I find very disturbing.

EM: Yes. Now, going back to your school career. Do you remember the name of your public school, you probably graduated in eighth grade?

SS: Yes, it was P.S. 226.

EM: Okay and it was probably around the corner, like everything else.

SS: Absolutely, a block and a half away, and then I went to Lafayette High School.

EM: Okay, and are you friendly with anyone from those days?

SS: No.

EM: Now, I know you married young, but did you have a first job?

SS: Yes, my first job was for Merrill Lynch, P.S. Fenner
      &Smith down on Wall Street, and I worked there maybe
      three months, because then I was pregnant.

EM: So you were married before you even worked.

SS: Yes.

EM: Okay, so let's—

SS: Wait a minute—that isn't true; I worked for a year.

EM: So this was your first job.

SS: Yes.

EM: Okay, so you worked for a year. Can you remember how
      much it paid?

SS: Oh, God, no, but it was probably no more than twenty dol-
      lars a week, or some—ridiculous.

EM: And what kind of work did you do at that job?

SS: It had something to do with programming. I really don't
      remember.

EM: Well, we're getting lovely background.

SS: Yes, we're getting rain and it sounds beautiful. I love rain.

EM: And we're getting chimes, and it sounds lovely. So, did
      you go to any college at all in your life?

SS: Yes, when my son started kindergarten, and my daughter
      started nursery school, I lived on Staten Island, and I en-
      rolled with trepidation in Staten Island Community Col-
      lege and I took one course. I was really nervous about it,
      because I thought, here I'm going into a university; every-
      body's gonna be so bright and so smart, and what an eye
      opener that was. And the first course was sociology. It was
      just—I was afraid to raise my hand, I was afraid to say an-
      ything, and I was very fortunate, because the instructor
      must have seen that here's somebody who was like at least
      ten years older than the rest of the students coming to her
      class. And after class, she called me up to talk to her and I
      thought, "This is it—kiss of death, finished." And she said
      to me, "You have so much to impart. Please, let's hear

more from you." And that was the beginning of a fast track with colleges.

EM: So you ultimately graduated?

SS: Yah. What I did was from the one course I went to fifteen credits and then I continued in the summer and I finished community college in a year and a half and then I decided that I would continue and get my bachelor's degree. So, I knew it was going to be one of the city universities. Living on Staten Island, I had to pick one that was within the bus route, the express bus that went from Staten Island into Manhattan, and it just so turned out to be John Jay College of Criminal Justice. I enrolled; I was there maybe three weeks when I found out that the college was moving up-town to across the street from Lincoln Center. And so I panicked, and my husband said to me, "You drive the car? Take the car into New York, and just continue—you'll park in a parking lot and just go to college." And that's how it all began.

EM: So you eventually received a degree in—

SS: At John Jay College, a Bachelor's of Science in Psycholo-gy, or I should say, Deviant Psychology, and then I en-rolled to Graduate School, and I was accepted at Hunter College for a degree in Vocational Rehabilitation.

EM: And you got that degree.

SS: Got that degree, and while I was finishing up my degree, the last six weeks was an internship, and I was at Bellevue Psychiatric Hospital. Abe Bean was the mayor there. I was working with people who, of course, had intellectual prob-lems. It was called a workbench where you gave them kind of "work" to do, so that they would feel productive, and then you started it all over again. I did a lot of counseling with the people there, and what happened was the city had a crisis, and the city was going to shut down because there were—lack of funds, and so the job that I was going to be

hired for, I was no longer hired. I finished up at Hunter
College, this was the summer, and I took the Lsats, and
passed the Lsats, I thought I would go to law school, and
my husband said to me, "You know, we have two kids that
we have to put through college also. Don't you think you
should go out and get a real job now?" So, I said, "Well, I
really don't know what I want to do." And he came up
with this great idea, "You know, the pharmaceutical industry is starting to hire female medical representatives. I read
about it in one of the journals. Why don't you look into
something like that?" And I said to him, "Honey, if you
want me to do that, then you go get me the applications,"
which he did. I filled out three applications, one for Eli
Lilly, one for Merk, Sharp and Dome, and one for Abbott
Laboratories. All three called me, to come in for an interview, but Merk's interview was really close, it was in Pe-
terborough, New Jersey, we were living on Staten Island at
the time, and so I decided to go for the interview. Went for
the interview and they hired me right there and then on the
spot, so that was my start as a medical representative. I had
to go to West Point, Pennsylvania, at the corporate head-
quarters for six weeks to do training. Training was very
vigorous, very involved, all the drugs that Merck had, I
had to learn about the competitor's drugs, I had to do a lot
of chemistry—it was very, very difficult. And I was hired,
and I had a piece of Bergen and a piece of Passaic County
as my territory. And that was 1970.

EM: And how long did you do that?

SS: I did that 'til 1975 and then I got cancer, and so there was
no contract at the time and if you could no longer do the
job you were hired for, you could no longer be part of the
company. So being a woman it was really the first of the
first, having cancer was one of the first of the first, and had
I been a male, with, let's say, a myocardial infarction,

there'd be no problem. So I told them I would really like to work at Merck and company, which was in Rahway, New Jersey, in perhaps human relations, since I did have a Master's Degree in Vocational Rehabilitation, and I'm sure I could go through training, but they were kind of hesitant about doing this. I spoke with a labor attorney who said at the time, "There's no point in fighting this, they have their whole cadre of attorneys, and again, this would be like once—this has never happened before." So, they kept me on long-term disability for almost a year, and they were really very kind, I guess they were a little nervous, in retrospect, cause they also let me have the car, the company car. And in 1985 New York City was having a shortage of teachers, a crisis, and I thought, well, what the hell, let me see what happens, went down to the hiring hall in Brooklyn, told them what my degree was in, brought them my transcripts, and they said, "You'd be great for special education." So I told them I don't want to teach and they said no, high school would be great. I was hoping for Staten Island since I was living in New Jersey at the time, and they said no, Brooklyn and they sent me to a school in Sunset Park, and it's named John Jay High School, met with the AP [assistant principal] and Stuie said, "We have a great position for you, Special Education, you can teach "World of Work," you can teach Science, you can teach a lot of things, no problem." And so I was hired and I started working there. About a year later it was listed as one of sixteen worst high schools in New York City, of the five boroughs, and they started New York Working Department, and so I spearheaded that department, and the students that I had were picked and we taught them the "World of Work," "Work Studies." My office was furbished as an office, with a phone, and we had a photocopy machine, and I started the curriculum around teaching the

kids how to work in the real world, and at the same time
still teaching other classes. I did that for twelve years, and
then I left. It was really very difficult working with snow-
storms in New York City. New York City does not close
down its schools, going into the Holland Tunnel at five
o'clock in the morning was not so easy, and after twelve
years I reached the age where I was able to retire, without
a full pension but my medical benefits, and so I retired.
And I was home a couple of months and then Clinton was
president and he had the Welfare to Work Reform, and
Jewish Vocational Services in East Orange wanted to start
a program. I sent in my resume and I was hired and I
spearheaded that program and I did—we started a Welfare
to Work Reform through Jewish Vocational Services, they
were given the federal and the state grants. I did GED
Studies, unfortunately most of the people that came were
women, they had children, we had to arrange for day care.
It was really very difficult. It was very difficult for them
and it was very difficult for us, to get a program like this
off the ground, but it worked and it was great.

EM: Fabulous. So you did that—

SS: I did that for about three or four years, and then Montclair
High School was starting a program for incoming students
with Asperger's and ADHD and other kinds of problems
and one of the psychiatrists—one of the psychologists, excuse me, on the board who I knew very well, said to me,
"How would you like to do something like this?" And I
was really ready to leave Jewish Vocational Services, it
was off the ground, it was great, it was running, and I was
kind of ready for the next—

EM: Challenge.

SS: Challenge. I was there when my husband said, "Enough.
I'm ready to retire." He had a pharmacy in Brooklyn. And
he said, "I've worked enough, I've been in that pharmacy

since I'm twelve years old, I want to retire." And that's how we left the East Coast and we moved to Texas.

EM: So before we go into how you met your husband, let's go back a little bit; I want you to tell (again) about the question you asked your grandfather about why do people— you know, you said it related to the Torah, that you had this talk with your grandfather about, um, I guess an election, or not being fair to people?

SS: Oh, that was years later, I had said to him, "Why did Jewish people vote for Franklin Roosevelt? And he looked at me and said, "I don't know what you mean." And I said, "Well, weren't ships sunk at sea, wasn't there a quota of how many people could come into America? And he said, "Yes, but at that time we were just so happy that the war was over, and that the Great Depression was over, and people weren't hungry anymore, and America was going through its boom, and people didn't realize it." And he said, "Had we realized it then, we probably would have protested much more than whatever protested there was." And of course today now we know, we're more vocal, as I was vocal during the Vietnam era, vocal against the Vietnam War, and how we protested. We just didn't want that to happen.

EM: I wanted you to tell it because it shows that you were thinking of the silent people who were unable to speak for themselves, and your fellow Jews who were across the ocean and unable to speak for themselves.

SS: Yes. I mean they say "six million," but what about all those millions that perished in the ocean, that perished running, that just not only just died during the Holocaust in the crematoriums and in the camps, but died elsewhere. And what do we have for them? Unfortunately, Yad Vashem, the Wiesenthal Center came about and people started to want to know more and more about what happened during the war.

EM: And the people made their presence felt, even though they were no longer here, that they are a viable presence and it will come into your project. But first I want to go back, when you were young, you said you married young, how and when did you meet your husband, how old were you?

SS: We went to the same high school, we had similar friends, and that's how we met.

EM: So you feel like you knew him for a long time.

SS: Oh, yes. I knew him since I was sixteen and he was eighteen.

EM: Was he in the same class with you?

SS: No, he's two years older than me.

EM: And you said he'd been in this pharmacy down the street since he was twelve.

SS: His father owned the pharmacy. His father had a partner and they owned the pharmacy. They were not my pharmacy; they were about twenty-five blocks away.

EM: Okay, so it wasn't like you saw him every day since you were ten.

SS: No, not at all.

EM: So, you both—he had finished high school, you had finished high school and then did you get married?

SS: I got engaged when I was a senior. He was a junior in college, and we were married when he was in his senior year. And he worked and I worked. We had a very small apartment, and um, I was pregnant at the prom.

EM: (laughing) And married.

SS: Of course married.

EM: That's the trick. Now was it love at first sight?

SS: Yes, yes, yes.

EM: So do you remember that moment when you saw each other and just knew?

SS: No, just—

EM: You just loved each other.

SS: Right.

EM: Where were you married?

SS: We were married in Brooklyn at the Kingsway Jewish Center. We had a very large wedding.

EM: Okay, you were a teen-age bride.

SS: That I was.

EM: And you were a teen-age mother?

SS: I just had turned twenty-one.

EM: Did you have anything special in your courtship?

SS: No.

EM: You were both in the same place, you didn't have to write letters, travel or do anything like that?

SS: No.

EM: Did you have a honeymoon?

SS: Not really. We had four days. We took a ride up to Canada and came back. We had no money, we had a '49 Plymouth, and he had to get back to work and he had to study for his boards. He took the boards in September, so we never even thought of things like that.

EM: Where did you set up married life?

SS: In Brooklyn, in a small apartment.

EM: And you lived there until?

SS: We lived there until—we lived there for about three, four years and then we were able to move to an apartment not too far away from where his business was, and that was called a "junior four." So the kids had the big bedroom, and we had a very small bedroom. And we lived there until 1960, and then we bought a house on Staten Island. We had originally wanted to move to the Five Towns, but we didn't have enough money for a down payment, so we were able to put a down payment on a house in Staten Island.

EM: Okay. So we're going to leave the family here, and we're going to fast forward to you and Bob going on a trip.

SS: Well, our best and most memorable trip was in 1972. Hebrew University was commemorating its first school of pharmacy in Tel Aviv, and one of my husband's professors became the dean of that school. And so my husband's college, Brooklyn College of Pharmacy, LIU, was putting together a tour, and both our children went to yeshiva, and we felt that this would be a great thing to do, and my aunt, who I was very close with, her youngest son was being *Bar Mitzvahed* in July, and we thought it would be great for him to be *Bar Mitzvahed* at the *Kotel*—we would all be there together. And that was our first trip to Israel.

EM: Special.

SS: Oh, it was very, very special. Extremely so.

EM: Well, let's fast forward to another trip that didn't start—it may have started in Israel, but it was a Prague trip, the one that we're going to talk about.

SS: In October 2012, our granddaughter Alexandra, was doing her fall semester at NYU in Prague. My husband and I decided we would take a trip to Prague. It was over *Sukkot*, and the Chabads in Eastern Europe are really very close with the kids on campus. So the kids were building the *Sukkah* at Rabbi Barrish's synagogue in Prague, and that's how we got involved with Chabad in Prague. We were there during Sukkot and it was during one of the *Seudahs* [festive meals] of *Sukkot* that Rabbi Barrish told the story of Rabbi Koves from Hungary who went to Russia and found these Torahs that were stolen by the Nazis. He was not able to get them out of Russia, but perhaps with some American help, maybe it would work. And I turned to my husband and I said, "Wouldn't that be a great thing to be able to do?" And he looked at me and he said, "I worked all my life. I want to go home and play my golf. You want to do it? You do it. I give you my full blessing." And that's how it all turned around. We came back, and unfortunately, a few months later my husband got very sick, and everything was on hold. He passed away December 27, 2014. In February, 2015, I invited Rabbi Koves from Budapest to come to speak at the Boca Raton Synagogue and tell about the Torahs that are sitting in this library in Nizhny Novgorod in Russia and from here on in it just took off.

EM: We should say that Nizhny Novgorod [formerly Gorky] is basically a military town.

SS: That is correct. It is 400 kilometers southeast of Moscow. The Torahs went to Nizhny because the soldiers from Russia that were going west collided with the Germans in Budapest who were going east. This was on a train going to Berlin, Judaica and artwork, and they, the Russian soldiers took two or three cars, they took it and brought it to Nizhny, unloaded it and put the artwork in the library, and the Judaica in the museum—no, excuse me, the artwork in the museum and the Judaica in the library, locked it up and it sat there, because after the war, don't forget, Russia was under Communist ruling. A rabbi from Hungary, a Rabbi Frolich, in 1980 did go out to Nizhny. He did in fact go into the library, but he could not do anything with the Torahs. Again, Communist rule sat and did nothing. Rabbi Frolich probably had spoken about it, and that's how Rabbi Koves several years later, many years later, went out to Nizhny to see if in fact this is true, because in the late 1990s we had a lot of Holocaust restitution going on, attorneys were doing great work, the Swiss banks, the art work, everything was open, *trags* of Judaica, stolen art, the Wiesenthal center, Yad Vashem, there were all sorts of claims rights, so forth and so on, all these attorneys from all over the world, but by the year 2000 everything kind of came to a halt, and it did not go further than Germany.

EM: When did you first see the Torahs?

SS: May 5, 2015, I went to Russia.

EM: And there is a clip of that. And it's very stirring.

SS: Yes.

EM: I'd like to touch on a moment that was stirring to the viewer as well as it must have been to you. When it shows you seeing the Torah, it shows you beginning to cry.

SS: Oh, of course. I cried because—I don't know whose Torah this was, and I cried for joy, and I cried for sorrow, and my greatest hope would be that this Torah would be restored to the shtetl or to the family that prayed with this Torah, that gave up their lives for this Torah, that everybody gave up their lives for.

EM: We should say something about the origin, or what's thought to be the origins of these Torahs. They were confiscated later in the war, so they're thought to be from Hungary?

SS: We thought originally they were Hungarian, but we now know, or we found out later through the eyes of five various scribes, that the Torahs are not from Hungary, that they are—one is a Sephardic Torah, one is a Torah written in the Alter Rebbe style, and we're talking about from the Chabad, from the original Chabad. We have another Torah that [is] from Czechoslovakia. There are ten Torahs with names on them that are clearly not Hungarian names, so the scribes can tell by the style of writing where the Torahs originated from.

EM: And would you hold this up, Sibyl? [EM hands her a paper] This was how I was introduced to the Torah; there was a program called "Torahs—let's see what they say: "Boca Raton Synagogue Restores Torahs to their Glory" and Sibyl spoke—that's when I first remember—I did hear Rabbi Koves, but mostly I heard you. [EM points to the paper] This is a picture of one of the Torahs, and this was the beginning of my involvement in the project. Now, there's one more thing—

EM: When did you first—I was going to ask you when the most stirring moment of the project was.

SS: Seeing the Torah. I mean, it was an unbelievable thing. We went into the library, and into the back room, and there's this woman, of course, at the desk, and I'm with Rabbi Bergman, who is the Chabad rabbi of Nizhny Novograd [sic] and he speaks no English, speaks Russian and Hebrew, I speak only English. So, he spoke to her, they had a little "what-to-say," and then, what happened was, she opens up this door, and there, lying one on top of another, are these cardboard cartons, stacked high, with numbers on them. And he just pointed to one of them, and she took it out, brought it into the front room, laid it on a desk, opened up the box, and there was a Torah. And it was unbelievable, just unbelievable.

EM: Now to go from the sublime to the ridiculous, what was the most discouraging part of the project?

SS: Not being able to take all of them at one time. [Laughing]

EM: So, what message to the Torahs and their saga hold for future generations?

SS: Without the Torahs, we are not a Jewish people. The Torah is—is the thread that binds us, the Torah is a book of ethics, the Torah is the mainstay of Judaism, the Torah is read on a Monday, on a Thursday, on a Saturday. It is read at a Bar Mitzvah, at a Bat Mitzvah. It is danced with on Simchas Torah. The Torah is—it's what HaShem, God gave to Moses for us, the people. But it symbolizes all people, be it Jewish and non-Jewish. Laws, our own constitution, things come from our Torah. The New Testament looks back onto the Torah. It is just the mainstay of life. It is our bread, it is our water, it is our existence.

EM: And how would you say that the Torah symbolizes and unites the people of the communities that were lost with us and the future?

SS: It is the only thing left of those communities that one can lay their eyes on. It is the—when one sees it, one can witness what it's all about. It's one thing to look at rubble; it's another thing to see the written word. We all know that we can go to a cemetery, and there are plenty of cemeteries and plenty of shtiebels in Eastern Europe, where you can barely read the stones, or whatever, but these Torahs—you can read them, you can see them. It is so important to keep them alive.

EM: And you have kept them alive with your wonderful Torah project, and you continue to. There will be the next episode, which will be very exciting—can you tell what's coming up?

SS: Well, to start with, I started a foundation, the Jewish Heritage Foundation, and through this foundation and the board of directors, board of advisors, I was very fortunate—many people wanted to come and help restore the Torahs. One Torah in particular has been restored by one family. This Torah will be going on the March of the Living, this Torah will be read by his son for the first time at the Kotel in Jerusalem in June [2016]. I mean, it's amazing to think that this Torah is alive, it's coming alive! And it symbolizes all that was destroyed, or they tried to destroy, they could not destroy. We have a scribe that has restored the Torah. It was in pretty good condition, so it didn't take a lot of work. So this Torah is going on this March [of the Living]—a second Torah, another family has dedicated it in memory of their parents. That Torah will also go on the March of the Living, and the first Torah, the last four words will be completed at the synagogue in Krakow where the scribe is coming from Jerusalem to do it, and it will be read on Thursday, May 5th [2016] in a synagogue, and I can't tell you the last time that Torah was read in a synagogue; we have no idea, but what a wonderful thing to think of!

EM: Yes, and we look forward to many, many more fabulous experiences with you and the Torah.

SS: Thank you.

EM: All right, I'm going to move over and I'm going to ask you, first of all, to say the web site—it's www—

SS: It's www.holocausttreasures.com, and there is a Facebook, which is www.facebook.com/stolenjudaica.com.

EM: And I bid you farewell from Heritage Biography International, which iswww.heritagebiographyinternational.com, and as I say, if it's the early part of the 20th century, please get in touch with me, we'd love to help you tell your special story, and if it's much later down the road, we bid you greetings from the past. Be well.

SS: Thank you.

EM: Thank you so much. [smiles, hugs and kisses]

Sibyl Silver Interview April 2018

EM: Good morning.

SS: Good morning.

EM: I'm here today, April 17, 2018, with my friend and my associate, my dissertation associate. We are continuing the ongoing saga of the Nizhny Novgorod Torahs. And, Sibyl's going to fill in a few details about her grandfather who came here, and then we're going on to some philosophical insights. I'm going to take my position now as an interviewer. (EM moves out of the range of the camera to a seat opposite Sibyl.) Okay, Sibyl, first of all, can you elaborate just what you know about your grandfather, the one who came here from Russia.

SS: He was born in Vilna, which is Lithuania, in the late 1880s, the early 1890s. At the age of sixteen, he came to

America, settled here, he came because he ran away—he did not want to go into the Red Army—because of conscription. He came here to America, how he met my grandmother I have no idea, met my grandmother, settled in Brooklyn, went to Cleveland, went to Chicago, went to Philadelphia, came back to Brooklyn. His three daughters were born in Cleveland, Ohio, but they came back to Brooklyn and they were educated in the public schools in Brooklyn, New York.

EM: So his name was—his first name was—

SS: Philip Cohen, but his real name when he came on the boat, when he came to Ellis Island, his name was Raphael Kahn, and they made him Philip Cohen.

EM: Okay, so his Jewish name was Raphael, and I think you mentioned something about a name Ivan—or not. Okay, not. And he came from Vilna. And that's the only thing you know about him. And avoiding conscription was an issue.

SS: Yes.

EM: All right, and just to orient our viewers, you are widowed, your late husband Bob we've talked about, he began the project with you, and you have two completely grown children.

SS: Grown, married children—four grandchildren.

EM: And the grandchildren live on the East Coast.

SS: Yes, they all live on the East Coast and are at various stages of their educational and professional levels.

EM: Okay, so you're a matriarch. Let's go into some of the more philosophical observations that are always interesting to find out. How would you describe your affiliation with Judaism in terms of Orthodox, Reform, Conservative, Traditional, Secular, Cultural?

SS: I was raised in an Orthodox home, my husband was not. When we married, he had to work on Saturdays, and so, my kitchen was always kosher, I started to—I wasn't a Sabbath observer in the real sense of being a *Shomer Shabbos* person where I did not drive on Saturday. However our children went to an Orthodox Yeshiva.

EM: Well, that's pretty Orthodox, and did you in some way observe the Sabbath? Did you go to services?

SS: Um, when we had the children, the children and myself—not their father—went to synagogue.

EM: Okay, so there was Sabbath in their life—did you have Friday night family dinners?

SS: Yes, but not all the time with my husband.

EM: Have you personally encountered any anti-Semitism in your public or personal life?

SS: Oh, yes. Our first home was on Staten Island. The children were not enrolled in day school; my son was enrolled in kindergarten, and the first PTA meeting was held erev Yom Kippur. I went to the school, complaining, and they said, "We can't change our rules just for a couple of Jews. I then went to the local church, because I felt maybe something could happen, and they too kind of told me, "This is the way it is." So I decided—I spoke with my husband, and we decided that we'd take our son out of public school and although it was an economic hardship, we enrolled him into the day school, the only [Jewish] day school that was on Staten Island for kindergarten, and then fortunately that spring, Young Israel broke ground and moved down the street from where I lived, so it was a no-brainer, because I then belonged to Young Israel of Staten Island.

EM: And you continued to have your children in Jewish Day School?

SS: Yes, they stayed. They never went to public school—they did go to public high school.

EM: Has your outlook on religion changed any in the course of your life?

SS: I think with age and with change, politically, and I think we all have different feelings at different times in our lives.

EM: Would you say you feel more invested in religion as you aged, or less—

SS: No. no.

EM: In your family holiday rituals from your childhood, what do you remember as being celebrated?

SS: We always had Seders.

EM: Were they large family Seders, small family Seders?

SS: The family was—my grandparents were—their relatives were all over the United States, so it was—a small family, the nuclear family.

EM: Now what role does the existence of the state of Israel play in your life?

SS: I've always been a Zionist; I'm a philanthropist when it comes to Israel, especially the Israeli Defense Fund. I've been to Israel many, many times—we took our children to Israel. I feel whatever happens to Israel affects every Jew all over the world.

EM: Now have you ever lived in Israel?

SS: No.

EM: Would you ever make *Aliyah?*

SS: That's interesting. When the professor of my husband's school of pharmacy became—one of my husband's professors in Brooklyn College of Pharmacy, Long Island University, he became Dean of the first school of pharmacy in Tel Aviv, and a lot of us went for the dedication. My son was twelve at the time, our daughter was eleven. We went, and we were really enthralled, we thought, well, maybe this would really be a good life for the children, and we really spoke about it, and my husband spoke to his professor and he said to him, "You know what? There are hundreds of pharmacists here. We really need you to pick beans.

Your wife we can use, because I had a Master's in Vocational Rehabilitation at the time, we could use her. So my husband said, "You know what? We're goin' back to the States." And that was the only time we had ever discussed making *Aliyah*.

EM: Yes, so *parnassah* was a factor.

SS: Of course.

EM: Is there something you like especially or dislike especially in Israel? You said you visited—

SS: No, no. It's great. I have no negatives, no positives. Everything is perfect.

EM: Do you have any family in Israel?

SS: No.

EM: Now, how has the igniting of your Jewish spark, this beautiful Torah project, how has it affected your own view of your place in American culture?

SS: I don't know if I'm there yet.

EM: Well, you do have a Facebook page, and you are affiliated with a university on the project, and you have a certain visibility. I think you're very modest—I would say it's made you a figure in Jewish American culture.

SS: Yes, you're right. Yes, I mean, the Torahs went on the March of the Living, the Torah was dedicated to the Bronx High School of Science, they have a Holocaust museum there, the Torahs have played a role . . . .

EM: In Jewish American life, so in that way you have played a role—you are playing a role.

SS: I'm very low key about it—I'm—you know—extremely.

EM: Yes, you are low key about it, but you are a persona. I mean, when I told my husband I was coming here to talk with you he said, oh, the lady with the Torahs? Yes, the lady with the Torahs. Now, this is last but not least—what do you see as the future of Judaism in America and Israel?

SS: That's a tough question, because I see a lot of intermar-
        riage which dilutes the amount of Jewish babies born, if
        the mother has not converted, and even with intermarriage
        and the baby being born to a Jewish mother, it not neces-
        sarily means that the child will be raised as a Jew, as in a
        house where both father and mother are Jewish. I see that
        the Holocaust has become less and less important; it is not
        an integral part of history in our public schools, which I
        think is really wrong. We do have Holocaust museums, but
        does it really attract our youth? And I think this is a very,
        very important factor, and I see that, well, in the Reform
        movement, soccer played on Saturday is more important
        than going to synagogue on Saturday. And the conserva-
        tive synagogues—how many kids after they're Bar and Bat
        Mitzvahed and have their $100,000 party continue going?
        And how many parents continue being members of syna-
        gogues? I think this is where we lose a lot of our Jews. So,
        I don't know if Judaism is as strong as I would want it to
        be in America.

EM: You did mention of course the Orthodox component. How
        does this factor in?

SS: Well, I don't know if—we can't say a hundred per cent if
        Orthodox offspring stay Orthodox. We do not know that.

EM: Now what about the future of Judaism in Israel?

SS: Well, you know, there's Judaism and there's Judaism.
        There's the *Haredi,* and there's the Israelis. The Israelis
        are a completely different kind of Jew than the *Haredis*
        are, so I can't make any statement about that. I do know
        that we must have the state of Israel; going forward, Amer-
        ica's best ally is Israel, and America should be the best ally
        of Israel, and Israel America, very, very important, and it
        should be the world.

EM: I'm going to come back. I want to thank Sibyl again for all her input and insight, and we will go further and forward. Thank you so much.

SS: My pleasure.

Bibliography

Aderet, Ofer. "Arab-Jewish Refugees Still Dream of Compensation, Nearly 70 Years On" Ha'aretz: https://www.haaretz.com/israel-news/.premium-1.734217. 30 Jul 2016 4:46 PM.

Anderson, Benedict. *Imagined Communities: Reflections on the Origin and Spread of Nationalism.* Rev. ed. London: Verso, 2006.

Andrews, William L. ed. *Journeys in New Worlds: Early American Women's Narratives.* Madison: U of Wisconsin P, 1990.

Ashcroft, Bill, Gareth Griffiths, and Helen Tiffin, eds. *The Empire Writes Back.* 2nd ed. London and New York: Routledge, 2010.

_____, eds. *The Post-Colonial Studies Reader.* 2nd ed. London and New York: Routledge, 2008.

Barnavi, Eli, ed. *A Historical Atlas of the Jewish People: From the Time of the Patriarchs to the Present.* Rev. ed. New York: Schocken Books, 2002.

Beal, Timothy K. *The Book of Hiding: Gender, Ethnicity, Annihilation and Esther.* New York: Routledge, 1997.

Ben Shahar, Tal. "Habits of Happiness." Boca Raton Synagogue, Boca Raton. 16 February 2014. Lecture.

Beauvoir, Simone de. *The Second Sex.* Trans. Constance Borde and Sheila Malovany- Chevallier. New York: Vintage, 2011.

Berman, Rochel U. *Dignity Beyond Death: The Jewish Preparation for Burial.* Jerusalem: Urim Publications, 2005.

Berman, Rochel and George. *A Life of Leadership: Eli Zborowski, From the Underground to Industry, to Holocaust Remembrance.* Jersey City: KTAV Publishing House, Inc., 2011.

Beverly, John. *Testimonio: On the Politics of Truth.* Minneapolis: U of Minnesota P, 2004.

Bhabha, Homi K. *The Location of Culture.* London and New York: Routledge, 2006.

_____, *Nation and Narration.* London and New York: Routledge, 1990.

Bierer, Linda M., et al. "Elevation of 11B-Hydroxysteroid Dehydrogenase Type 2 Activity in Holocaust Survivor Offspring: Evidence for an Intergenerational Effect of Maternal Trauma Exposure." Psychoneuroendocrinology, vol. 48, Oct. 2014, pp. 1-10. EBSCOhost, doi:10.1016/j.psyneuen.2014.06.001. Web.

Bierer, Linda M., Heather N. Bader, Nikolaos P. Daskalakis, Amy L. Lehrner, Iouri Makotkine, Jonathan R. Seckl, Rachel Yehuda. Elevation of 11β-hodroxysteroid dehydrogenase type 2 activity in Holocaust Survivor offspring: Evidence for an intergenerational effect of maternal trauma exposure. www.elsevier.com/locate/psyneuren. (2014) 48, 1-10. Web. August 2017.

Bordo, Susan. *Unbearable Weight: Feminism, Western Culture, and the Body.* Berkley: UC Press, 2003.

Braziel, Jana Evans and Anita Mannur, eds. *Theorizing Diaspora: A Reader.* Malden, MA: Blackwell Publishing Ltd, 2003.

Brenner, Athalya. *Ruth and Esther: A Feminist Companion to the Bible.* Sheffield: Sheffield Academic Press, 1999.

Buffalo Jewish Review. 107.24. Mar 6, 2015/15 Adar 5775: 16.

Bures, Frank. "The Secret Lives of Stories." *Poets&Writers* Jan./Feb. 2013: 34-39.

Cesaire, Aime. *Discourse on Colonialism.* Trans. Joan Pinkham. New York: Monthly Review Press, 2000.

Chakrabarty, Dipesh. *Provincializing Europe: Postcolonial Thought and Historical Difference.* Princeton: Princeton UP, 2000.

Chansky, Ricia Anne and Emily Hipchen, eds. *a/b: Auto/Biography Studies* 32.2. London: Routledge, 2017.

_____, *The Routledge Auto/Biography Studies Reader.* London: Routledge, 2016.

Charlemagne, https://www.brainyquote.com/quotes/charlemagne_182029

Chatterjee, Partha. *The Nation and its Fragments: Colonial and Postcolonial Histories.* Princeton: Princeton UP, 1993.

Christine de Pizan. *The Book of the City of Ladies.* Trans. Rosalind Brown-Grant. London: Penguin, 1999.

Cixous, Hélène, Keith Cohen and Paula Cohen. "The Laugh of the Medusa." Signs, 1.4. (1976): 875-893. Web.

Cohen, Lara Langer and Jordan Alexander Stein, eds. *Early African American Print Culture.*

Cohen. The Rev. Dr. A., ed. *The Five Megilloth.* London: Soncino P, 1984.

Cohen, Robin. *Global Diasporas: An Introduction.* 2nd ed. London and New York: Routledge, 2008.

Conforti, Y. (2015), State or Diaspora: Jewish History as a form of National Belonging. Studies in Ethnicity and Nationalism, 15: 230-250. doi: 10.1111/sena. 12150. Web. 04 Feb. 2016.

Dalley, Stephanie. Esther's Revenge at Susa. Oxford: OUP, 2007.

Danailova, Hilary. "A Museum of Biblical Proportion," *Hadassah Magazine* Nov./Dec. 2017: 52-55.

Derrida, Jacques. *Of Grammatology.* Trans. Gayatri Chakravorty Spivak. Baltimore: The Johns Hopkins University Press, 1997.

Domnitch, Larry. *The Cantonists: The Jewish Children's Army of the Tsar.* Jerusalem: Devora Publishing Company, 2003.

Douay-Rheims Catholic Bible www.drbo.org. Web.

Douglass, Frederick. *Narrative of the Life of Frederick Douglass.* New York: Dover Publications, Inc., 1995.

Du Bois W.E.B. (William Edward Burghardt). *The Souls of Black Folk.* Chicago: Dover Publications, Inc. 1994.

Dufoix, Stéphane. *Diasporas.* Trans. William Rodarmor. Berkley: U of California P, 2008.

Eakin, Paul John, ed. *American Autobiography: Retrospect and Prospect.* Madison: U of Wisconsin P, 1991.

Eisenstein, Bernice. *I Was a Child of Holocaust Survivors.* New York: Riverhead Books, 2006.

_____, *I Was a Child of Holocaust Survivors.* Eisenstein, Bernice narr. National   Film   Board   of   Canada,   2010.   Film. http://www.youtube.com/watch?v=lePogWeW9Do.

The 'Fainting Paintings'. http://www.womeninthebible.net/ paintings_esther.htm.

Fanon, Franz. *Black Skin, White Masks.* Trans. Richard Philcox. New York: Grove Press, 2008.

Feiler, Bruce "The Stories That Bind Us." *New York Times* 15 March 2013. 1-6. "This Life" Web. 24 June 2018.

_____, *The Wretched of the Earth.* Trans. Constance Farrington. New York: Grove Press, 1963.

Fishman, Sylvia Barack. "Reading Esther: Cultural Impact on Responses to Biblical Heroines." Hadassah International Research Institute on Jewish Women at Brandeis University, Working Paper. February 2002.

Freadman, Richard. *This Crazy Thing a Life: Australian Jewish Autobiography.* Crawley: University of Western Australia Press, 2007.

Fohrman, Rabbi David. *The Queen You Thought You Knew: Unmasking Esther's Hidden Story.* USA: OU Press, 2011.

Gabara, Rachel. *From Split to Screened Selves: French and Francophone Autobiography in the Third Person.* Stanford: Stanford UP, 2006.

Gandhi, Leela. *Postcolonial Theory A Critical Introduction.* New York: Columbia UP, 1998.

Gilroy, Paul. *The Black Atlantic.* Cambridge: Harvard UP, 1993.

Ginzberg, Louis. The Legends of the Jews. Trans. Boaz Cohen. The Jewish Publication Society of America, 1913. Rpt. 1992.Web.

Gold, Steven J. *The Israeli Diaspora.* Seattle: U of Washington P, 2002.

Goldberg, Efrem. "From the Rabbi's Desk." Boca Raton Synagogue Weekly. 4-11 Dec. 2015.

Goldberg, Rabbi Judah, MD. "Zionism When the State Disappoints You." Boca Raton Synagogue, 17 Dec. 2016. Lecture/Sourcesheet.

Hamilton, Nigel. *Biography: A Brief History.* Cambridge: Harvard UP, 2007.

_____, *How To Do Biography: A Primer.* Cambridge: Harvard UP, 2008.

Hanhart, Robert. "Esther." A New English Translation of the Septuagint. New York: Oxford UP, 2007. 425-440. Web.

Hardt, Michael, and Antonio Negri. *Empire.* Cambridge: Harvard UP, 2000.

Hegel, G.W.F., *Phenomenology of Spirit.* Trans. A.V. Miller. Oxford: Oxford UP, 1977.

Henson, Josiah. *The Life of Josiah Henson.* Bedford. Applewood Books, 2002.

Hirsch, Marianne. *The Generation of Postmemory.* New York: Columbia UP, 2012.

_____, POSTMEMORY.org.

Hoffman, Eva. *After Such Knowledge: Memory, History and the Legacy of the Holocaust.* New York: Public Affairs, 2004.

Horowitz, Elliott. *Reckless Rites: Purim and the Legacy of Jewish Violence.* Princeton: UP, 2006.

Hipchen, Emily and Richa Anne Chansky, ed. *a/b: Auto/Biography Studies* 32.2. London: Routledge, 2017. Print.

Jolly, Margaretta, ed. *Encyclopedia of Life Writing: Autobiographical and Biographical Forms.* 2 vols. Chicago: Fitzroy Dearborn Publishers, 2001.

Katz, Steven T. *Post-Holocaust Dialogues: Critical Studies in Modern Jewish Thought.* New York: New York University Press, 1983.

Kitov, Eliyahu. *The Book of Our Heritage.* Rev. ed. 3 vols. New York: Feldheim Publishers,1978.

Kenny, Kevin. *Diaspora: A Very Short Introduction.* NY: Oxford UP, 2013.

Lejeune, Philippe. *On Autobiography.* Ed. Paul John Eakin. Trans. Katherine Leary. Minneapolis: U of Minnesota P, 1989.

Loomba, Ania. *Colonialism/Postcolonialism.* New York: Routledge, 2005.

Loomba, Ania, Suvir Kaul, Matti Bunzl, Antoinette Burton, and Jed Esty, ed. *Postcolonial Studies and Beyond.* Durham and London: Duke UP, 2005.

Luckert, Steven. *The Art and Politics of Arthur Szyk.* Washington: United States Holocaust Memorial Museum, 2002.

Mackey, Robert. "In a Dance Remix of Netanyahu's Speech, Two Echo: 'Iran—Haman." New York Times: http://nyti.mes/1ExrhhK. 6 Mar. 2015. Web. 7 Mar. 2015.

Marshall, Carl and David. *The Book of Myself.* New York: Hyperion, 2007.

McLuhan, Marshall and Bruce R. Powers. *The Global Village: Transformations in World Life and Media in the 21ˢᵗ Century.* New York: OUP, 1989.

McLuhan, Marshall and Quentin Fiore. *The Medium is the Massage: An Inventory of Effects.* Berkeley: Gingko Press, Inc., 1996.

Memmi, Albert. *The Colonizer and the Colonized.* Trans. Howard Greenfield. Boston: Beacon Press, 1991.

_____, *Decolonization and the Decolonized.* Trans. Robert Bononno. Minneapolis: U of Minnesota P, 2006.

_____, *Portrait of a Jew.* Trans. Elisabeth Abbott. New York: The Orion Press, 1962.

Miller, Tricia. *Jews and Anti-Judaism in Esther and the Church.* Cambridge: James Clarke & Co, 2015.

_____, *Three Versions of Esther: Their Relationship to Anti-Semitic and Feminist Critique of the Story.* Leuven: Peeters, 2014.

Moore, Carey A. *Daniel, Esther and Jeremiah: The Editions.* Garden City: Doubleday, 1987.

Morad, Tamar, Dennis Shasha and Robert Shasha, eds. *Iraq's Last Jews: Stories of Daily Life, Upheaval, and Escape from Modern Babylon.* NY: Palgrave Macmillan, 2008.

Morris, Rosalind C. *Can The Subaltern Speak? Reflections on the History of an Idea.* New York: Columbia UP, 2010.

Mulvey, Laura. "Visual Pleasure and Narrative Cinema. *Screen 16.3.* (1975): 6-18. Web.

Musleah, Rahel. "Virtual Survivors: The Future of Holocaust Testimony." Hadassah Magazine Nov./Dec. 2017: 53.

Olney, James, ed. *Autobiography: Essays Theoretical and Critical.* Princeton: Princeton UP, 1980.

_____, *Memory & Narrative: The Weave of Life-Writing.* Chicago: U of Chicago P, 1998.

_____, *Metaphors of Self: The Meaning of Autobiography.* Princeton: Princeton U. Press, 1981.

_____, ed., *Studies in Autobiography.* New York: OUP, 1988.

Patkin, Izhar. "You Tell Us What to Do." Boca Raton Museum of Art. History Becomes Memory. 11 Sept. 2015-10 Jan. 2016. Exhibit.

Poletti, Anna, and Julie Rak, eds. *Identity Technologies: Constructing the Self Online.* Madison: U of Wisconsin P, 2014.

Porter, Monica. "A secret Japanese history." *The Jewish Chronicle:* https://www.thejc.com/lifestyle/features/a-secret-japanese-history-1.60751. Web. 14 July 2016. 26 November 2017.

Porter, Roger J. and H.R. Wolf. *The Voice Within: Reading and Writing Autobiography.* New York: Alfred Knopf, 1973.

Rich, Adrienne. "Compulsory Heterosexuality and Lesbian Existence." *Feminist Theory: A Reader. 3rd ed.* New York: McGraw-Hill, 2010.

Rubin-Dorsky, Jeffrey, and Shelley Fisher Fishkin, eds. *People of the Book: Thirty Scholars Reflect on Their Jewish Identity.* Madison: U of Wisconsin P, 1996.

Said, Edward W., *Culture and Imperialism.* New York: Vintage, 1994.

_____, *Orientalism.* New York: Vintage Books, 1979.

Sacks, Jonathan. *The Dignity of Difference.* London: Bloomsbury Publishing, 2014.

_____, *To Heal a Fractured World.* New York: Schocken Books, 2005.

_____, *The Jonathan Sacks Haggada.* Jerusalem: Koren Publishers, 2016.

Scherman, Rabbi Nosson, ed. *The Tanach: The Artscroll Series/Stone Edition.* New York: Mesorah Publications, 1996.

Scherman, Rabbi Nosson and Rabbi Meir Zlotowitz, eds. *The Complete Artscroll Siddur.* New York: Mesorah Publications, Ltd., 1991.

_____, *Artscroll Youth Megillah.* New York: Mesorah Pub., 1988.

_____, *The Chumash: The Artscroll Series/Stone Edition.* New York: Mesorah Publications, 2001.

Segev, Tom. "Now It Can Be Told" Ha'aretz: https://www.haaretz.com/now-it-can-be-told 1.184724. 6 Apr. 2006 12:00 AM. Web. 3 Jan. 2018.

Shavit, Ari, author, *My Promised Land: The Triumph and Tragedy of Israel. Fresh Air.* Narr. Terry Gross. Natl. Public Radio. WHYY, 18 Nov. 2013. Radio.

Singh, Amritjit, and Peter Schmidt, eds. *Postcolonial Theory and the United States: ace, Ethnicity and* Literature. Jackson: University Press of Mississippi, 2000.

Smith, Sidonie and Julia Watson, eds. *Reading Autobiography: A Guide for Interpreting Life Narratives.* 2nd ed. Minneapolis: University of Minnesota Press, 2010.

Sor Juana Inéz de la Cruz. *Poems, Protest and a Dream: Selected Writings.* Trans. Margaret Sayers Peden. New York: Penguin, 1997.

Spivak, Gayatri Chakravorty. *The Post-Colonial Critic: Interviews, Strategies and Dialogues.* New York: Routledge, 1990.

_____, A *Critique of Postcolonial Reason.* Cambridge and London: Harvard UP, 1999.

Stanton, Elizabeth (1895). *The Woman's Bible: A Classic Feminist Perspective.* European Pub Co. Web.

Stowe, Harriet Beecher (1878). *Bible Heroines.* Fords, Howard & Hulbert. Retrieved Nov. 30, 2015: n. pag. Web.

Thiong'o, Ngugi wa. "A Family Affair." Florida Atlantic University John D. MacArthur Campus, Jupiter. 30 January 2015.

_____, *Theory and the Politics of Knowing.* New York: Columbia UP, 2012.

Trend, David. *Worlding: Identity, Media, and Imagination in a Digital Age.* Boulder: Paradigm Publishers, 2013.

Tull, Patricia K. Esther and Ruth. Louisville: Westminster John Knox Press, 2003.

Turkle, Sherry. *Life on the Screen: Identity in the Age of the Internet.* New York: Simon & Schuster, 1995.

Watt, Mary A. "Christopher Columbus and the Divine Comedy: Odyssey and Revelation in the New World Project." Twentieth Annual Connie De Marco Distinguished Lecture in Italian Studies. Jaffe Center for Book Arts in the Wimberley Library at Florida Atlantic University, Boca Raton. 20 Nov. 2013. Lecture.

Wiesel, Elie. *A Jew Today.* Trans. Marion Wiesel. New York: Vintage, 1979.

_____, *The Jews of Silence: A Personal Report on Soviet Jewry.* Trans. Neal Kozodoy. New York: Schocken Books, 2011.

_____, *The Night Trilogy: Night; Dawn; Day.* Trans. Marion Wiesel. New York: Hill and Wang, 2008.

_____, *Open Heart.* Trans. Marion Wiesel. New York: Schocken Books, 2012.

Wolf, Howard. *The Autobiographical Impulse in America: Essays on The Crisis of Humanism in Contemporary Culture.* Delhi: Academic Foundation, 1993.

Wolfe, Alan. *At Home in Exile: Why Diaspora is Good for the Jews.* Boston: Beacon Press, 2014.

Wollstonecraft, Mary. *A Vindication of the Rights of Woman.* London: Penguin Books, 2004.

Yerushalmi, Yosef Hayim. *Zakhor: Jewish History and Jewish Memory.* Seattle: U of Washington P, 1996.

Zaeske, Susan. "Unveiling Esther as a Pragmatic Radical Rhetoric". *Philosophy & Rhetoric* 33.3 (2000): 193–220. Web.

Zlotowitz, Rabbi Meir. *The Family Megillah.* New York: Mesorah Publications, 1994.

Index